What Money Can't Buy

What Money Can't Buy

Family Income and Children's Life Chances

SUSAN E. MAYER

Harvard University Press

Cambridge, Massachusetts
London, England
1997

Library of Congress Cataloging-in-Publication Data
Mayer, Susan E.
What money can't buy : family income and children's life chances /
Susan E. Mayer
p.   cm.
Includes bibliographical references (p.   ) and index.
ISBN 0-674-58733-2 (alk. paper)
1. Children—United States—Social conditions.   2. Children—
United States—Economic conditions.   3. Social mobility—United
States.   4. Income—United States.   5. Poor children—United States.
6. Poverty—United States.   7. Poor—United States.   8. Public
welfare—United States.   I. Title.
HQ792.U5M39   1997
305.23′0973—dc20
96-34429

To my children, Jason David and Elizabeth Lucille

Acknowledgments

This book presented me with difficult methodological, substantive, and political issues. Any progress I have made in resolving these issues has invariably resulted from the help of colleagues and friends.

The W. T. Grant Foundation provided the major financial support for this book. Funding from the Carnegie Corporation made it possible for me to complete the work that appears in Chapter 8 on the effect of welfare benefit levels on children's outcomes.

Three people have made unusually large contributions to this book. David Knutson and Timothy Veenstra labored tirelessly and beyond all reasonable expectations to do most of the data analysis. They not only spent too many nights and weekends tethered to the computer, but they also read and reread the manuscript, checking tables and other information for accuracy. Their technical and substantive suggestions have greatly improved this work.

Christopher Jencks has been a mentor and friend for more than ten years. Nearly all of our conversations over this time have in one way or another helped shape my approach to social problems and, therefore, the ideas in this book. More directly, he read the entire manuscript, much of it more than once, making suggestions about the methodology used, the interpretation of the results, and the prose. I could not exaggerate my debt to him.

Although I promised them anonymity, I am very grateful to the many educators who took the time to talk to me. These interviews were invaluable in shaping my arguments. I found the dedication and deep concern that these teachers, administrators, and counselors expressed for the disadvantaged children in their charge deeply touching and inspiring. I thank Lynnie Case, Susan Greenwald, Vicki Krugman, and Jan Mathis for helping me arrange these interviews.

I have benefited immensely from the free trade in ideas at the University of Chicago's Irving B. Harris Graduate School of Public Policy, where I have been on the faculty since 1989. My colleagues Robert

Michael, Charles Glaser, and Larry Lynn provided especially thoughtful and detailed comments on an early version of the manuscript.

I have also been lucky to maintain ties with faculty and students at Northwestern University, where I received my Ph.D. At Northwestern I am especially indebted to Greg Duncan, who was editing a book on this same topic as I was finishing my manuscript. The work that he and his colleagues were doing forced me to confront many issues that I might otherwise have ignored. Tom Cook also provided especially helpful comments on many aspects of the book. Mary Driscoll provided valuable feedback on an earlier draft. Other current and former Northwestern students who provided data analysis and substantive critiques of my statistical techniques include David Harris, Judy Levine, Meredith Philips, Scott Winship, and David Rhodes.

Others who have read part or all of earlier versions of this manuscript and provided helpful comments include Andrew Cherlin, Chris Winship, Mary Corcoran, Peter Gottschalk, and Larry Radbill.

As discussants at conferences and seminars, Amy Butler, Charles Manski, and Frank Levy supplied very useful comments. Arloc Sherman shared valuable feedback, especially on the literature review. I am also grateful to Greg Hanna for the hours he spent tracking down books, articles, and data in the library. My son, Jason Ocken, shaped many of my arguments by often disagreeing with my conclusions and pressing me to defend my ideas.

Finally, I thank my colleagues and students, and most of all my husband, David, and my daughter, Elizabeth, who endured more neglect than was fair while I wrote this book.

Contents

1

Introduction

Poor children have more than their share of problems. They usually weigh less than rich children at birth and are more likely to die in their first year of life. When they enter school, poor children score lower on standardized tests, and this remains true through high school. Poor children are also absent from school more often and have more behavior problems than affluent children. Poor teenagers are more likely than teenagers from affluent families to have a baby, drop out of high school, and get in trouble with the law. Young adults who were poor as children complete fewer years of schooling, work fewer hours, and earn lower wages than young adults raised in affluent families. As a result, children raised in poverty are more likely to end up poor and in need of public assistance when they become adults.

No social scientist believes that income is the sole determinant of how children turn out, but most believe that parental income has an important influence on children, and some believe it is the single most important influence on children's life chances. Indeed, many argue that other factors that increase the risk of failure among children, such as growing up in a single-parent family, are hazardous mainly because they decrease parental income. When I first began to write this book, I too believed this. At one time I was a young single mother without much money. I know what it is like not to be able to afford a pair of jeans or a birthday cake for your child, to have to borrow money to pay a doctor's bill, and to worry about a child left home alone after school because there is no money for child care. To paraphrase Sophie Tucker, I have been poor and I have been not so poor and not so poor is better. But my belief in the importance of income to children's well-being was not based on personal experiences alone; it was also based on a large body of social science research.

Although the empirical studies with which I was familiar did not agree on how much influence parents' income had on any particular measure of children's well-being, none suggested that its effect was negative, and the best evidence suggested that it was quite important for many outcomes. My own preliminary research also showed that parental income had a large effect on teenage childbearing, dropping out of high school, and children's eventual educational attainment, even after I held constant characteristics such as parents' race, education, and age. Empirical evidence also suggested that the effect of income on children's outcomes was usually what statisticians call "nonlinear," meaning that an extra dollar would help poor children more than it would help rich children. If this were the case, transferring income from the rich to the poor would usually help poor children more than it would hurt rich children.

I recognized, of course, that many Americans discounted the importance of income, arguing that how children turn out largely depends on their parents' moral character, social skills, intelligence, and other characteristics. If this were true, increasing the income of low-income families might not help their children. But the evidence I had seemed to show that income had a greater effect on adults' character than character had on income. Furthermore, whereas most Americans now believe that income transfers discourage work and marriage, my reading of the research convinced me that such effects were quite small. Compared with other ways of helping low-income children, increasing parental income through income transfer, child tax credits, child support payments, and the Earned Income Tax Credit (EITC) seemed like simple, effective, and efficient ways to help more children grow up to be productive, law-abiding citizens.

As it turned out, however, the relationship between parental income and children's outcomes is more complicated than I first imagined. In most cases, additional parental income does improve children's chances for success. But parental income is not as important to children's outcomes as many social scientists have thought. This is because the parental characteristics that employers value and are willing to pay for, such as skills, diligence, honesty, good health, and reliability, also improve children's life chances, independent of their effect on parents' income. Children of parents with these attributes do well even when their parents do not have much income.

This conclusion flies in the face of the common liberal claim that "the poor are just like everyone else except that they have less money." But this claim has always been a half-truth. Almost no one believes that the average welfare recipient is just like the average CEO or the average schoolteacher. The rich and the poor have far more in common than the rich generally admit, but giving poor parents more cash will not make them just like the well-to-do in all respects. The crucial question, therefore, is whether the things that extra money can buy make a big difference to children. When extra money prevents hunger or homelessness, or when it buys medical care and other necessities, it can make a big difference to children. But in the United States most poor families can meet these basic material needs through a combination of Food Stamps, Medicaid, housing subsidies, government income transfers, and private transfers of cash, goods, and services. Under these circumstances the question is seldom whether money for basic necessities would help children, but usually whether money for goods and services beyond some minimum would significantly increase a child's chances for success.

In this book I assess the effect of parental income on young children, teenagers, and young adults. I look at young children's cognitive skills and behavior problems, whether teenagers drop out of high school, whether teenage girls have babies, whether young women become single mothers, the number of years of schooling completed by young adults, young men's wages and earnings, and what I call male "idleness"—the chance that a twenty-four-year-old male who is not in school did no paid work in the previous year. Each of these variables is described in detail in Appendix A.

I experimented with a variable that counted women as idle if they had no children and were neither in school nor working. This proved to be unrelated to parental income. I also omitted some other measures of children's well-being that appear to be uninfluenced by parental income, including measures of verbal memory and scholastic competence. These may appear unrelated to parental income because they are poorly measured.

Although this list of outcomes covers only a few of the many possible measures of children's well-being, it includes most of the measures that social scientists have studied in the past, and most of those that policy makers and legislators now worry about. Some conspicuous omissions are violent crime, suicide, and drug use, which are not reliably measured in any of the surveys I analyzed.

The data for estimating the effect of income come mainly from two large longitudinal surveys, the Panel Study of Income Dynamics (PSID) and the National Longitudinal Survey of Youth (NLSY) mother-child files. These data and the particular samples I use are also described in Appendix A. The PSID has followed a national sample of families since 1968, and has accumulated detailed information on their children's educational attainment, childbearing, marital status, and labor-market success, but it has little information on children when they were young. The NLSY, in contrast, has followed children born to a national sample of women who were between the ages of fourteen and twenty-one in 1979. Almost all these children were still quite young in 1992, which was the most recent year for which data were available when I wrote this book. In a few cases I use data from various years of the decennial Census and the March Current Population Survey. I also interviewed teachers, counselors, school administrators, Head Start workers, and social workers from schools in Michigan, Illinois, Georgia, and New Mexico. These are not a representative sample of people who work with children, but a diverse group of educators who work with an even more diverse group of children. I use insights from these interviews throughout the book.

This book is about the effect of parental income on all children, not just poor children. Nonetheless, the history of policies for poor children in the United States provides a useful framework for understanding how Americans have thought about the relationship between income and children's life chances. Chapter 2 shows that over the last two hundred years welfare policies in the United States have vacillated between trying to improve the material well-being of poor children and trying to improve the moral character of their parents. The cyclical nature of America's policies is the result of a basic dilemma facing those who make policies for poor children. Most Americans are sympathetic to poor children; they do not believe they should go hungry or live in squalor because their parents are poor. But Americans are also reluctant to give money to poor adults for fear of rewarding the very behavior that made them poor.

In the beginning of the nineteenth century, "outdoor relief" provided destitute families with food, shelter, and small amounts of cash to meet their basic material needs. But as the nineteenth century progressed, more Americans began to believe that destitution resulted largely from moral weakness. They argued that outdoor relief reinforced the very behaviors that gave rise to poverty. For the next hundred years states tried to break the cycle of pauperism by improving the moral character of poor families. Initially they tried to punish the behaviors that lead to pauperism by requiring destitute children and adults to enter almshouses if they wanted help. Later they tried to remove children from the influence of their pauper parents by placing them in "orphan asylums" or foster care. When this proved expensive, they provided small sums of money for destitute mothers to care for their children at home, but only if the mother provided what the state considered a "suitable" home.

The Great Depression altered Americans' views about the importance of income to children's well-being. Widespread economic deprivation eroded support for the view that low parental income was evidence of weak moral character. Instead, Americans began to think that poverty hurt children because poor parents could not purchase the goods and services that their children needed. They argued that children who came to school hungry could not compete with those who were well fed, and children whose families could not afford decent housing or medical care had more than their share of serious illnesses, which interfered with both schooling and social adjustment. Congress created Aid to Dependent Children (ADC) in 1935 mainly to improve the material living conditions of poor children. At first states retained many rules governing the behavior of welfare recipients in an attempt to exclude mothers whose behavior they did not condone. But the emphasis on the material needs of families that had taken hold in the 1930s encouraged the growth of federal regulations that reduced local officials' discretion about which families to support. By the 1960s a combination of court orders and regulations had eliminated most of the rules governing the behavior of welfare recipients. Separate child-welfare agencies became responsible for dealing with families that neglected or abused children. For a brief period America's welfare policies were almost exclusively aimed at meeting the material needs of the poor. In this respect they had come to resemble the outdoor relief that existed early in the nineteenth century.

But dissatisfaction with outdoor relief was as strong in the 1960s as it had been in the early 1800s. The welfare bill of 1996 returned responsibility for poor families to the states, ended the entitlement to cash assistance, and required poor families to demonstrate suitability through work effort. Thus in many ways welfare policies at the close of the twentieth century resemble those at the beginning of the century. The real value of cash transfers to poor families declined steadily since the early 1970s. America instead tried to provide for the basic material needs of poor families with Food Stamps, Medicaid, housing subsidies, and other noncash programs.

The outdoor relief of the twentieth century, unlike that of the nineteenth century, was accompanied by programs that provided services for poor children, including child care, Head Start, compensatory education, and foster care. In one important way all these policies are like the orphan asylums and foster care of the nineteenth century: they provide help for poor children outside their homes. Since 1988 such programs have grown much faster than either cash or noncash assistance. Foster care has grown rapidly, and proposals to bring back orphanages to care for destitute children are now taken seriously.

We are likely to repeat the same cycle of policies over the next hundred years unless new information sheds light on the old questions of what money can and cannot buy. Thus this book is about what money can buy for children.

Chapter 3 examines the differences between rich and poor children's test scores, behavior problems, educational attainment, and young men's wages and labor-market participation. It also looks at the risk that rich and poor children will become teenage mothers, drop out of high school, or become single mothers. Taken in isolation, none of these measures provides a very good picture of how rich and poor children fare. Not all children who know a lot grow up to become prosperous adults, and not all slow learners grow up to be poor. Some children who grow up to earn high wages are still unhappy, whereas others are happy despite earning low wages. Some children get pregnant too early, or with the wrong person, but still become productive adults. Nonetheless, most people agree that children with high cognitive skills are likely to be better off than those with low skills; that teenagers who have babies and drop out of high school are usually worse off than those who do not; and that young adults with many years of education, steady jobs, and high wages are mostly better off than those with limited education, precarious jobs, and low wages. Most people also agree that it is better for individuals who have children to get married, and that stable marriages are better than unstable marriages. Not surprisingly, Chapter 3 shows that, on average, children from low-income families fare worse than those from high-income families on all of these outcomes.

Social scientists have developed at least two theories to explain these differences between rich and poor children. Most economists use a theory based on an investment model in which parents invest both time and money in their children's human capital. The children later reap the benefits of this investment in the form of higher wages, better marriage partners, and better lives. The investments parents make in their children include good housing near good neighbors and good schools, adequate medical care, and learning tools such as computers and books. All else being equal, families with more income can invest more in their children, so their children are more likely to succeed.

Most noneconomists explain the relationship between parental income and children's success using theories in which income initially affects the behavior of parents, which then affects their children. The "parental-stress" theory holds that poverty is stressful and that stress diminishes parents' ability to provide appropriate and effective parenting. The "role-model" theory holds that because of their position at the bottom of the social hierarchy, low-income parents develop values, norms, and behaviors that cause them to be "bad" role models for their children.

One variant of the role-model hypothesis holds that this kind of parental behavior, though dysfunctional for members of the middle class, is a rational response to long-term poverty. According to this theory, increasing parental income might not improve children's life chances in the short run, but it should help in the long run by changing parents' values and behavior. A stronger and more controversial version of the role-model hypothesis holds that among those enmeshed in a "culture of poverty," values and behavior will not change at all in response to income transfers.

All these theories try to explain why children's chances for success depend on their parents' income. But the fact that poor children fare worse than rich children does not suffice to prove that low parental income per se hurts children. Poor parents differ from rich parents in many ways besides their income. For instance, low-income parents usually have less education and worse health, and they are less likely to be married. Such differences could also explain most of the disparities in rich and poor children's life chances.

Chapter 4 provides evidence from what I call "conventional" models of the relationship between parental income and children's outcomes. These models control some but not all nonmonetary characteristics of parents. I call them conventional because they are the kind of model that researchers have usually used in the past. Social scientists also describe them as "reduced-form" models, because they try to estimate the effect we could expect to observe if we simply gave parents more money. Conventional reduced-form models suggest that whereas parental income has a relatively small effect on young children's test scores and behavior, it has a much greater effect on teenage childbearing, single motherhood, dropping out of high school, postsecondary education, and young men's labor-market success. Models of this kind have convinced most social scientists that how children turn out depends on their parents' income. It has also convinced some policy makers that raising the income of poor families through transfers or tax credits will help poor children succeed.

But though these studies control some relevant parental characteristics, they omit many others. As a result, such studies cannot persuade skeptics who believe that parental competence, values, or intelligence are what really affect children's well-being because they do not control all these parental traits. This book investigates what I call the "true" effect of income. By this I mean the effect controlling all parental characteristics, both observed and unobserved, that influence the parents' income and the children's outcomes. I find that for most outcomes the true effect of parental income is consistently smaller than estimates based on conventional methods.

No one strategy for controlling the unobserved parental traits that influence both income and children's outcomes can ever be completely convincing. Therefore, I use five strategies for estimating the true effect of parental income. First I look at income from different sources. If income helps children, a dollar from welfare should be as valuable as a dollar from parents' wages or a dollar from winning the lottery. But several studies seem to show that welfare income is less beneficial to children than income from other sources (mainly work). These studies raise the suspicion that welfare recipients differ in important but unmeasured ways from those who do not receive welfare, and that these differences affect their children's outcomes.

No source of income is completely unrelated to parental traits, but some sources are more strongly related to these traits than others. Unearned income from sources other than government transfers (such as income from child-support payments or interest), which I refer to as "other" income, is less strongly related to observed parental characteristics such as education and cognitive skills than either earnings or income from government transfers, so it is likely to be less strongly related to unobserved characteristics as well. Consequently, the effect of "other" income on children's outcomes should more closely approximate the true effect of money than does the effect of either earned income or government transfers. For most outcomes, the effect of "other" income is smaller than the effect of total income, even though this technique does not account for all the bias due to unobserved parental traits, because "other" income is not entirely unassociated with these characteristics.

My second strategy for estimating the true effect of income is to compare the apparent effect of parental income measured before an outcome, such as a teenager's having a baby or dropping out of high school, with the apparent effect of parental income after the outcome occurs. Annual income has a relatively stable or "permanent" component and an unstable or "transitory" component. The stable component is likely to be highly correlated with stable parental characteristics such as skill and motivation. The unstable component is by definition uncorrelated with stable parental characteristics. In most cases, income after an outcome occurs cannot affect that outcome. If income after the outcome appears to predict the outcome, this must mean that income after the outcome is a proxy for parental characteristics that existed before the outcome. If parental income when a child is twenty-five predicts both that child's quitting high school and parental income when the child was fifteen, the most likely explanation is that both measures of income were equally influenced by stable parental characteristics that also affect the child's quitting high school. More generally, the relative size of an outcome's correlation with income before and after an outcome can tell us how important stable but unmeasured parental characteristics are relative to income per se. I find that for most outcomes, these unmeasured parental traits account for a substantial amount of the effect of parental income.

According to what I have called the investment theory, if parental income improves children's outcomes then the things parents buy as their income increases ought to improve children's outcomes. My third strategy is to see if this is the case. Chapter 6 shows that poor families spend less on food and live in smaller homes that are in worse repair than affluent families. High-income parents have more cars, spend more on eating out, and are more likely to have health insurance than low-income parents. But whereas higher income yields better living conditions, better living conditions do not improve children's outcomes much. This is partly because relatively few American children experience the kinds of material deprivation that do them serious physical or social harm. Less serious material deprivations, such as not owning a car or not eating out often, seldom seem to leave permanent scars on children.

Some child-specific possessions and activities, such as the number of books a child has and how often a child visits a museum, do influence how well children score on cognitive assessments. But parents' income is only weakly related to whether children have these amenities. This is probably because these items cost so little that their distribution depends more on parents' tastes than on their income. Thus the amenities that are important to children's outcomes are weakly related to parents' income, whereas the amenities that are strongly related to parents' income are not very important to children's outcomes.

What I have called the "good-parent" theory holds that income improves parents' psychological well-being, which in turn improves their parenting practices. According to this model, as income increases, parents buy peace of mind. Chapter 7 shows that the relationship between family income and parents' psychological well-being is not so strong as many social scientists have thought. The relationship of parents' income to how they discipline their children, how often they talk with their children, how much television their children watch, and how often mothers read to their children is also weak. Thus it does not appear that parents' income appreciably influences children's outcomes through its influence on parents' psychological well-being or their parenting practices.

If parental income has a large influence on children's outcomes relative to other factors, trends in parental income should also predict trends in children's outcomes. My fourth strategy is to compare these trends. Chapter 8 shows that median parental income has increased since the 1950s, so the standard of living of children born in 1970 was higher than that of children born in 1960. Whereas some outcomes improved as parental income increased, others did not. Beginning in the early 1970s, income declined among poor parents but increased among rich parents, though few measures of children's success were redistributed to the rich. The fact that neither changes in the level nor changes in the distribution of children's outcomes parallel changes in parental income raises doubts about the importance of parental income per se. But many other things could have happened to affect these trends, so evidence of this kind cannot definitively show that the link between parental income and children's success is weak.

My final strategy for measuring the true effect of income is to look for exogenous sources of variation in income that are uncorrelated with parental characteristics. Variations in public policy are an obvious possibility. In the continental United States in 1992, the maximum Aid to Families with Dependent Children (AFDC) benefit for a family of three varied from a high of $680 in Connecticut to a low of $120 in Mississippi. AFDC almost exclusively served single-parent families. If parental income improves children's outcomes and all else is equal, children living in single-parent families should have had better outcomes in Connecticut than in Mississippi. Of course, all else is not equal when we compare Connecticut and Mississippi. We know this because outcomes for children in two-parent families, which cannot be much affected by welfare benefit levels, correlate with benefit levels. This happens because benefit levels correlate with state-to-state differences in educational policy, economic development, social attitudes, and other factors. All families are influenced by these factors, but only single-parent families are appreciably affected by the welfare benefit level. Thus if high welfare benefits help poor children, the gap in outcomes between children in single-parent and married-parent families should be smaller in states with high welfare benefits than in states with low benefits. Once I control all relevant state characteristics, the apparent effect of AFDC benefits on all outcomes is very small. In fact, higher benefits appear to widen the gap between children from one- and two-parent families for some outcomes.

None of these strategies would be completely convincing by itself. But all five strategies lead to the conclusion that conventional models overstate the importance of income to children's outcomes. They also show that the effect of income per se on most outcomes is smaller than many researchers have thought.

Chapter 9 discusses the implications of this research. The significance of the finding that income has a small influence on children's outcomes is likely to be misstated by those who want to believe that "income does not matter." It is therefore important to underscore a crucial fact: almost all the children in the samples I use, as well as most children in America, have had their basic material needs met. The results in this book imply that *once children's basic material needs are met*, characteristics of their parents become more important to how they turn out than anything additional money can buy. My results do not show that we can cut income-support programs with impunity; indeed, they suggest that income-support programs have been relatively successful in maintaining the material standard of living of many poor children.

Income transfers are one of a group of policies that I call "multipurpose." Such policies try to solve many social problems at once by changing one thing that seems common to them all. Multipurpose policies are in contrast to what I call targeted policies (such as Food Stamps), which more or less try to solve one problem with one program.

No one really expected that increasing poor parents' incomes would solve all the problems of their children. Instead, income transfers were expected to improve many outcomes a little. The cumulative effect of these improvements could be important.

Multipurpose policies are not easy to evaluate, and they will always be subject to political controversy. Social scientists cannot measure all the effects of such policies, so they are left to generalize from what they do measure to what they do not. Because by design the effect of a multipurpose policy on any one outcome is likely to be small, it will be easy to conclude that the policy is not worth the money. But someone will always be able to come up with an outcome that has not been assessed and argue that the effect of income transfers on that outcome will be large. Furthermore, when true effects are small, social science will often produce conflicting and unreliable estimates leaving a lot of uncertainty. Multipurpose policies might improve some outcomes but hurt others. Many people believe that income transfers improve poor children's behavior but make their parents less likely to work and marry. Although both effects are small, some people will give greater weight to the effects on adult behavior. They will want to reduce income transfers. Others will place greater weight on the effects on children. They will want to increase income transfers.

Furthermore, the fact that the influence of parental income is smaller than many social scientists and policy makers thought does not mean that income was not important in the past or that it might not be important in the future. As countries get richer, they often implement policies to reduce poverty among families hit by random catastrophes such as the death of a spouse, protracted illness, or job loss. When nations do this, poverty declines, but those who remain poor also become less like everyone else. When barriers to work are lowered, as they have been for both women and racial minorities in the twentieth century, those who still do not work are more exceptional than they were when these barriers were higher. Thus, as poverty rates are lowered and poverty becomes less dependent on bad luck, those who stay poor for long periods of time are increasingly likely to be those who suffer from multiple liabilities.

Faced with evidence that persistently poor parents differ in important ways from middle-income parents, some readers will want to help them and others will want to punish them. Historically, political conservatives have viewed the poor as willfully wicked and liberals have viewed them as helpless victims. It seems hard to believe that depression, alienation, and addiction are the results of human nature and that punishment can cure them. It is equally difficult to imagine what might really help persistently poor parents. To help parents, we must determine what kind of assistance they need. We have not expended much effort trying to do this, and when we have tried to find out what poor adults need, the services were often not available. The states and the federal government provide enough money for only a handful of welfare recipients to participate in job training and education programs, and those who do participate in such programs usually get only a few months of help. The government provides even less help when the problem is drug abuse, depression, or poor health. And it provides almost no help to the fathers of children on welfare. Instead of helping parents, we have increasingly concentrated on providing services for disadvantaged children outside their homes through Head Start, compensatory education, and other school-based programs. The juvenile justice system and child protective services also help troubled children and sometimes their parents, but usually only in a crisis.

Solving the social problems associated with poverty is not only a matter of changing the characteristics of the persistently poor; how individual characteristics manifest themselves in social behavior is partly determined by social structure and social institutions. Children get more education when they are required to stay in school until they are sixteen than when they are required to stay only until they are fourteen. Fewer mothers stay single when many men are "marriageable" because they have good jobs than when fewer men are marriageable because they are jobless or in prison. Fewer teenagers have babies when abortion is cheap and available than when it is prohibited.

I argue that when parents' income increases, children's material standard of living improves. But this improvement has little influence on children's test scores or behavior, on their educational attainment or labor-market success, or on teenage girls' chances of having a baby or becoming a single mother. We therefore have little reason to expect that policies to increase the income of poor families alone will substantially improve their children's life chances. Instead, parental characteristics associated with their income influence children's well-being. We have no direct way of knowing what these characteristics are. Because they are associated with parents' income they must be correlated with characteristics valued by employers, such as social adjustment, skills, enthusiasm, dependability, and hard work. In today's economy, parents with less than their share of these characteristics cannot make enough money to support themselves unless they get outside help. These same characteristics are valuable to children. Without outside help, parents who rank low on these characteristics find it hard to create an environment conducive to children's success.

As one teacher put it to me, "There are all kinds of poor. We have a lot of children of graduate students. They are poor in the economic sense only. They are rich in so many ways. We have the poor of Mexico and that is a lot poorer than anything here. Some of these kids have had nothing—no shoes, no clothes, no food. They move here when they are ten or so and they have had nothing, not even the most basic things. They are so poor they can be crammed twenty in a trailer with no food and babies all over the place, but they have a family unit. That's a different kind of poor than having no one there. We have the kids that are poor in all kinds of ways—poor in cognitive skill, lacking parents' support, and [economically poor]." This poverty "in all kinds of ways" is what Americans must now try to alleviate.

2

□ □ □ □ □

America's Response to Poverty

Most Americans agree on the general goal of equal opportunity for rich and poor children. They also agree that poor children should not suffer from hunger, homelessness, or lack of medical care. But they disagree about how to achieve these goals. This is nothing new: Americans have always disagreed about what to do about their poorest citizens. Every generation of reformers believes that it can solve the problems of poor children by devising new and improved policies, but none of these policies have eliminated poverty or closed the gap between rich and poor children's chances for success. In fact, the sequence of policies implemented over the last hundred years strongly resembles the sequence of policies implemented over the previous hundred years.[1] As Grace Abbott wrote in 1939, "We have proceeded along in a stumbling fashion, trying one method of care after another and often moving from bad to worse, and back again, in the search for a 'cure of pauperism'" (Abbott 1941, p. 9).

Policies for poor families with children are cyclical because Americans swing between the same two polar explanations of why poor children fail more often than rich children. I discuss these explanations more in the next chapter. Briefly, one explanation holds that the same factors that contribute to the low income of parents contribute to the failure of their children. Parents who are present-oriented, fatalistic, and unambitious raise children who are the same. Both generations tend to be jobless and poor. This theory implies that income support alone cannot prevent the ills that poor parents pass on to their children. This view dominated social policy from the early nineteenth century until the Great Depression, and it has resurfaced many times since.

The other explanation for poor children's failure emphasizes the material deprivations and parental stress that result from poverty. According to this view, children who are hungry, poorly housed, or suffering from untreated health problems cannot compete with children whose material needs are met. This theory implies that income support can cure many of the problems of poor children. It dominated social policy roughly from the 1930s to the mid-1970s, although versions of it were articulated before the 1930s and are often still heard today.

As first one explanation and then the other gains support, our ideas about the relative importance of income support and services for families also change. When public sentiment leans toward the "bad-parent" theory, legislators usually try to find policies to help poor children that by-pass their parents, either by providing services to children outside the home or—in extreme cases—by separating children from their parents altogether. When public sentiment leans toward the theory that money itself matters, legislators usually try to provide cash and noncash support to families so they can take care of their children at home.

Figure 2.1 is a schematic diagram of policies for poor families over the last two hundred years. There have been four basic kinds of policies.

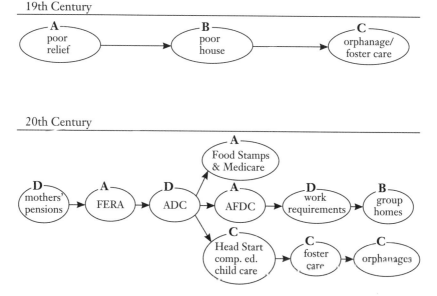

Figure 2.1 Policies for poor families with children

Those I designate with an A are policies that mainly provide cash and noncash transfers to improve the material well-being of poor families. Policies designated with a B require parents and children to live in group quarters as a way of discouraging the behaviors that supposedly make parents poor in the first place. Type C policies separate destitute parents from their children in an attempt to break the cycle of poverty. Type D policies provide supervision of poor parents who take care of their children at home. As Figure 2.1 shows, we cycled through A to C policies in the nineteenth century and began the twentieth century with Type D policies. In the middle of the twentieth century, we briefly returned to mainly income-support policies, but then began to repeat the cycle of the nineteenth and early twentieth century, apparently in reverse order.[2]

This history suggests that we have made little progress in our basic thinking about how to address the needs of poor children. This is because we have not learned much about the relative importance of parental income compared with other parental characteristics for children's success. Nor are we ever likely to resolve the dilemma posed by these alternate views of the poor unless we have more accurate information about the actual costs and benefits of the different policies we try.

From Moral Guidance to Income Support

Punishing Paupers

At the beginning of the nineteenth century, remnants of the English poor laws still dominated America's policies for destitute families. Towns and counties provided small sums of money, goods, and services to poor families. Officially, only evidence of need was required to receive such support from the "overseer of the poor," though many overseers probably enforced informal rules. Outdoor relief, as it was called, was largely intended to provide for the material needs of families. In Figure 2.1 this is a Type A policy.

Pauperism increased in the early 1800s. Americans blamed its growth on urbanization, immigration, and intemperance. But mostly they blamed it on outdoor relief (Katz 1986b, p. 16). Many Americans believed that destitution was the result of weak character, and that public help itself weakened character. Critics argued that such support led to "idleness" and "improvidence" and constituted "so many invitations to become beggars." They complained that the industrious poor were "discouraged by observing the bounty bestowed upon the idle, which they can only obtain by the sweat of their brow" (Katz 1986b, p. 17). In response, many cities and states began requiring destitute adults to enter almshouses or other institutions. The number of almshouses increased rapidly; for example, Massachusetts had 83 almshouses in 1824, 180 in 1840, and 219 in 1860 (Trattner 1989, p. 55).

Initially, destitute children were housed in the same almshouses as destitute adults alongside the aged, the infirm, and the insane. They were treated much the same as poor adults: they had to earn their keep or suffer. Boys were often assigned to indentured apprenticeships, and girls were sent to serve in wealthy households. Unlike outdoor relief, almshouses were not intended to improve the income or living conditions of the destitute. Advocates of almshouses claimed that they would promote work, temperance, and moral propriety among both adults and children. They argued that destitute children were brought up in "ignorance and idleness" in their own homes (Katz 1986b, p. 23). By contrast, in almshouses children's health and morals could be molded, preparing them for a productive future. Thus almshouses were mainly intended to deter adults and children from behaviors that would lead to destitution. This is a Type B policy in Figure 2.1.

At the same time that the number of almshouses was increasing, attitudes about the nature of childhood were shifting from "the certainty of children's evil to the probability of their good—and even the possibility of their perfection" (Trattner 1989, p. 105). In America the idea that children turned out badly because of society's influence was gaining credibility. In 1846 a minister, Horace Bushnell, published an influential book, *Christian Nature*, in which he argued that children were malleable creatures who could attain salvation through a healthful, nurturing environment, rather than a punitive life of labor. The view that children were "special beings" helped encourage the movement for compulsory public schooling and child labor laws. It also encouraged the view that almshouses were no place for children.

In 1861 Ohio passed the first statute requiring the removal of children from almshouses (Trattner 1989, p. 108). Over the next few years most states passed similar laws. Although Americans increasingly came to believe that children did not belong in almshouses, they remained convinced that a home with destitute parents was no place for them either. Disadvantaged children were increasingly placed in new children's institutions called "orphan asylums." The number of such institutions grew from 75 in 1861 to more than 600 by 1890. Between 1890 and 1900 alone at least 247 institutions for children were incorporated (Katz 1986b).

Despite their name, orphan asylums were not primarily for orphaned or abandoned children. A study of Philadelphia in the late 1800s found, for example, that most children confined to orphanages were there because their parents were either "too poor or too vicious" to care for them (Clements in Lindsey 1994, p. 14). In Figure 2.1 such institutions are Type C policies. Like their counterparts today, Americans in the mid-nineteenth century wanted to help poor children without helping their parents. They viewed parents' destitution as proof of their inability to provide a moral and healthful environment for their children. The cycle of pauperism could therefore be broken only by separating children from their destitute parents. Most destitute children were not institutionalized, of course, but this was the main publicly supported policy for such children, and it became increasingly common.

The logic of separating poor children from their parents did not require that they be institutionalized, however. Reverend Charles Loring Brace began a "placing-out" program in New York City in 1853. According to him, "Asylum life is not the best training for outcast children in preparing for the practical life. In large buildings, where a multitude of children are gathered together, the bad corrupt the good, and the good are not educated in the virtues of real life" (Trattner 1989, p. 110n). Brace's program and the others that followed its lead placed destitute, orphaned, and abandoned children with farm families in the Western states as a way of saving the children both from the influence of their destitute parents and from the corruption in orphan asylums.[3] Programs of this kind were the forerunners of today's foster-care system, except that today's system compensates foster parents in cash, whereas Brace's program merely offered them a child's labor. But states usually paid the costs of placing children in both foster care and orphanages.

As the number of children in both institutions and foster care increased, so did the costs to state governments. Critics began to argue that "it is poor economy to have a system operating in which children are being separated from their mothers" (Davis 1929, p. 375). Criticisms of the care children received in such placements also increased. Child advocates accused orphanages of providing cold, rigid, custodial care. Studies claimed that foster care created delinquents and criminals rather than upright citizens. Western states complained that the thousands of needy children sent there to foster care had become a drain on state budgets, because they grew up to become public charges, criminals, or otherwise in need of state aid. Some states passed laws prohibiting the placement of out-of-state children in foster care within their boundaries. Social workers, judges, and child advocates grew increasingly convinced that neither foster homes nor orphanages were conducive to children's moral development. The poor themselves complained that they did not want their children removed to distant farms where they were often never heard from again.

By the early twentieth century a new consensus had begun to emerge. According to this view, the best place for most destitute children was with their natural parents. To achieve this, government funds should be made available for at least some poor parents to care for their children at home.

Supporting "Suitable" Mothers

Many children were destitute because their fathers had died or deserted them. Although many widows with children and other single mothers did work, it was the belief of most Americans that when mothers work "the home crumbles" and the "physical and moral well-being of the mother and children is impaired and seriously menaced" (Leff 1973, p. 397). Thus women with no husbands to support them were not necessarily expected to support their children without outside help.

In 1911 Missouri and Illinois established the first statewide programs to aid needy children living in their parents' homes. By 1920, forty states had enacted similar legislation. These programs were known as "mothers' pensions," "mothers' aid," or "widows' pensions," because only families in which the father was permanently absent due to death, desertion, imprisonment, or insanity were eligible. Americans expected men to work, and they believed that cash assistance to families in which men lived would discourage such work. Thus though mothers' pensions marked a return to the outdoor relief that states had abandoned over the previous century, the relief now came with strings attached. Mothers' pensions are Type D policies in Figure 2.1.

The suspicion that poverty was a sign of weak character remained strong. Even supporters of mothers' pensions seldom believed that poor single mothers could be good parents without supervision. Almost all states required that mothers' pensions be limited to mothers who provided a "suitable home." Advocates of mothers' pensions viewed them as child-welfare programs, not income-support programs. Most Americans still believed that the moral environment had more impact on children than the material environment. Legislators, therefore, gave more attention to how mothers behaved than to how well they met their children's material needs. The programs were largely staffed by specialists in child welfare, who routinely visited mothers, overseeing the children's "health, education, dietetics, and home care" (Bell 1965, p. 11).

In most states supervision of mothers was a central rationale for switching from orphan asylums and foster care to mothers' pensions. Frank Loomis, the secretary of the Newark, New Jersey, Children's Bureau, summarized this point: "So long as the child remains in his home, the State supervises him in many ways which are discontinued if the child is removed to an institution" (Katz 1986b, p. 129). State legislators believed that giving destitute mothers money would be wasteful unless they could reasonably assume that "children will have a home which will provide at least the conditions necessary to make possible moral, physical, and mental development" (Nesbit in Bell 1965, p. 7).

Rules defining a suitable home varied by state. In some states tubercular parents or those who scored too low on intelligence tests were ineligible for aid. Mothers were also disqualified for crime, drunkenness, being a "poor disciplinarian," use of tobacco, and failing to provide religious instruction to children. Some families were forced to move from what social workers considered "morally questionable" neighborhoods to what they considered wholesome neighborhoods (Leff 1973, p. 412). But the most common reason for denying aid to families was either that the mother had an illegitimate child or that she had (or was suspected of having) an "improper" relationship with a man. In five states only widows could receive aid. In thirty-six states mothers who had been deserted were eligible as well. In twenty-one states divorced mothers were eligible. In only eleven states were unwed mothers even potentially eligible for mothers' pensions (Davis 1929). Even when divorced, deserted, and unwed mothers were eligible for aid, states often used suitable-home rules to deny them benefits. As a result, 82 percent of families receiving cash through mothers'-pension programs were headed by widows in 1931 (Leff 1973, p. 414). Of the forty-six thousand families receiving mothers' pensions, only fifty-five were headed by unmarried mothers (Heclo 1992).

Because of their vagueness, suitable-home rules were easily adapted to local and regional norms. Few black mothers received any aid, and in some Southern counties blacks were completely barred from receiving mothers' pensions. Overall, only 3 percent of all pensions went to black mothers in 1931 (Leff 1973, p. 414).

Because most mothers' pensions went to white widows who were certified as "suitable" by local social workers, it was easy for most white Americans to believe that these transfers supported only the truly needy and deserving poor. Consequently, mothers' pensions enjoyed widespread support. They did, however, have detractors, and their arguments sound familiar: mothers would spend their money recklessly; the money would "repress the desire for self-help, self-respect, and independence"; it would encourage fathers to desert their children; it would discourage "the great principle of family solidarity, calling upon the strong members of the family to support the weak" (Leff 1973, p. 404). Most supporters of women's suffrage favored mothers' pensions, but the militant wing of the movement argued that they would damage the cause of equality between the sexes by glorifying a mother's place in the home and discouraging women from work and independence. Detractors also argued that poor widows from other countries or other states would flock to the states that provided mothers' aid, and thus drain their budgets. Nonetheless, mothers' pensions retained support until the 1930s.

The Cycle Repeats

The Great Depression changed the way Americans viewed poor children and their parents. Mass unemployment meant that the poor were no longer a morally corrupt fringe; they were one's neighbor, one's friend, or oneself. The Great Depression demonstrated to many Americans that poverty was sometimes the result of bad luck rather than weak character, and that the social and economic forces that created poverty were often beyond the control of individuals.

During the Depression, many states ran out of money to fund mothers' pensions. Between 1929 and 1932, a third of the nation's private charities closed for lack of funds (Trattner 1989, p. 249). Nonetheless, President Herbert Hoover opposed federal aid to families, giving the same reasons as opponents of government transfers today: federal aid would stifle voluntary giving, demoralize recipients, discourage work, and create bloated, politicized bureaucracies. But though the idea that all Americans could earn a living if they tried had been popular when the economy was expanding, Hoover's insistence that this was still true in the early 1930s cost him his job.

Hoover's successor, Franklin D. Roosevelt, created the Federal Emergency Relief Administration (FERA) to coordinate federal welfare policy. FERA was intended to provide "sufficient relief to prevent physical suffering and to maintain living standards" (Patterson 1986, p. 57) through cash grants and a surplus commodity program. This was strong recognition that the material needs of families were important.

Because neither states nor private charities could afford to help all impoverished citizens, FERA assumed responsibility for many of the nation's children. It was not staffed by social workers intent on reforming the character of the poor (although one provision required local relief administrators to employ at least one experienced social worker); rather, it was staffed by civil servants who believed that the poor needed food and shelter, not moral guidance. In her presidential address before the National Conference of Social Workers at the end of the Depression, Grace Coyle noted, "There is no reasonable doubt that poverty itself is responsible for increased illness, physical and mental, that unemployment breeds unemployability, that crowded housing undermines family life, that under-nourished children will grow into incompetent adults" (Trattner 1989, p. 270). The role of state aid to poor families shifted from supervising poor widows to providing mass economic assistance to families. FERA administered financial aid uniformly, with no rules regarding suitable recipients other than that they come to a relief station and pass a means test. Until FERA was phased out, the United States had briefly recreated outdoor relief.

In 1935 the federal government passed the Social Security Act, establishing ADC. The act made the Social Security Board responsible for federal financial aid to families, and the Children's Bureau in the Department of Labor responsible for children's social services (Hanlan 1966). This was the beginning of a trend toward separating financial aid for families from social services for their children—a trend that eventually led to the split in policies shown in Figure 2.1.

The main goal of ADC, like FERA, was to improve the material well-being of families, not the behavior of parents. The Social Security Board noted that "homes in which dependent children now live do not, in many instances, conform to a minimum standard of decency and health or provide a minimum opportunity for a child's welfare. These conditions frequently result directly or indirectly from economic pressures . . . and may be eliminated by adequate assistance and services" (Bell 1965, p. 33). Thus the Board believed that in most cases poor mothers could raise their children adequately if they had the money to do so.

Although the Social Security Act emphasized financial help for poor families, it allowed states to retain many of their suitable-home rules and to set their own benefit levels. In most states families could not appeal a decision denying them aid. Partly for this reason, relatively few families, especially in the South, actually received aid before World War II. Only 360,000 families were on the ADC rolls in 1940—less than 1 percent of all American families. Nine states, five of them in the South, had fewer than 1,000 families on their roles (Piven and Cloward 1971, p. 117). Thus taxpayers could continue to feel confident that they were helping only truly needy and deserving families. This was especially important in the South, where resistance to federal aid to poor families was strong. Although the rhetoric of ADC emphasized material support for families, most states retained suitable-home rules. Therefore, I label this policy D in Figure 2.1.

The 1939 amendments to the Social Security Act placed some widows under Social Security rather than ADC. Eventually Social Security covered most widows, making ADC mainly a program for children whose mothers were divorced, abandoned, or never married. These were, of course, the mothers many states had previously considered unsuitable. States could, however, still use suitable-home rules to limit eligibility for ADC, and some Southern states renewed their efforts to assure that recipients were "worthy."[4]

This balance persisted until the 1960s, when the program was re-named Aid to Families with Dependent Children. Soon after that, lit-igation and pressure from both the welfare rights movement and the civil rights movement led the federal government to bar most of the nonfinancial eligibility rules that states had established, including al-most all suitable-home rules. In 1966 Congress passed the "Fleming rule," which required that children not be denied welfare benefits solely because they had been born out of wedlock, unless an alternative for their care, such as an orphanage or institution, was found. Since such placements were expensive, states were deterred from using illegitimacy to deny benefits. Social workers' discretion in deciding who could re-ceive benefits was greatly diminished when the Supreme Court declared their unannounced visits unconstitutional in 1969. The Court also struck down state-residency rules. The last vestiges of "moral guidance" were removed from welfare policies. The sentiments of the 1930s had finally taken hold, and once again for a brief time welfare became much like outdoor relief, an income-support program with few strings at-tached.

As AFDC came to resemble the outdoor relief of the early 1800s, programs to help poor children only while they were temporarily away from their parents became increasingly popular. Cultural and psycho-logical explanations for the failure of poor children helped to shift the emphasis of child-welfare advocates away from income support for poor parents toward education and social services for their children. Psy-chologists, educators, and children's advocates maintained that depri-vation in early childhood significantly limited child development, and that environmental stimulation could improve young children's cog-nitive growth. Thus early-childhood education and compensatory ed-ucation after children entered school could assure that poor children and rich children had the same opportunity to learn. If government policy could no longer either educate or cajole mothers to raise their children properly, the institutions that served children could still com-pensate for a deficient home life. Thus Figure 2.1 shows that in the 1960s, as the ability of social workers to certify AFDC recipients de-clined, antipoverty programs split into Type A programs, which were intended to improve the material needs of poor families, and Type C programs, which provided services to children while they were away from home.

No-strings-attached income transfers were short-lived. Suitable-home and administrative rules had been used to hold down the welfare rolls. When they were removed, the rolls grew. The number of AFDC recipients increased from 3.1 million in 1960 to 4.3 million in 1965, 6.1 million in 1969, and 10.8 million in 1974 (House Ways and Means Committee 1993, p. 685; Patterson 1986, p. 171). The rate of growth slowed once those who had been denied benefits were absorbed into the rolls: in the twenty years between 1972 and 1992, the number of recipients grew by only 28 percent, mainly reflecting population growth (House Ways and Means Committee 1993, p. 688).

Suspicion about the moral character of welfare mothers had always been widespread, but it intensified once local officials were unable to certify the character of recipients and the welfare roles increased. The militant tone of the welfare rights movement made it difficult to see welfare recipients as helpless, destitute mothers in need of a handout. The fact that many mothers of young children were now working at least part-time also made it hard to defend welfare for mothers who did not work.

Reinventing Moral Obligation

Until the 1960s, Americans' main concern about mothers' behavior had been whether they were sexually promiscuous, not whether they worked. Although many mothers did work, the mothers'-pension movement of the turn of the century promoted the principle that "to be the breadwinner and the home-maker of the family is more than the average woman can bear" (Leff 1973, p. 397). ADC was designed to "release from the wage earning role the person whose natural function is to give her children the physical and affectionate guardianship necessary . . . to rear them into citizens capable of contributing to society" (National Conference on Social Welfare cited in Garfinkel and Mc-Lanahan 1986, pp. 101–102). Stripped of the ability to regulate sex, legislators turned to regulating work.[5] Consequently, work requirements are labeled Type D in Figure 2.1

In 1967 AFDC was revised to require recipients to participate in job training and search for "suitable" jobs. The growing number of women in the labor market encouraged the notion that even single mothers could earn enough to support their families. But work policies for welfare recipients were never rigorously enforced, partly because alternative child care arrangements for their children were expensive. As a result, the proportion of single mothers who work has not changed much. In 1987, 54 percent of female heads of families worked, compared with 55 percent in 1980 and 52 percent in 1968 (Moffitt 1992). Meanwhile, the proportion of married mothers who worked rose from 37 percent in 1968 to 47 percent in 1980 and 53 percent in 1987 (Moffitt 1992). The fact that labor-force participation increased for married but not single mothers has contributed to the suspicion that welfare discourages single mothers from working.

Concern that welfare discourages work had historically rested on the belief that work is a moral virtue. In the mid-1980s Lawrence Meade (1986) argued that reciprocal obligations are essential to social order, and that the changes in welfare rules in the 1960s had undermined the moral authority of the state, especially its right to regulate the behavior of those who depended on it for income. Meade did not argue, as I have, that the state's inability to certify that welfare recipients were trying to help themselves undermined support for welfare. He argued that requiring work in return for welfare would help restore social order by setting clear standards of behavior. He called for a return to regulating recipient behavior for many of the same reasons that had led legislators to impose suitable-home rules in the early part of the century; namely, that the poor could not be trusted to do the right things without supervision. This view emphasized the obligations of the state as well as the recipients of its goodwill.

At the same time that legislators were trying to impose work requirements on adult welfare recipients, they continued to pursue policies aimed at providing more services to poor children outside the home, such as Head Start and compensatory education. Although these programs help children who live at home, I label them Type C programs, because they provide services to children only while they are away from home. Foster care is, of course, more similar to the nineteenth-century Type C programs. After Reagan's election, many welfare programs appeared to be in real danger. Recognizing the political sympathy evoked by children and the futility of lobbying for increases in cash transfers to their parents, child advocates built their agenda on the direct-service model of the War on Poverty. After 1980 child advocates' recommendations for increasing income transfers to poor families were usually little more than an afterthought. They usually promoted income increases indirectly by recommending additional child care funds so more poor mothers could work, or by recommending laws requiring absent parents to pay child support.[6]

In the 1960s liberals had supported child care, compensatory education, and other services because they believed that they would improve poor children's chances for success. Conservatives were less enthusiastic about such programs, partly because they did not believe that the programs would work, and partly because they believed that even if they did work they would cost too much. But in 1988 George Bush ran on a platform that advocated expanding Head Start to reach all eligible children. Bush also proposed expanding the school lunch program and the supplemental food program for Women, Infants, and Children (WIC). Many of these programs had suffered budget cuts during the early 1980s, but they enjoyed increased funding during Bush's administration.[7]

Moderate Republicans had come around to the liberal point of view on child-welfare programs for at least three reasons. First, research convinced many people that these programs worked. Second, the strategy for helping poor children by providing money to the institutions they use rather than to their parents is consistent with conservatives' beliefs about the character of poor parents. In order to promote these programs, child advocates had to claim that they were needed. To make this claim they had to point to the inadequacy of poor parents, or at least some poor parents. Neither researchers nor advocates intend to blame poor mothers for their children's cognitive and social problems; indeed, if they were to blame anyone, most would probably blame governments for stingy cash transfers or public schools for not being sensitive to the special needs of disadvantaged students. But the relationship between children's failure and their parents' ignorance and neglect is one that conservatives have long emphasized.

A third reason conservatives and liberals more or less agreed on expanding programs for poor children outside the home was that both groups felt that single mothers should work. When mothers go to work, there must be some provision for their children. Most liberals have supported both work and training requirements and child care allowances for poor families for the last twenty-five years. Conservatives have been more reluctant.[8] Once it became clear that poor single mothers could not find jobs that would pay enough to cover their child care costs, however, many moderate conservatives began to support federal expenditures for child care. As I show below, programs that provide child care for low-income families have been among the fastest-growing government programs for children.

During the 1980s, eliminating what had once been called home relief was again on the political agenda. But the alternatives that reformers had proposed in the nineteenth century—removing children from their families or supervising their mothers—were no longer viable options. Distrust of government had led liberals to restrict its role as an enforcer of moral values. Attempts to impose work requirements were too expensive. Instead, the government wrote checks and handed out food, housing, and medical care. Few Americans were happy with this "amoral" approach to handouts; some wanted to reimpose moral requirements, others wanted to end handouts entirely.

Since 1980 our commitment to providing income support to families with children has diminished steadily. The purchasing power of AFDC benefits declined by 12.7 percent during the 1980s and continues to decline. In contrast, our willingness to help poor children while they are away from their families has increased. The number of children in foster homes rose from 4.4 per 1,000 in 1980 to 5.9 per 1,000 in 1990. Government funding for child care is growing rapidly. Even our willingness to support "group homes" reminiscent of the almshouses of the 1900s has increased. In some cities homeless shelters for families with children have become permanent housing, and some politicians have proposed that poor teenage mothers be required to live in group homes, where they can be supervised in order to qualify for public assistance. Proposals to increase the number of orphanages are now taken seriously.

Changes in Government Expenditures on Poor Children

Government expenditures are not a perfect gauge of either policy makers' sentiments or the adequacy of policies. The need for expenditures changes over time, as does the efficiency with which the money is spent.

Nonetheless, trends in expenditures provide important information about the priority that legislators assign to programs of various kinds.

Table 2.1 shows trends in federal expenditures on poor children and their families for three types of programs: cash transfers, noncash transfers, and services for children outside the home. It shows expenditures for 1975, 1980, 1988, and 1992. I begin with 1975 because it is the earliest year for which information for many of the programs is available. Since several programs grew during the Bush administration, I show expenditures for 1988. For many programs 1992 is the last year for which information is available as I write this book.

Ideally, Table 2.1 should also include state and local government expenditures for poor families. The federal government contributed only about half of the total amount spent for AFDC and Medicaid. Many of the other programs listed in Table 2.1 require states to match federal expenditures. States and localities also have some programs directed at poor children that have no federal funding and do not appear in Table 2.1. Unfortunately, no national data on state and local programs currently exist. Even accounting for federal expenditures is difficult, because the federal government does not keep track of how states use all the federal money they receive.[9]

Two important changes dominate trends in social-welfare spending for poor families with children since the early 1970s. The first, which is well known to those who study these things, is that expenditures for cash transfers to such families increased at a much slower rate than expenditures for noncash transfers. The second, which is not so well known, is that expenditures on programs that provide services for poor children outside the home have increased rapidly since 1988.

Cash Assistance

Measured in constant 1992 dollars, federal expenditures for AFDC decreased slightly between 1975 and 1980, then increased by 16.3 percent between 1980 and 1992.[10] Overall, real federal expenditures for AFDC increased by 10.3 percent between 1975 and 1992, but the average monthly number of AFDC recipients increased by 21 percent, from 11.1 million to 13.4 million (House Ways and Means Committee 1993, pp. 690–691).[11] Because the share of AFDC expenditures contributed

Table 2.1 Federal government expenditures on poor children by year in millions of 1992 dollars[a]

Program	1975	1980	1988	1992
Cash assistance				
AFDC	12,473.0	11,829.9	12,300.3	13,754.0
Emergency assistance	172.2	186.6	305.2	267.0
SSI	236.3	433.8	729.3	1,715.2
Total	12,881.5	12,450.3	13,334.8	15,736.2
Noncash assistance				
Food stamps	6,373.9	9,037.3	9,454.6	13,754.0[b]
Medicaid	5,114.8	7,115.8	10,367.4	19,398.5
Housing assistance	4,270.5[c]	6,114.3	10,854.8	12,160.1
WIC	459.5	867.5	1,565.8	1,873.5
Total	16,218.7	23,134.9	32,242.6	47,186.1
Programs for children outside the home				
Head Start	993.6	1,256.9	1,435.5	2,201.8
Compensatory education	6,804.4	5,480.0	4,793.1	6,170.9
Child care	2,023.3[c]	1,635.6	1,545.8	1,997.5
Child nutrition	5,077.4	5,774.8	5,103.0	6,111.1
Foster care and adoption	315.1	529.2	1,176.0	2,429.4
Child welfare services	123.0	97.5	284.9	273.9
Total	15,336.8	14,774.0	14,338.3	19,184.6

Sources: House Ways and Means Committee (1993); Bixby (1990); *1982–83 Statistical Abstract of the United States; 1988 Statistical Abstract of the United States; 1990 Statistical Abstract of the United States; 1993 Statistical Abstract of the United States.*

a. Dollar amounts are inflated using the PCE fixed-weight price index (*1993 Statistical Abstract of the United States,* table 768). Amounts include administrative expenditures unless otherwise noted.

b. Number is for 1977.

c. Estimated.

by the federal government remained fairly constant and administrative expenditures declined only slightly, the real benefits per recipient decreased. The decrease per family was even larger, because AFDC families got smaller.[12]

The decline in real AFDC benefits per family appears to have accelerated in recent years. The decline in the average monthly benefit between 1990 and 1992 was greater than the decline between 1975 and 1980 or between 1980 and 1985. Not one state increased AFDC benefits enough to keep up with inflation between 1990 and 1993, and thirty-seven states either failed to increase AFDC benefits at all or reduced them (House Ways and Means Committee 1993, p. 666).

States can also provide emergency assistance to families with a 50 percent federal match if it is necessary to "prevent a child from destitution." Federal expenditures for emergency assistance grew throughout the 1970s and 1980s, but declined between 1988 and 1992. Much of this assistance is provided in the form of shelter and medical care rather than cash. The increase in emergency assistance during the 1980s was mainly due to states' increasing use of emergency assistance to house homeless families with children. Consequently, treating emergency assistance as if it were all cash overstates the growth in cash transfers.[13]

Before 1996 AFDC and emergency assistance were the only two programs that transferred cash on the basis of financial need alone. Supplemental Security Income (SSI) provides income to needy aged, blind, or disabled persons including children. Only 518,000 children received SSI payments in 1992 (House Ways and Means Committee 1993, p. 842), compared with 9.2 million children who received AFDC that year. But the proportion of poor children who receive SSI is increasing rapidly. Expenditures for children on SSI increased sevenfold between 1975 and 1992.[14] I have no way of knowing how many parents of poor children received SSI. SSI benefits were higher than AFDC benefits, and are increased annually to keep pace with inflation. More than a fifth of children who receive SSI live in hospitals and other institutions or with foster families.

Two programs, the EITC and the Child Care Tax Credit, increase the income of poor parents who work. Both are fast-growing programs, and before the Republican Party turned to the right in 1993–1994, both enjoyed considerable support because they provide an incentive for low-income parents to work. The EITC is means-tested, but it is not just for poor families. In 1993, when the poverty threshold for a family of three was $11,522, only 20.4 percent of expenditures for the EITC went to families whose income was under $10,000. Another 55.8 percent went to families whose income was between $10,000 and $20,000 (House Ways and Means Committee 1993, p. 1060). Less than half of the tax expenditure for EITC probably goes to officially poor families.

The Child Care Tax Credit accounts for about 60 percent of government expenditures for child care (Robbins 1991). It is not limited to poor families either. The credit is limited to the amount of a family's tax liability. Since poor families pay few taxes, the main beneficiaries of the tax credit have been middle-income families. According to one estimate, less than 1 percent of all tax-related child care benefits go to low-income families (Robbins 1991).

Both child care tax credits and the EITC are income-transfer programs. But they also give low-income parents an incentive to place their children in someone else's care for a large part of the day.

Noncash Assistance

Table 2.1 shows that as cash transfers to poor families declined between 1975 and 1980, expenditures on all noncash programs increased. Between 1975 and 1992, real federal expenditures for noncash transfers to poor families increased by 191 percent. This increase was due in part to the rapid increase in the cost of medical care. It was also partly due to the decrease in cash benefits available to families, since Food Stamps, housing subsidies, and some other noncash benefits increase as cash income declines. But much of the increase in noncash benefits was due to expanded eligibility or more generous benefits.

Medicaid provides free or subsidized health care for all AFDC recipients (as well as some others with low incomes, mainly the elderly, disabled, or "medically needy"). In 1986 Congress extended Medicaid coverage to pregnant women and children under the age of six whose family income was less than 133 percent of the poverty line. In 1988 it required states to extend Medicaid coverage for up to one year to former AFDC recipients who became ineligible for AFDC because their earnings from work increased. In 1991 Congress extended Medicaid to cover all poor children born after 1983. As a result of these changes, two-thirds of children living below the poverty line received Medicaid in 1991 (House Ways and Means Committee 1993, p. 1639), compared with about half in 1987 (U.S. Bureau of the Census 1990, table 148), even though the 1991 changes in eligibility were probably not fully implemented in that year.[15]

Congress also expanded the Food Stamp program repeatedly during the 1970s.[16] Both the number of Food Stamp recipients and the benefits they received grew slowly from 1981 to 1985, because the 1981 Omnibus Reconciliation Act delayed inflation indexing and limited eligibility. Congress liberalized Food Stamp eligibility in 1985, easing limits on assets and several forms of cash assistance and removing address requirements that had prevented the homeless from receiving Food Stamps. The Hunger Prevention Act of 1988 again increased Food Stamp benefits across the board. But most of the increase in expenditures on Food Stamps has been due to an increase in the number of eligible families and a decline in their real income. Measured in 1992 dollars, the maximum Food Stamp allotment for a family of four was $369 in 1975 and $370 in 1992 (House Ways and Means Committee 1993, p. 1632). Because of the decline in recipients' income, however, the average amount a person actually received was $64.50 in 1991 compared with $44.10 in 1972.

Expenditures on housing for poor families also increased rapidly in the 1980s, because of an increase both in the number of households receiving subsidies and in the subsidy per household.[17] The total number of households receiving federal housing assistance increased from 3.2 million in 1977 to 5.5 million in 1992. In constant dollars, the average per unit outlay increased from $2,680 in 1977 to $4,240 in 1993 (House Ways and Means Committee 1993, p. 1676).[18] The outlay per unit increased partly because federally subsidized units set tenants' rent at 30 percent of their income. Thus whenever tenants' real income declines, whether because of a decline in wages or in cash transfers, housing subsidies increase.

WIC provides nutritional counseling and vouchers for specific kinds of food for pregnant, postpartum, or lactating women and to infants and children up to age five who are "at risk" for nutritional deficiencies. Real expenditures for WIC increased by 116 percent between 1980 and 1992.[19]

Programs for Children outside the Home

Besides cash and noncash transfers to parents, three other major groups of programs try to help poor children: education programs, health and nutrition programs, and child protection and welfare programs. These programs provide money to institutions, such as schools, that try to compensate for deprivations at home, rather than providing money to the child's family to reduce those deprivations. Expenditures for such programs declined between 1975 and 1988, largely because of the decline in expenditures for compensatory education and child care programs. But expenditures on these programs increased by more than a third between 1988 and 1992.

Head Start is the best-known education program for poor children. Table 2.1 shows that real expenditures for Head Start have increased steadily since 1975.[20] Compensatory education services are supposed to continue Head Start's effort in elementary school, but they have never been as popular as Head Start. Real federal expenditures for compensatory education declined by 29.6 percent between 1975 and 1988 and then rose by about the same amount between 1988 and 1992.[21]

Estimates of the number of federal programs providing some form of child care range from twenty-eight to forty-six, depending on how child care is defined. Although Congress requires the states and the Department of Health and Human Services to compile information on child care services supported by the government, neither the number of children served nor the amount of federal expenditures is known. Furthermore, we can only guess at what proportion of federal expenditures for child care goes to the poor. Table 2.1 shows expenditures on child care from major funding sources, but it omits many smaller sources of funding.[22] Prior to 1988 the main source of child care funds was the Title XX Social Services Block Grant; because it failed to grow, federal expenditures on child care failed to grow. But federal expenditures on child care increased by nearly 30 percent between 1988 and 1992, mainly because of new legislation. New child care programs for AFDC families were enacted in 1988 as part of the Family Support Act's effort to get welfare recipients to work. Two additional programs (the At-Risk Child Care Program and the Child Care and Development Block Grant) were passed in 1990. These are still in the early stages of implementation. The Social Services Block Grant continues to be an important source of child care expenditures.

Under the National School Lunch Program, the School Breakfast Program, and the Child and Adult Care Food Program, the federal government provides both cash and surplus food to subsidize meals served in schools and child care facilities.[23] The Summer Food Service Program and the Special Milk Program also provide nutritional assistance to children. Real federal expenditures on these child nutrition programs increased between 1975 and 1980, declined from 1980 to 1988, then rose after 1988.

Federal expenditure for foster care and adoption increased fourfold between 1975 and 1992.[24] Under Title IV of the Social Security Act, this money supports any child in foster care whose biological family would have qualified for AFDC had the child not been removed from the home. The number of such children decreased from an average of 106,869 a month in 1975 to 100,272 a month in 1980. After that the number began to climb, reaching 167,981 in 1990 and 222,315 in 1992. Thus between 1980 and 1992 the number of children receiving transfers through Title IV more than doubled.[25]

The federal government also provides a 75 percent matching grant for state services that protect the welfare of children by trying to "provide substitutes for the functions parents have difficulty in performing."[26] These services include placing children in adoptive homes and assuring adequate foster care. But they also include preventing children from unnecessary separation from their families and restoring children to their families when possible. As a result, not all this money goes to services for children outside the home. No information is available on exactly how this money is used by the states or how many children are served (House Ways and Means Committee 1993, p. 889); nor could I find information on the proportion of expenditures used to preserve families. Real federal expenditures for this program have declined since 1988.

Overall, programs designed to help children outside the home grew by 25 percent in real dollars between 1975 and 1992. Expenditures for these programs increased by 30 percent between 1988 and 1992 alone. If we were to count child care tax credits and the EITC as transfers that support services for children outside the home, these increases would be even greater. Expenditures for cash assistance grew by 22.2 percent between 1975 and 1992, and even before the 1994 elections they were expected to grow very slowly or not at all over the next several years. Expenditures for noncash programs grew by 208 percent between 1975 and 1992, with most of this growth in the 1980s. Growth in expenditures for these programs is likely to be much slower in the foreseeable future.

To understand how these shifts in expenditures have affected children, we need to know how much we can improve poor children's chances of becoming competent, successful, considerate adults if we transfer, say, an extra $1,000 per year in cash or goods and services to their parents, and how much we can improve these same children's life chances if we spend $1,000 on the diverse institutions that serve them outside the home. The remainder of this book examines the likely effect of cash transfers to families.

3

How Rich and Poor
Children Differ

Young children are the poorest age group in the United States. In 1991, 12.4 percent of persons age sixty-five and older were officially classified as poor, compared with 21.1 percent of children under the age of eighteen. Child poverty rates grew from 14.9 percent in 1970 to 19.9 percent in 1990, with both years marking similar points in the business cycle (U.S. Bureau of the Census 1993, tables 736 and 739). Child poverty rates in this country are astonishingly high compared with the rates in other rich industrial countries. In the mid-1980s (the latest period for which data are available), 20.4 percent of children in the United States were poor, compared with 9.3 percent in Canada, 7.4 percent in the United Kingdom, 4.6 percent in France, 2.8 percent in Germany, and only 1.6 percent in Sweden (House Ways and Means Committee 1993, p. 1453).

In addition, poor children in the United States fare worse than more affluent children on almost every measure of well-being for which we collect data. There is no question that poor children suffer in the United States and that the nation is diminished by the wasted opportunity and productive effort that result from child poverty. High rates of child poverty and the social problems associated with it are the basis for the intuition that increasing the incomes of poor parents will help their children. But the grim facts of child poverty alone tell us little about what would help poor children. This is why Americans continue to debate the usefulness of income-support policies.

Measures of Children's Well-Being

No one measure neatly summarizes what we mean by children's well-being or life chances. What we study about children reflects what adults think is important for children, and what adults think is important depends on who they are. Policy makers, social scientists, and parents are unlikely to agree on a concise list of factors that define children's well-being. Even if they did agree on such a list, they would assign the various items on the list different weights. These days policy makers mainly want to know whether parents' income influences children's chances of depending on the government for help once they are grown up. Thus they are mostly interested in outcomes related to children's economic self-sufficiency, not their happiness or self-realization. For parents, the fact that their children become economically self-sufficient is seldom enough. They may want their children to prosper economically, but they may also be interested in their children's moral character, happiness, or social conscience.

Social scientists who study the effect of income on children's well-being emphasize different aspects of well-being depending on their discipline. Educators and developmental psychologists usually focus on children's cognitive test scores and behavior problems. Sociologists sometimes focus on "deviant" behavior among adolescents, such as teenage childbearing, dropping out of high school, and delinquency, or else on educational attainment and economic success in adulthood. Economists usually study the effect of parental income on adolescent labor-force participation and young adults' wages or family income. Thus different disciplines focus not only on different outcomes but also on different developmental stages.

Different disciplines also use different methods to study these relationships. Developmental psychologists tend to use small convenience samples, and they often try to approximate experimental conditions. Sociologists and economists who study the effect of income prefer large, nationally representative samples, and they usually rely on statistical inference rather than experiments to test hypotheses. As I discuss below, different disciplines also have different theories about why children's outcomes are correlated with their parents' income. Because academic disciplines focus on different outcomes and use different theories and methods, it is difficult to get a full picture of how much parents' income influences children's chances for various kinds of success.

How Large Are the Differences?

In response to debates about equal opportunity in the 1960s, social scientists began estimating the correlation between parents' income and children's (usually sons') earnings or income. In a rigid caste society the intergenerational correlation of economic well-being would approach one, whereas in a society characterized by equal opportunity and no genetic effects on earnings, the correlation would be closer to zero.

Estimates of the correlation between father's income in a randomly selected year and son's income in a randomly selected year are .20 or less (Becker and Tomes 1986; Behrman and Taubman 1990; Behrman et al. 1980; Sewell and Hauser 1975). But estimates of the correlation between parental income averaged over several years and sons' income averaged over several years are between .40 and .60, suggesting much less intergenerational mobility (Altonji and Dunn 1991; Gottschalk 1992; Solon 1992; Zimmerman 1992).[1] This finding underscores the importance of the number of years over which income is measured, a point to which I return in the next chapter.

A correlation of .45 between parents' and children's income implies that when parents have income at the fifth percentile of the income distribution, only 6 percent of their children will grow up to have family incomes above the median. Forty percent of their children will have family incomes in the bottom 10 percent of the income distribution. Findings such as this have encouraged the idea that parental income influences children's income and other outcomes correlated with income.

Table 3.1 shows children's outcomes by their parents' income. The NLSY includes two measures of young children's cognitive skills, the Peabody Picture Vocabulary Test Revised (PPVT) and the Peabody Individual Achievement Tests (PIAT). The PPVT is one of the most widely used and extensively validated tests of "receptive" vocabulary. Children are shown a series of four pictures and asked to choose the one that matches a word spoken by the interviewer. The PPVT can be viewed as a scholastic aptitude test for verbal ability or as an achievement test for vocabulary. It correlates well with measures of intelligence

Table 3.1 Children's outcomes by parental income group

Children's outcomes	Parents' income quintile					Mean SD
	Poorest	Second	Third	Fourth	Richest	
Test scores for five- to seven-year-olds						
PPVT	88.3	91.3	97.0	97.2	101.8	94.5 (16.5)
PIAT math	96.9	98.8	101.1	102.1	104.4	100.7 (12.5)
PIAT reading	101.9	102.9	105.6	107.1	108.2	105.1 (12.2)
BPI	109.7	108.2	106.4	104.9	103.7	106.5 (14.2)
Adolescent outcomes (in percentages)						
Girls who become teenage mothers	40.0	25.3	18.3	12.2	4.9	20.2
Teens who drop out of high school	34.1	22.8	15.9	7.5	6.5	17.3
Young-adult outcomes						
Years of education at age twenty-four	11.7	12.2	12.8	13.3	13.8	12.8 (1.9)
Years of education for high school graduates	12.6	12.9	13.2	13.5	14.0	13.3 (1.7)
Male workers' hourly wages (1992 dollars)	8.57	9.89	11.37	12.90	12.60	11.06 (6.34)
Male workers' annual earnings (1992 dollars)	16,772	20,860	23,306	26,168	26,168	22,639 (14,230)
Percentage of twenty-four-year-old men "idle" for the year	16.7	11.4	7.2	10.1	7.7	10.5
Percentage of women who become single mothers by age twenty-four	47.4	33.4	19.7	15.3	7.5	24.5
Income for twenty-four-year-old household heads (1992 dollars)	23,820	29,411	30,827	32,714	34,756	30,160 (19,253)
Percentage with welfare income	10.8	7.4	4.9	3.1	0.5	5.5

Sources: Estimates for children's test scores were computed from NLSY mother-child files by David Knutson. Estimates for other outcomes were computed from PSID data by Timothy Veenstra. For five- to seven-year-olds, income is measured in the year before the child took the assessment. For adolescent and young-adult outcomes, income is measured when children were fourteen years old. Wages and earnings are for men ages nineteen to thirty.

and is a good indicator of academic achievement.[2] The PPVT was normed on a national sample in 1980, and the norming was refined in 1990. It was then standardized to have a mean of one hundred and a standard deviation of fifteen.

Table 3.1 shows that the mean PPVT score for the NLSY sample of children who were five, six, or seven years old in 1986, 1988, or 1990 is 94.5, or 5.5 points lower than the national average. This is probably because the children of NLSY respondents were born to relatively young mothers. (The mean age of mothers at the child's birth was 21.5 years for the five- to seven-year-olds in the NLSY compared with about 23 years in the PSID.) This means that children of advantaged mothers are undersampled in the NLSY. It also means that the income distribution is somewhat more compressed in the NLSY. The gap in test scores between high- and low-income children might be somewhat understated as a result.

The PIAT measures the academic achievement of children in kindergarten through twelfth grade; in Table 3.1 I use the parts of the exam that measure math skills and reading recognition. Like the NLSY, the PIAT has been extensively validated. The PIAT assessments were normed in 1970 and standardized to have a mean of one hundred and a standard deviation of fifteen. Among five- to seven-year-olds in the NLSY, PIAT reading scores are 5.1 points higher than the national average in 1970. The average PIAT math scores for the NLSY sample are close to 100, which is higher than expected in this sample. These results reflect the fact that reading and math scores have improved since 1970.[3]

The PPVT and PIAT scores reported throughout this book are age-adjusted standardized scores.[4] For most analyses in the NLSY I use this sample of five- to seven-year-olds. I do not include older children because in the NLSY older children were born to especially young mothers; I do not include younger children because test scores for them are less reliable.

Young children who live in the poorest 20 percent of households (whom I refer to as low-income) score lower than the richest 20 percent of young children (whom I refer to as affluent) on all three measures of cognitive ability, but the size of the difference varies from test to test. Low-income children score 13.5 points (more than four-fifths of a standard deviation) lower than affluent children on the PPVT. At age six this represents about nine months of cognitive growth for an average child. Low-income children score 7.5 points lower (more than half a standard deviation) on the PIAT math assessment, and 6.3 points lower on the PIAT reading assessment.

The NLSY also includes a Behavior Problems Index (BPI). The BPI is based on mothers' reports of their children's behavior. Interviewers ask a mother whether her child "clings to adults," "cries too much," "has sudden changes in mood," "feels worthless or inferior," "worries too much," and so on. Higher scores indicate more behavior problems. The BPI was normed separately for boys and girls on a national sample in 1981. It is standardized to have a mean of one hundred and a standard deviation of fifteen. Table 3.1 shows that the NLSY sample averages more behavior problems than the national average. This is consistent with the lower scores on the PPVT, and it at least partly reflects the fact that these children are born to young mothers. Low-income children score 6.0 points higher than affluent children on the BPI. This difference might reflect class differences in mothers' interpretations of their children's behavior as well as differences in children's actual behavior.

Table 3.1 shows the likelihood that a girl will have a baby before she turns twenty and the likelihood that a teenager will drop out of high school.[5] For these two adolescent outcomes I measured parental income when the child was fourteen years old. The next chapter shows that parental income measured in only one year is not as strongly correlated with children's outcomes as parental income averaged over a longer period. Because parental income is measured in only one year in Table 3.1, the numbers understate the differences between children who grow up in low- and high-income families. Nonetheless, these differences are quite large. Forty percent of low-income teenage girls have had a baby before their twentieth birthday compared with only 4.9 percent of affluent girls. The dropout rates for high- and low-income teenagers differ by 27.6 percentage points.

According to Table 3.1, by the time children are twenty-four years old, those who lived in affluent households as adolescents average 2.1 more years of school than those who lived in low-income households at the same age. Among those who graduated from high school, low-income children averaged 1.4 fewer years of schooling. Young male workers who grew up in low-income households earn an average of

$8.57 per hour (in 1992 dollars), compared with $12.60 for those who grew up in affluent households. Their earnings, which are the product of their wages and the number of hours they work, are only 64 percent of the earnings of those who grew up in affluent households. Men raised in low-income households are much more likely than those raised in high-income households to be "idle" (neither in school nor working) when they are twenty-four years old. Nearly half of all women raised in low-income households become single mothers before their twenty-fifth birthday, compared with 7.5 percent of those from affluent households.

Among twenty-four-year-olds who head their own households, those raised in low-income households have 32 percent less household income than those raised in affluent households. Among these same twenty-four-year-olds, 10.8 percent of those raised in low-income households receive welfare, compared with less than 1 percent of those raised in affluent households.

Given these differences, it is no wonder that Americans are concerned about poor parents and worried about what to do for their children. Table 3.1 also shows, however, that income is not the sole determinant of any outcome. Even if the poorest children did as well as the median child, 18 percent of teenage girls would still have babies, and nearly 16 percent of teenagers would fail to graduate from high school. One-fifth of twenty-four-year-old women would still have been single mothers, and more than 7 percent of men would spend their twenty-fourth year idle.

Why Parental Income Might Be Important

Americans disagree about the relative importance of parental income and other parental characteristics in shaping children's outcomes. Folk theories do not always correspond with social science theory, but in this case the ideas of the educators I interviewed summarize the main theoretical positions of social scientists on the importance of income. Two theories of the relationship between parental income and children's well-being dominate social science. I refer to them as the "investment" theory and the "good-parent" theory. These theories lead to different predictions about how additional parental income influences children.

The Investment Theory

Some people argue that money is important because it buys the things that children need, such as food and medical care. Most Americans agree that children whose basic material needs are not met have a hard time acquiring the skills that help them succeed. One teacher told me, "We have kids who have no food. We had two kids we knew were not getting any food at home. They were only getting the breakfast and lunch at school. We called [the state] Social Services and they said, 'Well that's ok. They are getting two meals a day.' Can you believe that they said that? We gave those kids peanut butter and bread every week." An assistant principal in a mostly middle-class school in the South gave this example: "We had a little girl who had a toothache—her tooth was just rotting, and it really hurt. We couldn't find anyone to see her because Medicaid doesn't pay for dental. How could she learn in school?" Her colleague was more blunt, "You can't do without money, can you?"

The investment theory dominates economics and is usually associated with Gary Becker and his colleagues (Becker 1981; Becker and Tomes 1986). In this theory the relationship between parents' and children's economic success is the result of biological and other endowments that parents pass on to their children, combined with what parents invest in their children. Endowments include both genetic endowments, such as a child's sex and race, as well as "cultural" endowments, such as the value parents place on their children's education. Parents invest both time and money in their children's "human capital," especially by investing in their education, but also by purchasing health care, good neighbors, and other "inputs" that improve children's future well-being.

How much parents invest in their children is determined by their own values and norms, their ability to finance investments (which is influenced by their income and their access to capital), and the availability of alternative sources of investment, such as government programs. Since the return on investments depends on children's biological endowments, these also influence how much parents are willing to invest.

The investment theory holds that children raised in affluent families succeed more often than those raised in poor families, both because rich parents pass on superior endowments and because they can invest more in their children. In theory, income transfers (or other policies that equalize access to capital) could equalize parents' investments in their children. If investments were equal, the remaining differences in the life chances of children would be due to endowments and "luck." Since endowments are all the things parents pass on to their children, including biological, social, and psychological attributes, the remaining differences might be quite large unless, as some social scientists believe, income transfers could also equalize parents' social and psychological attributes.

As Becker and others have noted, government transfers to parents might be an inefficient way to increase investments in poor children. Parents are likely to spend at least some transfer income on themselves or on other goods and services that do not increase their children's human capital. One study finds that, on average, households spend only about 38 percent of their income on children. The remaining 62 percent is spent on the adults (Lazear and Michael 1988). This is partly because of short-term egalitarianism. In many realms children, at least before adolescence, need less than adults. They eat less and their clothes and entertainment cost less. Thus if a family tries to ensure that all members' needs are met equally, it will spend more on adults than on children. In addition, parents are not completely altruistic in their expenditure decisions. This same study finds that rich parents allocate a smaller proportion of their expenditures to children than poor parents. The fact that poor parents spend a higher fraction of their money on their children implies that transferring income from rich to poor parents would increase the aggregate amount spent on children. But it is not clear that this would result in improved child outcomes. If the additional money spent on children went for fast food or fancy gym shoes, the long-term benefits to children might be small.

Even if the government provides specific goods and services, such as education, to improve children's human capital, parents are likely to redirect some of what they would have spent on providing these things to other forms of consumption that do not improve their children's human capital. For example, if the government provides free health care for children, parents will switch some of what they would have spent on health care to other forms of consumption. Thus though transferring income or noncash benefits to parents will likely increase investments in low-income children, it will also increase the amount low-income parents spend on themselves. The political attractiveness of transfers depends on one's willingness to finance poor parent's expenditures on themselves in order to increase expenditures on children. This in turn depends on how much additional expenditures on children improve their outcomes.

The Good-Parent Theory

In contrast to the investment theory, the good-parent theory holds that low income reduces parents' ability to be good parents, not because poor families have less money to invest in their children, but because low income decreases the quality of nonmonetary investments, such as parents' interactions with their children. This in turn hurts children's chances for success. One teacher I talked to used her own experience to make this point. She explained that at one time she had been a single mother with two children. "Money is an issue, I mean it makes a big difference. I can remember being in school and what I was really thinking about was whether a check was going to bounce. I can remember, my kids were sick and I knew their father was supposed to pay for their medical things, but I knew he wouldn't pay unless I paid it first, then hasseled him to get it back. I worried, was it worth doing that? Do they really need to see the doctor? Are they sick enough? It was hard. Being poor is not easy."

There are at least two versions of the good-parent theory: the parental-stress version and the role-model version. The parental-stress version, which dominates psychology, holds that poverty is stressful and that stress diminishes parents' ability to provide "supportive, consistent, and involved parenting" (McLoyd 1990). Poor parenting, in turn, hurts the social and emotional development of children, which limits their educational and social opportunities. This theory implies that transferring income to poor families should alleviate stress, improve parenting, and thus improve children's outcomes.

The transactional theory of child development is a closely related elaboration of the stress theory (Parker et al. 1988; Sameroff and Chandler 1975; Scarr and McCartney 1983). It holds that children's characteristics, such as their cognitive ability, temperament, and health, shape their responses to the environment, and that these responses in turn transform the environment. A student teacher made this point. In describing why some children fail and others succeed, she said, "Well I know that it's not always just the parents. I come from a home, I mean my parents are always on me about my work, and they expect the same from my brothers and sisters. But my sister is determined she's just not going to do what she's supposed to. Every night my daddy, he'd say, 'Let me see your homework,' and she'd say, 'Oh we didn't have any today.' He'd call the teachers. I mean he knew she had to have some homework. It came to a point where there was nothing he could do. They went to counseling. They tried everything. But they couldn't take her hand and make her do it. So I know it isn't just the parents."

The example psychologists often use to describe the transactional theory is a child born prematurely to a poor single mother. The premature birth and the prospect of rearing a child alone with little money depress the mother. Because the child is immature, she is often passive. The child's passivity makes the mother feel inadequate, which deepens her depression. Because she is depressed, the mother is unresponsive to the child. The child gets little stimulation from the environment, and eventually stops seeking it. This further deepens the mother's feelings of inadequacy. By the time the child is two or three years old, she is behind in language and cognitive development (Parker et al. 1988). But no one factor in this scenario is the sole "cause" of the developmental delay—the child's low birth weight, her mother's depression, and the family's poverty all play a role.

This reasoning has led to the notion that children's success depends on the number of "risk factors" they face. Risk factors include such things as a poor home environment, poor health, and poverty. Some researchers treat poverty as a "marker" for risk factors, that is, as a correlate but not necessarily a cause of risks such as stress, poor health, weak social support, and maternal depression (Parker et al. 1988). Others treat poverty as a cause of such risks (Houston et al. 1994). The distinction is important. If poverty causes depression, transferring income to parents can alleviate their depression. But if parents who are depressed are poor because depression makes it hard to earn a living, transferring money to them will not reduce their depression. In this case we would have to treat parental depression directly.

Psychologists differ as to the relative importance of various risk factors. Some seem to believe that all risk factors are equally important. In the example of the premature child, they view the mother's poverty and the child's birth weight as equally important, because changing either would change the child's development by the same amount. Had we transferred money to the mother, she would have been less anxious about her child's birth and, therefore, less depressed and more responsive to the child. Yet a medical intervention that increased the child's birth weight would have gotten the same result, because the child would then have been more responsive, leading the mother to be less depressed and more responsive in return. Others suggest that because all risk factors are equally important, interventions must address all of them simultaneously. Advocates of this approach suggest interventions that address the material, emotional, and psychological needs of poor families.

Some researchers try to estimate the relative importance of various risk factors, usually by estimating their additive effect. If risk factors are additive, each one has the same effect regardless of other characteristics of parents and their children. The transaction theory suggests, however, that poverty interacts with other factors. When risk factors interact, the effect of a risk factor depends on other characteristics of parents and children. For example, an additive model assumes that parental depression has the same effect on children regardless of parents' income. An interaction model assumes that parental depression is more (or less) harmful for children when their parents are poor. No data set has enough cases to estimate all the potential interactions implied by such hypotheses.

The role-model version of the good-parent theory also emphasizes parents' interactions with their children, but it does not necessarily imply that poor parents are stressed. Instead, it usually holds that because of their position at the bottom of the social hierarchy, low-income parents develop values, norms, and behaviors that are "dysfunctional" for success in the dominant culture. This could be because the parents are unusually stressed, because their deviant values help reduce stress, or for reasons that have little to do with stress.

A common variation of this hypothesis is that behaviors which appear to be dysfunctional from the point of view of the middle class are in fact a rational response to poverty. An assistant principal in a school in which nearly all the students are economically disadvantaged described it this way: "A lot of time the parents want to have expectations for their kids. But they think it doesn't do any good to have expectations if you don't think it's ever going to be in the reach of the child. So they don't follow through. Lack of hope. That is one of the most profound things. Simply the lack of hope. You take most of the parents that we work with and they would like to hope that their child will go to college, but they don't really see a way that they are going to make that happen."

A teacher in an affluent suburb of Chicago who tutored students on the impoverished west side of the city saw the same thing. "The expectation there was that your kid—no matter how bright your kid was—he was going to fail. I mean that was the expectation. To be streetwise was a much better value. Most of them thought that they were going to live in that part of the city where they had been brought up for the rest of their lives. And that was just the way it was. It was almost like it was preordained was the feeling I got from the parents and the kids. They had the idea that . . . no matter what they did they were going to fail." If parents believe that their children cannot succeed in school, not valuing education will reduce feelings of failure. Since children tend to model their own values and behavior on those of their parents, parents' "dysfunctional" values and behaviors are transmitted to their children. As a result, poor parents are "bad" role models for their children. If generations of irregular employment and discrimination result in street skills seeming more valuable than academic skills, parents will be more likely to encourage their children to acquire street skills than to study or stay in school.

This version of the good-parent theory implies that neither increasing parents' incomes nor providing parents with the means to invest in their children's human capital is likely to improve children's life chances in the short run. Instead, parents' values, attitudes, and behavior must be changed, a process that is likely to require a permanent change in the opportunity structure. This version of the role-model hypothesis is usually called the "culture of poverty" hypothesis and has been politically controversial. Conservatives argue that if parental values and norms account for both parents' poverty and the failures of their children, transferring income to poor parents without changing their attitudes and behaviors will not only fail to help poor children but could actually hurt the children by reinforcing the parental values that result in poverty. They argue that the values and attitudes of the poor will change only in response to the right incentives. Liberals agree that the incentives should be changed, but by this they usually mean that the government must work to change the structural circumstances that reinforce "dysfunctional" values and behavior, including racism, economic segregation, and segmented labor markets. Once the structural changes create a "level playing field," parents will change (Ogbu 1981; Wilson 1987).[6]

The role-model hypothesis applies mainly to families experiencing long-term poverty. For families experiencing short-term poverty, stress is likely to be high but changes in basic values are likely to be rare. Indeed, the role-model hypothesis often assumes that low-income parents change their values over the long run precisely because this is an effective way of reducing the stress caused by economic stringency and deprivation.

All these theories try to describe how income influences children's outcomes. But it is possible that the problems associated with poor children are a result not of low income but of parental characteristics that cause their income to be low and also influence their children's outcomes. In this view, parents' attitudes, values, and behavior influence children's chances for success. One teacher at a school in Georgia was typical of those with this view. She told me emphatically, "The amount of money that somebody makes does not determine [how well his or her child does in school]. It's what they do with their money and the time they spend with their children." She attributed her own success growing up in a family without much money to parents who had high expectations for her. "They were responsible. They made sure I was clothed and fed, and then they expected me, when I went to school, to do well. They checked up on me to make sure I was doing well. They were involved in school. They always went to PTA. They kept up with my report cards. They expected me to behave. They wanted more for me than they had."

Some folk theories still hold that poverty improves character. A young student teacher thought her family's poverty led her to a college education. She explained that because of her family's poverty, "I didn't fit in (with other children) style-wise. I've never fit in style-wise, I mean—clothes-wise. So I decided to fit in with the smart crowd. That's why I made good grades and all. I thought if I can't fit in with a crowd that is popular and has money, I'll fit in with this other crowd." Nevertheless, almost no empirical evidence supports the idea that poverty benefits children.

Figure 3.1 is a schematic overview of these theories about how parental income affects children's outcomes. It shows that observed parental characteristics (X) affect both parental income (I) and children's outcomes (O). Many parental characteristics that we cannot measure, what I call unobserved parental characteristics (Z), also affect both parental income and children's outcomes. The investment theory holds that income affects children's outcomes by affecting a family's consumption and investments in its children (C). The parental-stress theory holds that income affects parents' psychological well-being (P), which in turn affects children's outcomes.

Children from low-income families score lower on tests of cognitive skill than children from affluent families, are more likely to have babies as teenagers or become young single mothers, and are more likely to drop out of high school and receive fewer years of education. Young men raised in low-income families work fewer hours and earn lower wages than those raised in affluent families. Social scientists have developed several hypotheses about why poor children fare worse than affluent children, most of which imply that parental income per se affects children's outcomes.

All the social science theories about the influence of parental income on children's outcomes recognize that poor parents differ from rich

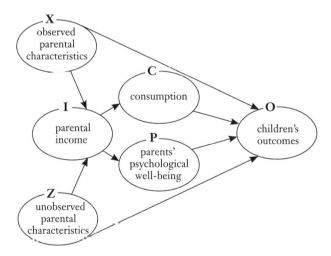

Figure 3.1 Heuristic income model

parents in many ways besides their income. In order to determine the true relationship between parental income and children's outcomes, we would need to compare children whose families have different incomes but are alike on all the characteristics that affect both parental income and children's well-being. The next chapter reviews studies that have tried to do this using conventional statistical models.

4

Conventional Estimates of the Effect of Income

No one thinks that low income is the only cause of poor children's problems. Low-income parents differ from high-income parents in ways other than income. For example, low-income parents have less education and fewer skills than high-income parents. These factors influence how much they earn and their children's chances for success. When social scientists try to estimate what would happen if poor parents' income increased, they usually try to compare children whose families differ in their income but are alike on at least some of these other factors.

In the first part of this chapter I review what other researchers have found when they have tried to estimate the effect of income on children's outcomes controlling some parental characteristics. I refer to the results of these studies as "conventional reduced-form" estimates. A reduced-form model is one that does not try to identify the mechanisms through which income affects children's outcomes. It just tries to estimate what would happen if families were simply given additional money. A reduced-form estimate, therefore, omits living conditions including neighborhood characteristics, parents' psychological well-being, and other mechanisms linking income to outcomes. By conventional I mean estimates that control some but not all the parental characteristics that affect both parental income and children's outcomes (independent of their effect on parental income). I refer to such models as conventional because they are the ones most researchers have estimated. Figure 4.1 is a schematic representation of a conventional reduced-form model.

Many of these studies have found that parental income has an important effect on children's outcomes, but because they do not control all the parental characteristics that could influence both parents' income and children's outcomes, they are likely to overstate the true effect of income. Nonetheless, in the second part of this chapter I use the data described in Chapter 1 to produce my own conventional reduced-form estimates, because these provide an invaluable baseline for assessing whether my samples are typical or atypical.

What Other Studies Show

For simplicity, I consider only studies that control at least two parental characteristics that are likely to affect both income and children's outcomes.[1]

With one exception, recent studies that control parental characteristics and measure parental income over five or fewer years show that a 10 percent increase in parental income increases children's earnings by 1.3 to 2 percent, with a median effect of 1.8 percent.[2] The exception, Behrman et al.'s (1980) estimate of 6 percent, is considerably larger than any of the others. The authors attribute this to the length of time over which they measure both parental income and children's earnings. They find that a 10 percent increase in one year of parental income increases children's earnings during young adulthood by 1.6 percent. The same increase in parental income averaged over 10 years increases children's earnings averaged over the same number of years by 6 percent.[3]

Like others, Shea (1995), using PSID data, finds that a 10 percent increase in fathers' income increases sons' income by 2.2 percent once

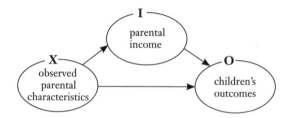

Figure 4.1 Conventional reduced-form model

fathers' education, occupation, race, and whether the sons live in a city and in the South are controlled. Then, however, Shea compares sons whose fathers were members of unions with sons with the same observable characteristics whose fathers were not union members. He argues that men who belong to unions receive higher wages than men with similar characteristics who do not belong to unions. If parental income influences children's income, children of union fathers will have higher nonunion incomes than children whose fathers were not union members, since this "union premium" is mostly due to luck. Shea finds that once he controls fathers' union status, the effect of fathers' incomes on sons' nonunion incomes drops to close to zero.

Previous research suggests that a 10 percent increase in parental income averaged over several years increases children's education by between .02 and .11 years.[4] To give some perspective to this difference in education, consider that in 1990 the difference in median years of education between blacks and whites was only .30 years, a difference that appears to have large social and economic consequences.

Parental income influences educational attainment by affecting both high school graduation and years of secondary schooling. One study finds that parental income has hardly any influence on teenagers' chances of dropping out of high school (Haveman et al. 1995). But another finds that parental income has a large effect on teenage girls' chances of dropping out (Shaw 1982). It found that when family income doubled from $4,000 to $8,000 (1967 dollars), the chance that white teenage girls in intact families with mothers who had graduated from high school will drop out of high school decreased from 13 percent to 8 percent. The same change resulted in a decrease from 30 percent to 19 percent for black girls. The declines were even greater for girls whose mothers had not graduated from high school.

The one study I could find that estimates the effect of parental income on teenage childbearing (Haveman et al. forthcoming) finds that parental income has hardly any effect on teenage out-of-wedlock childbearing.

One study tries to estimate the effect of parental income on children's cognitive test scores and behavior problems. Blau (1995), using NLSY mother-child data, finds that a $10,000 (1979 dollars) increase in parental income measured over the child's entire life increases the child's PPVT score by 12.8 percent of a standard deviation, the PIAT math score by 10.6 percent of a standard deviation, the PIAT reading-recognition score by 14.3 percent of a standard deviation, and reduces the score on the BPI by 19.8 percent of a standard deviation. Blau uses several techniques to control unobserved parental characteristics. First, he compares siblings whose parents' income changed. If parental income influences children's outcomes, siblings who are raised when income is higher ought to score higher. This model controls parental characteristics that remain the same over time. Second, Blau compares cousins whose mothers were both in the NLSY sample. He assumes that this controls unobserved parental characteristics common to sisters. He finds that these techniques for controlling unobserved parental characteristics usually reduce the apparent effect of income.

I was unable to find any studies that estimate the effect of parental income on young children's cognitive test scores, single motherhood, or male idleness.[5] But several studies estimate the effect of living in a family whose income is below the official poverty threshold.

Poverty or Income?

Many studies assess the effect of parents' "poverty ratio" rather than the effect of their income on children's outcomes. The poverty ratio (or the income-to-needs ratio, as it is sometimes called) is a family's total income divided by the U.S. government's poverty threshold, which varies according to a family's size and the age of its members. A poverty ratio less than one means that a family is officially poor. The adjustments for age built into the poverty line are quite small, but the adjustments for size are very large. When families of three or more double in size, their income must increase by 85 percent to keep their poverty ratio constant. This adjustment is not based on either a sound theoretical rationale or solid empirical findings.[6]

Determining how much a change in household size alters a family's income needs requires an equivalence scale that shows how much money families of different sizes need to be equally well off. But no one adjustment makes families equally well off in all respects. Scales that try to equalize adults' subjective well-being require small adjustments for household size (Rainwater 1974; Vaughn 1984), whereas scales that try to equalize households' material well-being or consumption require larger adjustments (Lazear and Michael 1988; Mayer and Jencks 1989;

Van der Gaag and Smolensky 1981). Social scientists disagree about whether the adjustments implied by the poverty thresholds are too large or too small.

Table 4.1 shows how much more income a family would need if its size doubled from, say, three to six members for the children's outcomes to remain unchanged. It shows, for example, that if family size doubles, family income would have to increase by 205 percent for children's PIAT reading scores to remain the same. If we want to adjust income for household size in a way that equalizes cognitive test scores, teenage childbearing, dropping out of high school, or male idleness, the size adjustment implied by the poverty thresholds is too small. In fact, the equivalence adjustments in Table 4.1 imply that for cognitive test scores

Table 4.1 Percentage increase in income required to offset the effect on children's outcomes of doubling household size

Children's outcomes	Percentage increase
U.S. poverty line	85
Test scores at age six	
PPVT	154
PIAT math	128
PIAT reading	205
BPI	48
Adolescent outcomes	
Probability of teenage childbearing	98
Probability of dropping out of high school	95
Young-adult outcomes	
Years of education	83
Years of education for high school graduates	76
Male workers' hourly wages	9
Male workers' annual earnings	27
Probability of male idleness	117
Probability of single motherhood	85

Sources: Estimates for children's test scores were computed from NLSY mother-child files by David Knutson. Estimates for other outcomes were computed from PSID data by Timothy Veenstra. Size adjustments are the absolute value of b_1 / b_2 from the following model:

$$O = b_1 \, (\log)\text{Income} + b_2 \, (\log)\text{Family Size},$$

where O is a child's outcome.

For five- to seven-year-olds, income is measured in the year before the child took the assessment. For adolescents and young adults, income is measured when children were fourteen years old.

and male idleness, family income must more than double to offset the effects of doubling family size. It follows that doubling family size is more detrimental to these outcomes than halving family income.

It is hard to believe that adjustments this large are solely due to the reduction in economic resources reaching any given child. When a family doubles in size it does not need to double the space it occupies, the number of televisions or cars it owns, or the amount of food it buys. This is why the official poverty thresholds rise less than 100 percent when family size doubles. The very large income adjustments required to offset an increase in family size presumably reflect the fact that parents cannot give children in large families as much time and attention as they could if the family were small. Offsetting these costs may require more than a proportional increase in income. If we want the poverty line to be a proxy for material well-being, the size adjustments of the poverty thresholds may be about right (Mayer and Jencks 1989). But if we want the poverty line to be a proxy for broader aspects of children's life chances, these adjustments might be too low.

The fact that the importance of family size varies so much from one outcome to another implies that family size and income should not be concatenated into one measure, such as a poverty ratio, unless we know exactly what we want to measure. Substituting the poverty ratio for parental income will exaggerate the importance of income to children's well-being in some cases, because the effect will be inflated by the inclusion of family size. In other cases the opposite will happen. Nonetheless, when researchers estimate the effect of the poverty ratio on children's outcomes, they are mostly estimating the effect of income. This is because family size varies less than family income, at least among families with children.

Studies estimate that increasing parental income from less than the poverty line to between one and two times the poverty line—an increase of about 100 percent—is associated with an increase of .15 to .25 years of completed schooling.[7] Haveman et al. (1995) find that the same income increase reduces a child's chances of dropping out of high school by only one percentage point.[8] They also find that parental income has a very small effect on teenage out-of-wedlock childbearing.[9]

Studies that try to determine the effect of parents' income on children's cognitive test scores highlight more than others the difficulty of interpreting the effect of income. Children's cognitive ability is partly a result of genetics and partly a result of environment. Parents' income is due partly to their own genetic endowment, which they pass on to their children. Estimating the effect of parents' income on children's cognitive ability without controlling parental ability is therefore likely to overstate the importance of parents' income, because the apparent effect of income will be due in part to genes that parents pass along to their children. Because there is no agreement about how large the genetic component of cognitive ability is, the size of the bias is unknown.

Studies that control family-background characteristics such as mothers' education and family structure, but not parents' cognitive skills, find that increasing parental income from less than the poverty line to between one and two times the poverty line raises test scores of children by about one-third of a standard deviation (4.7 to 6.3 points, depending on the assessment and the age at which children are tested).[10]

The one study that controls mothers' cognitive test scores produces a much smaller estimate of the effect of income on children's scores. Korenman et al (1994) control mothers' AFQT (Armed Forces Qualification Test) scores, which are highly correlated with measured IQ. They estimate that the difference between children below the poverty line and those between 1.85 and 3 times the poverty line is 2.6 points on the PPVT, 4 points on the PIAT math, and 4 points on the PIAT reading recognition. Since the mean income for parents below the poverty line is less than a quarter of that of parents whose income is between 1.85 and 3 times the poverty line, this implies that doubling income results in an increase of less than 1 point in PPVT scores and 1.3 points in reading and math scores.[11]

Mothers' cognitive ability is likely to account for a considerable part of the apparent effect of income on children's cognitive scores. No study provides data on fathers' cognitive skills, but they may also account for part of the apparent effect of income. Scarr and Weinberg (1978) show that increasing family income by 1 standard deviation increases the IQs of parents' biological adolescents by .145 standard deviations. But the same increase in income appears to decrease adopted children's IQs by .027 standard deviations. The fact that income appears to affect biological children more than adopted children suggests that income may be a proxy for parental genes. Even for biological children, the effect of income is halved once parents' IQs are controlled. But controlling adoptive parents' IQs hardly changes the effect of family income on adopted children's IQs, which is negligible in any case. These findings should not be taken too literally—the sample was small and parental income is measured in only one year. The estimated effects of income on test scores were not statistically significant in their study, even for biological children. In addition, the socioeconomic status of the families in this study was unusually high. If the effect of income is strongest near the bottom of the income distribution, as seems likely, this study would not capture its effect.

The one study that estimates the effect of income on behavior problems (Korenman et al. 1994) shows relatively small effects.

The disparity in estimates is due to differences in the definition of income, the period over which income is measured, and which characteristics of parents and families are controlled. Differences can also depend on the data set and the way the outcome is measured.

All the reduced-form estimates of the effect of income and the poverty ratio on teenage out-of-wedlock childbearing and dropping out of high school are very small. But all these estimates are by the same researchers using one data set. I could find no estimates of the effect of parental income or the poverty ratio on a girl's chances of becoming a single mother or on male idleness.

Reviews of published research, such as the review in this chapter, might not provide a representative picture of the results that researchers have actually obtained. The true effect of income is the effect controlling all the parental characteristics that influence both parental income and children's outcomes. If true effects are small, researchers will sometimes get substantial significant effects, often get small statistically insignificant effects, and sometimes get small statistically insignificant effects with the "wrong" sign. But significant effects with the expected sign are more likely to be published than insignificant effects or effects with the wrong sign. Academic journals are reluctant to publish papers in which effects are not statistically significant. Such results are considered weak evidence, because they are consistent with the conclusion that the true effects are positive, negative, or zero, depending on one's prior expectation.

Researchers themselves also tend to have preferences for particular findings, both because they know what is easiest to publish and because they have theoretical and political agendas to promote. Since social scientists who write about the effect of income often select this topic because they believe income is important, they are inclined to believe results showing that income matters and discount results showing the opposite.

In addition, when true effects are small, estimates will be sensitive to what researchers control, so published estimates will vary a lot. Thus even if the true effect of income is small, a review of published papers is likely to find that though income usually has an effect in the expected direction, the size of the effect varies quite a lot. This is what I have found in my review of previous research.

Re-estimating the Conventional Model

In this section I estimate the effect of income using the same approach as most previous research. That is, I estimate the effect of income controlling observed parental characteristics that are likely to affect both parental income and children's outcomes. My conventional estimates do not control all the things that influence both parents' income and children's outcomes; therefore, like the other studies I reviewed, they are likely to overstate the importance of income. Nonetheless, they provide an important baseline for estimating the true effect of income.

Estimates that rely on only one year of parental income are likely to understate the impact of long-term or "permanent" income on children. It is useful to think of annual income as having two components. The first is a stable or "permanent" component. The second is an unstable or "transitory" component. Most economists believe that the transitory component of income has little effect on a family's living standard, because families will borrow against future income or draw down savings when income is low in order to keep consuming at the level of their permanent income. Conversely, when income is high, families will pay off their debts or save rather than consuming more. If all this were true, and if income affected children's outcomes by affecting their living standards, the transitory component of income would have no effect on children's outcomes once we controlled permanent income. Because a measure of annual income includes this transitory component, it will understate the effect of changes in the permanent component.

Estimating the true effect of parental income on children's outcomes is also complicated by ambiguity about whether other parental characteristics are causes or consequences of parental income. Some studies control factors (such as neighborhood characteristics) that at least partly depend on parental income and plausibly affect children's outcomes. Yet the bias introduced by controlling these "endogenous" factors is often small. Controlling neighborhood composition, for example, does not appreciably reduce the effect of parents' income on children's earnings or educational attainment.[12] In some cases estimates that control neighborhood effects are larger than those that do not. For example, Brooks-Gunn et al. (1991) control measures of neighborhood social composition and find that an increase in parental income from below the poverty line to between one and two times the poverty line is associated with a 2.8 percentage point reduction in teenage out-of-wedlock childbearing. Using the same data set, but not controlling neighborhood composition, Haveman et al. (1995) find that the same increase in parental income is associated with a decrease of less than one percentage point. When Duncan (1994) controls neighborhood characteristics, he finds that increasing parental income from below the poverty line to between one and two times the poverty line is associated with .34 additional years of schooling for white men, .17 years for black men, .30 years for white women, and .31 years for black women. With the exception of the estimate for black men, Duncan's estimates are larger than any of the estimates that omit neighborhood characteristics.

This means that living in a "bad" neighborhood does not account for much of the effect of parents' income on these outcomes. It suggests that some of the reduced-form estimates are low compared with other estimates.

The characteristics I control include parents' age at the birth of the child, family size, whether the child is black, and parents' education.[13] When I estimate the effect of income on cognitive test scores and behavior problems, I also control whether the mother is Hispanic, her score on the AFQT, and the child's sex and age. When I predict the probability of dropping out of high school and years of education, I also control the child's sex. When I estimate young men's labor force outcomes, I also control the year in which the child turned twenty and the county unemployment rate. Appendix A describes these variables in more detail.

It is not entirely obvious that all these factors are causally prior to parental income and should therefore be controlled. Everyone agrees that parents' race is not the result of their income. Mothers' education, AFQT score, and age when the child was born might depend on the grandparents' income, but they do not depend on the parents' own income. Since they could also influence children's outcomes independent of their effects on mothers' income, I, like many other researchers, controlled them.

Family size is a more ambiguous case. As we have seen, it has a strong effect on many children's outcomes. After the first sibling, children's test scores and educational attainment decline and teenagers' chances of having a baby increase. A couple's income can obviously influence how many children they decide to have. If family size depends on income, controlling it will lead to overestimates of the effect of giving parents more income, because some of the benefits of extra income will be offset by increased fertility. Parental income also depends partly on family size, however, because women with many children work fewer hours and earn lower wages than those with fewer children (Korenman and Neumark 1992). The number of children is less important to how much fathers work. The number of children also affects the amount of public assistance a poor family can receive. Most studies that try to estimate the importance of parental income therefore control family size, either explicitly or because they estimate the effect of the poverty ratio rather than income. I do the same. Fortunately, the relationship between income and number of children is relatively weak, so treating family size as endogenous does not greatly alter any of my findings.[14]

Unlike many of those whose studies I reviewed in the previous section, I usually do not control the marital status of parents. Children from single-parent families appear to fare worse than those from married-parent families on just about every measure of children's well-being. Previous research suggests that this is in large part because single-parent families are poorer than married-couple families (McLanahan and Sandefur 1994). The fact that single-parent families are poorer than married-parent families has led many researchers to assume that family income depends on parents' marital status. If that fact accounted for the entire correlation between income and marital status, we would want to control parents' marital status when we estimate the effect on children of giving parents more money. But men and women with low incomes are also less likely than those with high incomes to marry when they have a child, and when low-income parents do marry they are more likely to separate and divorce. Thus parents' marital status depends in part on their income. Consequently, controlling marital status could produce estimates of the effect of income that are too low.[15] Since I do not control parental marital status, the estimates in this and the following chapters may slightly overstate the effect of income.

Parents' beliefs, attitudes, and behavior also affect children's outcomes. But in the PSID these are sometimes measured concurrent with parental income and may well depend on it. Reverse causation is not a problem in the NLSY, where parents' traits are measured before they enter the labor market, but in the NLSY measures of parental attitudes and behavior are sparse. In the chapters that follow, I estimate the extent to which omitting such parental characteristics biases the estimated effect of income on children's well-being.

I usually estimate the effect of income using the natural logarithm of income as an independent variable. This transformation treats a 1 percent increase in income as if it had the same effect on children's well-being regardless of how much income families start with. In contrast, using untransformed income assumes that each additional dollar of parental income improves children's outcomes by the same amount, regardless of how much money the family starts with. Most people think that an extra $1,000 helps a family with $10,000 a year more than a family with $100,000 a year. This is likely to be especially true for children, because the fraction of family income earmarked for children's needs falls as income rises (Lazear and Michael 1988). Testing the validity of this intuition, however, requires a very large sample—far larger than either the NLSY or the PSID. Nonetheless, a nonlinear transformation of income usually explains more variance in an outcome than the linear form of income (see Appendix B). If this were true even with everything else controlled and total income remained constant, a more equal distribution of parental income would improve the overall well-being of children, since poor children would gain more from each dollar their parents received than rich children would lose for each dollar their parents had to give up.

Table 4.2 shows the effect of raising income from $15,000 to $30,000 (in 1992 dollars) on five-, six-, and seven-year-olds' cognitive test scores and behavior problems. In 1992 the poverty threshold for a family of four was $14,342, so this is roughly equivalent to moving a family of

Table 4.2 Effect of doubling income from $15,000 to $30,000 on five- to seven-year-olds' test scores and behavior problems

Children's outcome income measure	Mean (SD)	Estimated value at:		Difference	Sample size
		$15,000	$30,000		
PPVT					
Income previous year	94.8 (16.4)	94.2	95.0	.72	1,111
Income previous three years		93.8	95.5	1.65	1,154
Income previous five years		93.6	95.5	1.89	1,174
PIAT math					
Income previous year	100.9 (12.4)	100.3	101.0	.78	2,735
Income previous three years		99.9	101.1	1.14	2,884
Income previous five years		99.9	101.1	1.19	2,941
PIAT reading					
Income previous year	105.1 (12.2)	104.3	105.4	1.08	2,700
Income previous three years		103.9	105.7	1.72	2,842
Income previous five years		103.9	105.8	1.97	2,900
BPI					
Income previous year	106.6 (14.2)	107.2	106.4	− .83	2,683
Income previous three years		107.7	106.1	− 1.64	2,834
Income previous five years		107.8	105.9	− 1.96	2,889

Source: Estimated from NLSY mother-child files by David Knutson. All income coefficients are statistically significant at the .01 level, except the coefficient for the PPVT for one year of income. Sample includes children who were five to eight years old in 1986, 1988, or 1990. All equations control age and race of child, household size, mother's age at child's birth, mother's AFQT score, and mother's education, which were set at sample means when calculating the expected values in columns two and three.

Note: Because of rounding, column four is not necessarily equal to the difference between columns three and two.

four from the poverty line to twice the poverty line. Because other studies suggest that income averaged over several years is more important than income in any one year, Table 4.2 shows estimates using three different measures of parental income. The first measure for each assessment is the effect of income measured in the year prior to the assessment. The second measure is the effect of income averaged over the three years prior to the assessment, and the third measure is the effect of income averaged over the five years prior to the assessment. The full regression models used for these estimates are in Appendix B.

Income averaged over three years clearly has a greater effect than income measured in the year of the assessment, and income averaged over five years has a greater effect still. Doubling parental income from $15,000 to $30,000 in the survey year increases a child's PPVT score by .72 points. But the same increase in income averaged over five years increases the PPVT score by 1.89 points. Readers may not think this is surprising, since doubling income over five or six years is bound to have a greater impact on children than doubling income in only one year.[16] Note that these estimates are similar to the estimates of Duncan et al. (1994) and Korenman et al. (1994), which use income measured over thirteen years.

In 1992 the lowest maximum combined AFDC and Food Stamp monthly benefit for a family of three in the continental United States was $412 in Mississippi. The highest combined benefit was $851 in Vermont. If the results in Table 4.2 are accurate, raising benefits in Mississippi to the level in Vermont would improve the PPVT score of AFDC children in Mississippi by roughly 1.9 points. If benefit levels in Mississippi were increased only to the national median ($652), the test score for Mississippi's children would increase by about 1 point. Income would have to quadruple to increase the PPVT score by a quarter of a standard deviation.

Although it takes a large percentage increase in parental income to raise children's test scores, it does not take many actual dollars to do so for poor families. Some families report annual incomes as low as $1,000. If such reports are accurate, transferring $5,000 to these families would increase their incomes by a factor of six. This might raise their children's test scores by enough to be important, although there are not enough such children in the NLSY to be sure.

It is hard to believe that families living in traditional housing actually live on as little as $1,000 a year worth of goods and services. Families who report incomes this low often receive help from friends or family members. Sometimes the help is in the form of noncash gifts such as food or supplies for children, and sometimes it is unreported cash. Many mothers who receive welfare also fail to report some income from work. Edin and Lein (forthcoming) report that 23 percent of the income received by the welfare recipients they interviewed came from what they call network-based strategies for making ends meet. These include help from absent fathers or boyfriends, parents, and siblings. Because this income is often irregular and welfare recipients who report it can have their AFDC benefits reduced, it is unlikely that they report all this income to interviewers. In addition, there appears to be a lot of inadvertent reporting errors among very low income families (Mayer and Jencks 1993). When I average income over several years, reporting error is reduced. The lowest five-year average income reported by PSID families is about $4,600 in 1992 dollars. If we could eliminate from the sample individuals whose true income was much higher than their reported income, the effect of a change in income at the very bottom of the income distribution would probably be somewhat larger than it looks in Table 4.2. The combination of small samples and reporting error makes it impossible to know exactly what would happen if the income of the poorest 1 or 2 percent of all families doubled.

Table 4.3 shows the effect of doubling parents' income from $15,000 to $30,000 on teenage childbearing, dropping out of high school, educational attainment, male wages, male earnings, male labor-force participation, and single motherhood using this conventional model. The full model from which these estimates are calculated is in Appendix B. For teenage childbearing, parental income is measured over the five years before a teenager had a child; for teenagers who did not have a baby, it is measured when they were thirteen to seventeen years old. In the PSID it is impossible to determine accurately when a child drops out of high school, so I cannot measure income during the five years before a child drops out. Once children reach late adolescence, many begin to move out of their parents' home. Thus for dropping out and young adulthood outcomes, I measure income when children were thirteen to seventeen years old.

As the reader will by now expect, income averaged over five years has a much greater effect on each of these outcomes than income measured in only one year. Income measured over ten years has a somewhat greater effect than income measured in five years. These estimates are shown in Appendix B.

In the PSID, the more years of income we require, the fewer children

Table 4.3 Effect of doubling parental income from $15,000 to $30,000 on adolescent and young-adult outcomes

Children's outcomes	Mean SD	Estimated value at: $15,000	$30,000	Difference	Sample size
Adolescent outcomes					
Probability of teenage childbearing	.203	.385	.221	−.164	2,124
Probability of dropping out of high school	.173	.307	.179	−.128	4,003
Young-adult outcomes					
Years of education	12.79 (1.94)	11.95	12.50	.546	3,275
Years of education for high school graduates	13.31 (1.66)	12.67	13.06	.393	2,586
Male workers' hourly wages (1992 dollars)	11.56 (6.68)	8.78	10.59	1.80	954
Male workers' annual earnings (1992 dollars)	23,728 (15,048)	17,009	21,410	4,401	954
Probability of male idleness	.106	.122	.107	−.016	1,355
Probability of single motherhood	.244	.443	.265	−.178	1,741

Source: Estimated from PSID data by Timothy Veenstra. All income coefficients except those predicting male idleness are statistically significant at the .05 level. All equations control household size, race, parents' age at the birth of the child, and parents' education. Equations for labor-market outcomes control the county unemployment rate and age of child in 1989. Education equations control child's sex. All control variables were set to their sample mean when calculating the expected values in columns two and three. For teenage childbearing, income is measured during the five years before a teenage birth, or ages thirteen to seventeen for girls with no birth before age twenty. For other outcomes, income is measured when the child was thirteen to seventeen years old.

remain in the sample.[17] Since reliable estimates of the effect of income depend on both the accuracy of the income measure and the size of the sample, we want to use the smallest number of years that will accurately characterize a child's experiences. This is especially important for outcomes measured after children have grown up, because few PSID respondents were in the sample both when they were two and when they were twenty. Because the difference between the effect of income measured in one year and in five years is much greater than the difference between the effect of income measured in five years and in ten years, and the sample size is greater when I measure income in five rather than ten years, I use income measured in five years for most of the analyses in this book.

If the results in Table 4.3 are accurate, doubling parental income would reduce teenage childbearing, dropping out of high school, and single motherhood by more than a third. It would also increase years of education by more than a half a year, increase male wages by 20 percent, and reduce male idleness by 13 percent. But as I will show in the next two chapters, these estimates almost certainly overstate the importance of income.

My results for educational attainment are similar to those of the other studies I reviewed earlier. My findings imply that a 10 percent increase in parental income increases education by .08 years. The range in the studies I reviewed was .020 to .112 years. My findings also imply that a 10 percent increase in parental income leads to a 2 percent increase in sons' wages. The range in other studies was from 1.3 to 6.0 percent. But my estimate of the effect of income on teenage childbearing is greater than the estimate in the only other study that uses income rather than the poverty ratio (Haveman et al. 1995), even though both are based on PSID data. Haveman et al. estimate the effect of income on *unwed* teenage births, whereas in Table 4.3 I include *all* teenage births. Haveman et al. use untransformed income, whereas I use the logarithm of income. They control family structure and I do not. Their sample is much smaller (873 versus 2,121) because they use only children who were zero to six years old in 1968. These differences help explain why my estimates are larger than theirs. These results are, however, similar to Brooks-Gunn et al.'s (1991) results, even though their study controls neighborhood composition.

Changes in Parental Income

The permanent-income hypothesis holds that fluctuations in parental income will not affect children's well-being because they will not lead to fluctuations in consumption. This hypothesis depends on families' being both willing and able to smooth their consumption. Imagine two identical families, the Smiths and the Joneses, who both receive $800,000 between their children's tenth and twenty-sixth birthdays. Both families have a mean annual income of $50,000. The Smiths receive $25,000 per year while their child is ten to seventeen years old and $75,000 per year while the child is eighteen to twenty-five years old. The Joneses reverse this pattern, averaging $75,000 a year in the first period and $25,000 a year in the second. Setting aside the cost of borrowing, the permanent-income hypothesis suggests that both families are equally well-off. This is because the Smiths will borrow against future income during the first period and live as though they had $50,000. The Joneses will save $25,000 a year in the first period, also consuming as though they had only $50,000. As a result, both families will live in the same kind of home and the same kind of neighborhood. Both families will also make the same investments in their children and have the same expectations for them as adults. Consequently, if all else is equal, their children will have an equal chance of graduating from high school and their teenage daughters will be equally likely to have a baby.

Most people will find this extreme form of the permanent-income hypothesis unconvincing. The future is unpredictable, so lenders are reluctant to use future income as collateral. Conversely, families are often too optimistic or undisciplined to save against the risk of a downturn. Thus the Jones family will almost certainly live better than the Smith family while the children are ten to seventeen years old. People who believe that income is important to children will therefore expect more of the Jones children to finish high school and fewer of their teenage daughters to have a baby.

Because the permanent-income hypothesis seems unconvincing, at least in its extreme form, social scientists have proposed other hypotheses which hold that income changes do affect children's well-being. The remainder of this section will test these hypotheses.

Early Childhood Income versus Later Income

Some people think that parental income when a child is young is more important than parental income when a child is older. Others think the opposite. A very young child may experience more ill effects than an older child from poor nutrition, accidents, lead poisoning, respiratory illness, and other problems that accompany poor housing. But teenagers may be more sensitive than young children to the social effects of low income, and their college plans may depend on how much help they think they can get from their parents.

The idea that income is more important at some ages than at others assumes that parents cannot fully smooth their consumption over time. If income when children are very young is more important than income when they are older, children whose parents' income is high when they are young will fare better than children whose parents have the same "permanent" income but have less income when they are young. To test this hypothesis we can estimate the effect of the average annual increase or decrease in income (the "slope" of family income) over some specified period of time, controlling the parents' average income. If an upward income slope improves an outcome with average income held constant, children whose family income is low when they are young and higher when they are older fare better than children whose family income is relatively constant. If an upward slope hurts children's outcomes, children are better off in families whose income is higher when they are young than when they are old.

Table 4.4 shows the effect of both a 10 percent change in average parental income and a 10 percent annual increase in parental income. Appendix B explains the details of these estimates. For young children, average income and the slope of income are both measured over the five years before the assessment. For teenage childbearing, average income and the slope of income are measured over the ten years before a teenager has a baby, or from ages seven to seventeen for teenagers who do not have a baby. For other outcomes, income and the slope of income are measured when the child was seven to seventeen years old. Estimates in the first two columns are from the same equation, so the effect of the slope of income is net of the effect of the level of income, and the effect of the level of income is net of the slope of income.

Table 4.4 Effect of the slope of parental income on children's outcomes with mean income controlled

Children's outcomes	10% increase in mean income	10% annual increase in income	Sample size
Test scores for five- to seven-year-olds			
PPVT	.277	.029	1,029
PIAT math	.170	.123	2,582
PIAT reading	.298	−.013	2,551
BPI	−.341	−.104	2,535
Adolescent outcomes			
Probability of teenage childbearing	−.014	−.048	1,561
Probability of dropping out of high school	−.013	−.014	3,062
Young adult outcomes			
Years of education	.111	−.087	2,288
Years of education for high school graduates	.083	−.106	1,820
Male workers' hourly wages	.255	−.217	578
Male workers' annual earnings	579	−1,289	549
Probability of male idleness	−.003	−.001	928
Probability of single motherhood	−.015	−.060	1,210

Sources: Estimates for test scores were computed from NLSY mother-child files by David Knutson. Estimates for adolescent and young-adult outcomes were computed from PSID data by Timothy Veenstra. Mean income and the annual change in income is measured over five years for children's test scores and over ten years for other outcomes. All equations control household size, race, parents' age at the birth of the child, and parents' education. Equations for labor-market outcomes also control the county unemployment rate and age of child in 1989. Equations for test scores also control child's age and mother's AFQT score. Equations for education and test scores also control child's sex. Columns one and two are from the same equation. See Appendix B.

Table 4.4 suggests that a child whose family experiences a 10 percent average annual income increase scores no higher on the PPVT or the PIAT reading assessment than a child with the same average income but no upward or downward trend in income. Increasing parental income (a positive income slope) is, however, associated with a small reduction in behavior problems and a small increase in PIAT math scores, although only the latter is reliably different from zero.[18]

Unlike young children's test scores and behavior, adolescent and young-adult outcomes are more sensitive to recent income than to earlier income.[19] When I hold average income constant, growth in parental income appears to reduce teenage childbearing, dropping out of high school, and single motherhood. This supports the hypothesis that parental income during adolescence is more important for adolescent outcomes than parental income when children are younger. Growth in parental income appears to reduce years of education and young men's wages and earnings, however. This supports the hypothesis that parental income when children are young is more important to adult outcomes than parental income when children are adolescents. But the effect of the slope of income is small. These results suggest that a child whose parents average a 10 percent annual income increase receives about a tenth of a year less schooling than a child whose parents have the same income but experience no upward or downward trend in income.

These results might not represent the effect of parents' income growth per se. Whatever causes income to increase or decrease may also affect children's behavior. For instance, when parents divorce, family income usually drops. The decrease in income might hurt the children, but so might the mother's distress or the father's absence.

The three main causes of family income fluctuations are changes in parents' marital status, wages, and hours worked. Changes in wages are unlikely to affect children's behavior independent of their effect on parents' income. Changes in both the number of hours parents work and their marital status are, however, likely to have direct effects on children. When I re-estimated the models in Table 4.4 controlling these factors, however, the results hardly changed.

Table 4.4 thus tells a mixed story about the timing of parental income. For young children, the timing of parental income has a weak effect on assessment scores and behavior problems; what mainly matters is parents' average income. For teenage childbearing, dropping out of high school, and single motherhood, income in adolescence appears to be more important than income in early childhood. For educational attainment and male labor-force success, income during middle childhood is more important than parental income in adolescence (though the effects are trivial for male idleness and not statistically significant for male wages).

A Drop in Parental Income

Most researchers emphasize the harmful effects of chronic low income. They claim that it leads to coping strategies and material deprivations that are detrimental to children's behavior. In folklore, chronic low income can also lead to thriftiness and efficiency in home production, which then mute the effect of low income, but recent research seldom considers this possibility.

Other researchers (Elder 1974; Elder et al. 1984) emphasize the adverse effects of a loss of income. Anticipated income fluctuations should have little effect on children's outcomes if parents who expect income fluctuations save when their income is high and spend when it is low. Unanticipated income losses may hurt children for two reasons. First, if parents have no savings or if their savings run out, they will be forced to buy fewer or poorer-quality goods and services for their children. Second, an unanticipated loss of income may cause stress for both parents and children. Of course, income that drops and does not rise again is equivalent to a downward income slope. But a large income drop could have an adverse effect even if it was subsequently offset by an income rise.

Forty-one percent of five- to seven-year-olds in the NLSY sample experienced a drop in income of 35 percent or more between two adjacent years over a five-year period. In the PSID sample about a third of the children experienced an income drop of at least 35 percent between two adjacent years over a ten-year period. Since the NLSY sample covers five rather than ten years of parental income, the higher incidence of drops in the NLSY suggests that large decreases in income are more common among young parents than among older parents.[20] Table 4.5 shows that children who experience such a drop in income have slightly lower test scores and slightly more behavior problems than children with the same average income who do not experience such a drop. Teenagers who have experienced such a drop are also more likely to become teenage mothers, and slightly more likely to drop out of high school, but neither effect is statistically significant. A large drop in income appears to reduce years of education. For other young-adult outcomes the effect of a large drop in parental income sometime in the past ten years is often positive rather than negative, and in the case of idleness the improvement is even significant.

Table 4.5   Change in children's outcomes due to a 35 percent drop in parental
income with mean income controlled

Children's outcomes	Change due to income drop	Sample size
Test scores for five- to seven-year-olds		
PPVT	−.407	628
PIAT math	−.487	1,599
PIAT reading	.001	1,586
BPI	1.264	1,560
Adolescent outcomes		
Probability of teenage childbearing	.032	1,561
Probability of dropping out of high school	.012	3,066
Young-adult outcomes		
Years of education	−.256	2,291
Years of education for high school graduates	−.157	1,823
Male workers' hourly wages (1992 dollars)	.159	559
Male workers' annual wage (1992 dollars)	1,490	549
Probability of male idleness	−.065	928
Probability of single motherhood	.047	1,213

Sources: Estimates for five- to seven-year-olds were computed from NLSY mother-child
files by David Knutson. Other estimates were computed from PSID data by Timothy
Veenstra. For children's test scores, mean income and the income drop are measured over
five years. For other outcomes, mean income and the income drop are measured over ten
years. All equations control household size, race, parents' age at the birth of the child,
parents' education, change in parents' marital status, and change in parents' labor-market
hours. Equations for labor-market outcomes control the county unemployment rate and
age of child in 1989. Equations for test scores also control mother's AFQT score.
Equations for education and test scores also control child's sex.

At least some of these income drops were probably anticipated by
families. Unanticipated drops are therefore likely to have larger effects
than this table implies.

Income fluctuations do not appear to affect children's well-being. I
estimated a model in which I included both a family's average income
and the standard deviation of income over the same period. This specification assumes that what matters is the percentage change in income,
not the absolute dollar change. This corresponds to most people's intuition, since a $1,000 loss of income is probably more important to a
family whose income is $20,000 than to a family whose income is
$100,000. The standard deviation of family income did not have a large
or statistically significant effect on any outcome.

Taken together, this evidence shows that the effect of changes in parental income depends on the outcome, but parents' permanent income is always more important than the timing of income or income fluctuations.

5

The "True" Effect of Income

Despite evidence of the kind presented up to this point, many people believe that parental income does not appreciably affect children's life chances. They see high parental income as mainly a proxy for other parental characteristics, such as cognitive skills or a strong work ethic, that influence both children's behavior and parents' income. They do not expect children to benefit appreciably if, say, their parents suddenly inherit $50,000 or win the lottery. Nor do they expect children on welfare to be hurt much if the state legislature decreases welfare benefits by $100 a month.

Unfortunately, no survey measures all the parental characteristics that might affect children's outcomes. The PSID includes no measures of parenting practices. The NLSY provides better measures of parenting practices and cognitive skills, but it will not provide good information on teenage outcomes for another decade. Even if these surveys had more detailed data than they do, we would always have reason to worry about the things they fail to measure. Evidence from conventional models like those in the last chapter will never convince people who believe that money does not matter. In this chapter I try to estimate the true effect of income on children's outcomes. By the true effect I mean what would happen if we increased parents' income but changed nothing else.

To estimate the true effect of income, we must control all parental characteristics that influence both children's outcomes and parental income. There is no straightforward way to do this. I have tried five approaches. First, I use the effect of income from sources other than earnings and government transfers to measure the true effect of extra income. Second, I compare the apparent effects of parental income measured before an outcome has occurred with the apparent effect of income after the outcome. Third, I try to see whether the things parents buy as their income increases help children succeed. Fourth, I ask whether trends in parental income parallel trends in children's outcomes. Fifth, I ask whether children in states that pay high AFDC benefits fare better than children in states that pay low AFDC benefits. I also review evidence from the Negative Income Tax (NIT) experiments. This chapter discusses the first two strategies, The next three chapters discuss the others.

Figure 5.1 depicts the model I try to estimate. It shows that all the strategies I use in this chapter estimate the effect of income on children's outcomes controlling unobserved parental characteristics, which I have labeled Z.

The Source of Income

Imagine that the Smith family and the Jones family are both headed by a single mother with two children. Mrs. Smith gets $10,000 a year in child support and alimony from her ex-husband. Mrs. Jones gets $10,000 a year in welfare. If income influences children's outcomes, the Smith children and the Jones children should fare equally well, assum-

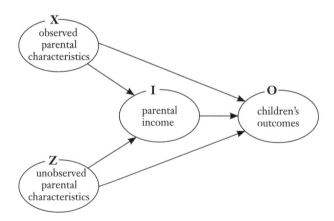

Figure 5.1 "True" reduced-form model

ing the families are the same in all other respects. The source of income should not matter: a dollar from welfare should have as great an effect as a dollar from child support or a dollar from winning the lottery.

If instead of welfare Mrs. Jones received the same amount of money from working, she would have to spend some of that money on transportation, child care, and other expenses associated with work. This is money she could not spend on better housing, piano lessons, or books. If such amenities improve children's outcomes, the Smith children might fare better than the Jones children. But some research finds the opposite. Whereas income from work appears to improve children's outcomes, welfare income appears to reduce their chances of graduating from high school (Haveman and Wolfe 1994; McLanahan 1985), their eventual years of education (Duncan and Yeung 1994; Hill and Duncan 1987), sons' earnings and hours of work (Corcoran and Adams 1993a; Corcoran et al. 1992; Hill and Ponza 1983b), and young children's test scores (Hill and O'Neill 1994). Other studies seem to show that among children in single-parent families, income from child-support payments improves children's educational attainment more than income from welfare or mothers' work (Graham et al. 1994; Knox and Bane 1994).

The fact that welfare income appears to harm children whereas income from other sources helps them can be interpreted in three ways. One interpretation is that incompetent parents are more likely than competent parents to apply for and receive welfare. Since we do not have information on competence, welfare income appears to be harmful. A second interpretation is that welfare reduces self-esteem and increases alienation, resulting in worse parenting. A third interpretation is that welfare receipt is a proxy for severe material deprivation. According to this reasoning, parents who receive welfare have fewer resources or a greater need for resources than those who report the same income but do not receive welfare. Welfare recipients could have fewer resources because they get less help from their family and friends, or because they have special needs, such as high medical costs. Whatever the correct interpretation, these studies raise the suspicion that welfare recipients differ in important but unmeasured ways from those who do not receive welfare, and that these differences affect their children's outcomes. They also suggest that we can only estimate the true effect of income if we have a measure of income that is not related to unmeasured parental characteristics.

Although no source of income is completely unrelated to parental traits, some sources are more strongly related than others. In the NLSY, for example, parental education correlates .466 with parents' earned income, −.293 with their income from government transfers such as welfare and unemployment compensation, but only −.005 with their income from sources other than earnings and government transfers. Mothers' AFQT scores are correlated .308 with earned income, −.322 with transfer income, but only −.083 with "other" income. Income from sources other than earnings and government transfers is also more weakly correlated with the mother's race and age when the child was born.[1]

If what I have referred to as "other" income is less strongly related to observed parental characteristics than either government transfers or earned income, it is also less likely to be correlated with unobserved parental traits. Nonetheless, its apparent effect on children's outcomes is likely to overstate the effect of money per se. The three largest sources of "other" income are child-support and alimony; interest, dividends, and rents; and inherited income. Both savings and having rich relatives are likely to be correlated with parental traits that affect children's outcomes directly. Child support and alimony are both proxies for marital dissolution, which can have an important negative effect on children's outcomes. When I estimate the effect of "other" income I control parents' marital status. As a result, the remaining variation in child support and alimony payments is likely to be a proxy for the absent parent's earnings, and is therefore likely to yield an upwardly biased estimate of the way money affects children. As I have noted, this is what previous research shows.

By contrast, the effect of "other" income would be biased downward if it were measured with more error than total income. Income from some sources is better reported on surveys than income from other sources. For example, studies show that respondents to the Current Population Survey (CPS) report 99.4 percent of their wages and salaries, 82.8 percent of SSI, 72.8 percent of AFDC, and 46 percent of workman's compensation. For sources of "other" income, they report 72.5 percent of net rent and royalties, 55.2 percent of interest, and 52.7 percent of dividends (U.S. Bureau of the Census 1992). If the PSID and NLSY were like the CPS, we would have good reason to think that measurement error in "other" income was a more serious problem than measurement error in total income.[2] I do not know how accurately income is reported in the NLSY, but the PSID appears to do a better job than the CPS of getting respondents to report both transfer income and "other" income. Depending on the assumptions I make, between 79 and 82 percent of "other" income is reported in the PSID, compared with 95.7 percent of total income.[3]

I do not know how accurate reports of alimony and child support are in either the PSID or the CPS. But since studies seem to show that among single parents, a dollar from alimony or child support improves children's educational attainment more than a dollar from earnings or welfare, it is hard to argue that this source of "other" income is measured with more error than earnings or welfare.

In the five years over which income is measured, all families in the PSID had at least some earned income, 86.6 percent had some unearned income, and 44.8 percent received some form of government cash transfer. In the three years over which income is measured for the younger families in the NLSY, 94.8 percent had some earnings, 60 percent had some government transfers, and 79.6 percent had some other income.

To see if income sources matter, I first regress each outcome on total income averaged over the five years prior to an outcome, controlling household size, race, child's age, and parents' age at the birth of the child, education, and marital status. Equations for labor-market outcomes also control the county unemployment rate; equations for children's test scores control mother's AFQT score; and equations for education and test scores also control child's sex. In order to compare the effect of a dollar from different sources, these regressions use total income in dollars, not its logarithm.[4] The first column in Table 5.1 shows that increasing total parental income by $15,000 would improve all outcomes. For example, it would increase children's PPVT scores by 1.129 points. It would reduce teenage girls' chances of having a baby by 8.7 percentage points and teenagers' chances of dropping out of high school by 5.5 percentage points. These changes are not as large as those for the conventional model reported in the last chapter because the estimates in Table 5.1 control parents' marital status and use a linear form of income.

The second column in Table 5.1 shows the change in each outcome due to a $15,000 increase in income when I replace the coefficient of

Table 5.1 Effect of increasing total income and "other" income by $15,000 on children's outcomes

Children's outcomes	Effect of increase in total income	Effect of increase in "other" income	Sample size
Test scores for five- to seven-year-olds			
PPVT	1.129	1.296	1,183
PIAT math	.531	−.053	2,955
PIAT reading	1.150	1.430	2,914
BPI	−1.149	−.097	2,904
Adolescent outcomes			
Probability of teenage childbearing	−.087	−.039	2,124
Probability of dropping out of high school	−.055	−.019	4,003
Young-adult outcomes			
Years of education	.230	.228	3,275
Years of education for high school graduates	.192	.209	2,586
Male workers' hourly wages (1992 dollars)	.72	.42	954
Male workers' annual earnings (1992 dollars)	1,687	1,435	954
Probability of male idleness	−.008	.023	1,355
Probability of single motherhood	−.092	−.038	1,741

Sources: Estimates for test scores were computed from NLSY mother-child files by David Knutson. Estimates for other outcomes were computed from PSID data by Timothy Veenstra. Estimates in column two were obtained from the following model:

$$O = b_1 I_e + b_2 I_o + b_3 I_g + b_4 X,$$

where O is a child's outcome, I_e is family income from earnings, I_o is other income, I_g is income from government transfers, and X is a vector of control variables including household size, parents' age at the birth of the child, marital status, and education, and child's race. Equations for labor-market outcomes control the county unemployment rate and age of child in 1989. Education equations control child's sex. Equations for test scores also control child's age and mother's AFQT score.

total income with the coefficient of "other" income from a regression that controls income from government transfers and earnings.[5] For most outcomes, the effect of "other" income is smaller than the effect of total income, and in one case, idleness, the sign of the coefficient reverses, suggesting that an increase in parental income increases male idleness. The PPVT and the PIAT reading assessment are notable exceptions, but in neither case is the effect of "other" income significantly different from the effect of total income. The effect of "other" income is about the same as the effect of total income on educational attainment and men's earnings.

This technique for estimating the true effect of income shows that conventional methods overstate the effect of parental income on children's behavior problems, teenagers' chances of dropping out of high school, teenage girls' chances of having a baby, young women's chances of becoming single mothers, and men's chances of being idle. The true effect of parental income on teenage childbearing is only 44.8 percent of the effect estimated using total income. The true effect is 41.3 percent of the conventional estimate for single motherhood, 34.5 percent of the conventional estimate for dropping out, and 58.3 percent of the conventional estimate for male wages. Furthermore, if the results in Table 5.1 are correct, increasing parental income increases a son's chances of being idle. This technique also shows that conventional estimates of the effect of income on some cognitive test scores and on years of education are not greatly biased, however.

As noted, this technique will not account for all the bias resulting from unobserved parental traits, because "other" income is generally associated with positive parental characteristics. Nonetheless, this technique suggests that conventional models may overstate the improvement in most children's outcomes from raising parental income.

Income before and after an Outcome

Under most circumstances, parental income after an outcome has occurred cannot affect the outcome. If it appears to have such an effect, it is probably because income after the outcome is a proxy for the parental characteristics that affect income both before and after the outcome.

Imagine that Mrs. Smith and Mrs. Jones each earn $15,000 per year while their children are growing up. But when the youngest child turns twenty-five, Mrs. Smith inherits a large sum of money. Mrs. Jones's income remains the same. If Mrs. Smith did not anticipate the inheritance, she could not have borrowed against it or saved less in anticipation of it when her children were growing up. Nor could her children have altered their behavior in anticipation of the additional income. Consequently, the inheritance could not have influenced her children's chances of graduating from high school or having a baby when they were teenagers.

If instead of an inheritance Mrs. Smith received a large, unexpected raise in pay when her child turned twenty-five, it would have no more influence on her children's adolescent behavior than the unexpected inheritance. But if Mrs. Smith got a raise because she was especially competent, and if parental competence reduces teenagers' chances of having a baby and dropping out of high school, the Smith teenagers would have been less likely than the Jones teenagers to engage in these behaviors. If we then tried to estimate the effect of parental income when the children were grown on their adolescent behavior, it would appear that the difference in outcomes was due to Mrs. Smith's raise, when in fact it was due to her being more competent.

A family's current level of consumption cannot be influenced by unexpected future income. But many economists argue that if Mrs. Smith expected a raise in the future or expected to get an inheritance one day, she would borrow money or save less when her children are young in anticipation of this future income. Thus, even though the Smith family and the Jones family had the same income when their children were growing up, the Smith children would have experienced a higher standard of living. According to this argument, parental income once the children are adults is a proxy for their standard of living as children. In addition, if the Smith children expected their mother to have more income in the future, they might change their behavior during adolescence. Even when families anticipate higher future income, however, they are usually uncertain about when they will receive the money and how much they will actually get. This makes borrowing against these future resources risky. Lenders are also reluctant to lend money in such circumstances. Therefore, it seems unlikely that families can borrow or save against income that they are likely to receive in the distant future.

Some research seems to demonstrate that current consumption is not responsive even to expected future income (Campbell and Deaton 1989; Carroll 1994; Viard 1993; West 1988). Other research seems to show the opposite (Altonji and Siow 1987; Bernanke 1984; Hall 1978). I will discuss these issues more in the next chapter. For now, I assume that under most circumstances parental income once children are grown up cannot influence young children's or teenagers' outcomes. If it appears to have such an influence, it is probably because future income is correlated with unmeasured parental characteristics.

As I discussed in Chapter 4, annual income has a relatively stable, or permanent, component and an unstable, or transitory, component. The stable component is likely to be highly correlated with stable parental characteristics such as skill and motivation. The unstable component is by definition uncorrelated with stable parental characteristics. Thus if the unmeasured stable parental characteristics that affect income also have a large direct influence on children's behavior, the coefficient of the stable component of parental income will be considerably larger than the coefficient of the unstable component.

To determine whether the conventional estimates in the last chapter are biased because they do not control important stable characteristics of parents, I constructed two income measures. What I call "Time 1 income" is parents' income during the five years before an outcome occurs. What I call "Time 2 income" is parents' income during five years following the outcome. For all outcomes, parental income during the first period can affect the outcome. With certain possible exceptions, which I discuss below, income in the second period cannot influence earlier outcomes.

For this analysis I measure children's outcomes in the NLSY in 1986. Time 1 income is, therefore, mean income in 1981 to 1985, whereas Time 2 income is mean income in 1988 to 1992. For teenage childbearing, Time 1 income is averaged over the five years before a teenage girl has a baby. For example, if a girl has a baby when she is fifteen, Time 1 income is measured when she was ten to fourteen years old. For a girl who reaches the age of twenty without having a baby, Time 1 income is measured when she was thirteen to seventeen years old. Time 2 income is the average parental income when the girl was twenty-three to twenty-seven years old. For all other outcomes, Time 1 income is measured when the child was thirteen to seventeen. For dropping out, Time 2 income is the average parental income when children were twenty-three to twenty-seven years old. I measure wages and carnings in 1983 and 1984, so Time 2 income is measured in 1985 to 1989.[6] Single parenthood, educational attainment, and male idleness are measured when children are twenty-four years old. For these outcomes, Time 2 income is measured when the child was twenty-five to twenty-nine years old.

This approach assumes that income measured before the outcome is a good gauge of the family's actual resources at that time. If Time 1 income were a poor gauge of family resources, either because of reporting errors or because families anticipated future income changes and decided to smooth their consumption, then income after the outcome might influence children's outcomes because it served as a proxy for resources at Time 1. If Time 1 income covered only one year, for example, Time 2 income might appear to influence an outcome because it would serve as a partial proxy for income prior to Time 1. If the measurement error in five-year income averages were a major problem, income averaged over ten years should predict outcomes substantially better than income averaged over five years. As we have seen, this is not the case.[7]

If income at Time 2 came from an inheritance that was foreseeable at Time 1, the family might have felt freer to borrow money to send a child to college. One way to test the hypothesis that income averaged over three to five years is a good measure of a family's actual resources during the relevant years of a child's life is to look at direct measures of the family's material living conditions, such as expenditures on food and housing, the number of rooms the family has in its home, and the number of automobiles it owns. I report these analyses in Chapter 7 and Appendix D. But Time 2 income does not appear to influence a family's living conditions during Time 1 in any consistent way. Thus if Time 2 income appears to influence children's behavior, it is probably because it serves as a proxy for stable parental traits that influence both parental income and children's outcomes, not because it is a proxy for unmeasured monetary resources at Time 1.

The statistical utility of my approach also depends on there being substantial changes in income between Time 1 and Time 2. If the two income measures were very highly correlated, observed changes might be largely noise, making them almost uninterpretable. The actual correlations between income at Time 1 and income at Time 2 range from .594 to .725, depending on the sample. These correlations are large by social science standards, but they are not large enough to suggest that income fluctuations are all noise. Because the measures of income are five-year averages, they contain relatively little measurement error.

Under plausible assumptions, the correlation between Time 1 income and Time 2 income roughly estimates the percentage of variance in the two income averages that could be traceable to stable parental characteristics. This figure varies from one analysis to another, both because different analyses cover parents of different ages and because of random sampling error. For the teenage childbearing sample, the two income measures correlate .626. This implies that 62.6 percent of the variance in the five-year income averages could be due to stable parental traits, whereas 37.4 percent is traceable to more transitory influences. If the apparent effect of parental income were entirely attributable to the fact that stable parental traits affected both parents' income and their children's outcomes, parental Time 2 income should be a perfect substitute for income at Time 1. In this case the correlation between an outcome and Time 1 income would be about the same as the correlation between the outcome and Time 2 income. If, in contrast, unmeasured parental traits had no direct effect on teenagers' behavior, the correlation between teenage childbearing and subsequent parental income should be about 62.6 percent of the correlation between teenage childbearing and Time 1 income.[8] Appendix C describes this model more fully.

To determine whether bias resulting from unobserved stable parental characteristics is statistically significant, I estimate an equation for each outcome in which I include income at both Time 1 and Time 2, as well as the measured characteristics in the conventional estimates of the last chapter. These include parents' education, child's race, and family size. If the coefficient of Time 2 income is statistically significant, the coefficient of Time 1 income in the conventional model is significantly biased by the omission of the stable parental characteristics, for which Time 2 income is a proxy. This is because Time 2 income can only affect an outcome through its correlation with parental characteristics that are omitted from the equation. Thus if the effect of Time 2 income is significant, the effect of the unobserved stable characteristics must also be significant. Although this test tells us whether the coefficient of Time 1 income is significantly biased, it does not tell us how large the bias is.

The coefficient for Time 2 income was not statistically significant for the PPVT or the PIAT math assessment. Nor was it statistically significant for teenage childbearing, men's wages, or male idleness at age twenty-four. This does not mean, however, that the effect of Time 1 income on these outcomes is unbiased; it means only that I do not have enough cases to determine with confidence whether these coefficients are biased. The effect of parental Time 2 income was statistically significant for the other outcomes.

Although Time 1 income is not significantly biased for some of these outcomes, an estimate that takes into account bias from omitted variables is still a better estimate of the true effect of income than estimates that do not take this bias into account. Therefore, Table 5.2 estimates the size of the bias in conventional estimates of the effect of parental income on young children's cognitive test scores and behavior problems shown in Table 4.2.[9]

The first two rows show the correlation of each outcome with Time 1 and Time 2 income. The third row shows the correlation between Time 1 income and Time 2 income. Row 4 shows the standardized regression coefficient of Time 1 income for each outcome, controlling parents' education, family size, mother's age at the birth of the child, mother's AFQT score, the child's race, age, and sex. These coefficients are smaller than the coefficients in row 1 because these observed traits account for much of the difference in children's test scores. Row 5 shows the standardized coefficient of Time 1 income, controlling both measured and unmeasured stable parental characteristics.

Table 5.2   The "true" effect of parental income on five- to seven-year-old children's outcomes

Estimate	PPVT	BPI	PIAT math	PIAT reading
(1) Correlation with Time 1 income	.326	−.130	.215	.180
(2) Correlation with Time 2 income	.286	−.129	.187	.169
(3) Correlation between Time 1 and Time 2 income	.605	.616	.615	.607
(4) Conventional standardized coefficient	.105	−.135	.057	.136
(5) "True" standardized coefficient	.126	−.002	.073	−.012
(SE)	(.089)	(.079)	(.062)	(.043)
(6) Number of cases	903	986	1,005	988

Source: Calculated from NLSY mother-child files by David Knutson. See the text for a description of the model and the income variables. The equations for the conventional standardized coefficient control household size, race, mother's age at the birth of the child, mother's AFQT score, mother's education, and child's sex.

The estimates in Table 5.2 are in standardized form. In the case of the PPVT, for example, the correlation of .326 with income at Time 1 means that a child whose family income is one standard deviation below the mean has a PPVT score .326 standard deviations below the mean. When we control race, household size, mother's education, and mother's AFQT score, the effect falls to .105 standard deviations. When we control all stable parental characteristics that affect income, it rises slightly, to .126, a change that, as I noted earlier, is statistically insignificant.

These coefficients suggest that, all else being equal, high parental income hardly affects children's behavior problems or PIAT reading scores. But these estimates are subject to random sampling error. The standard errors of these estimates are shown in parentheses. (Appendix C explains how I estimated the standard errors.) Taking into account the standard errors suggests that the true effect of parental income on the PIAT reading-assessment and BPI scores could range from a small negative effect to a small positive effect.

The estimated true effect of income on the PPVT and PIAT math scores is slightly greater than the conventional estimate. In neither case is the change large enough to be of much practical importance. In both cases the effect is clearly small.

Table 5.3 estimates the size of the bias in conventional estimates of adolescent outcomes, educational attainment, and single motherhood. Some of the outcomes in Table 5.3 are dichotomous. The methodology I use in this section is not ideal for such outcomes because it assumes that extra income has the same effect on people with, say, high and low probabilities of dropping out of school. Nonetheless, if the standardized estimate from a conventional model is a third greater than the "true" standardized coefficient, we can assume that the estimate from a conventional logistic regression will also be a third greater than the "true" estimate from a logistic regression. Therefore, I use the correlation approach to assess the extent of bias, but I use the results from logistic regressions to determine the point estimates.[10]

Table 5.3 shows that the true effect of income on teenage childbearing is two-thirds the conventional estimate.[11] The true effect of parental income on dropping out of high school is only 48.1 percent of the conventional estimate, and the true effect of parental income on single motherhood is 47.7 percent of the conventional estimate. Al-

Table 5.3 The "true" effect of parental income on adolescent outcomes, educational attainment, and single motherhood

Estimate	Adolescent outcomes		Years of education		Single motherhood
	Teenage motherhood	Dropping out of school	All	High school graduates	
(1) Correlation with Time 1 income	−.294	−.297	.364	.274	−.310
(2) Correlation with Time 2 income	−.263	−.272	.312	.202	−.283
(3) Correlation between Time 1 and Time 2 income	.726	.710	.689	.671	.685
(4) Conventional standardized coefficient	−.173	−.179	.186	.141	−.176
(5) "True" standardized coefficient	−.114	−.086	.168	.222	−.084
(SE)	(.103)	(.072)	(.066)	(.058)	(.055)
(6) Sample size	1,221	2,273	1,853	1,489	969

Source: Calculated from PSID data by Timothy Veenstra. See the text for a description of the model. Time 1 income is measured when children were thirteen to seventeen years old for all variables except teenage childbearing. For teenage childbearing it is measured over the five years before a teenage birth, or from ages thirteen to seventeen for those who had no teenage birth. Time 2 income is measured when children were twenty-three to twenty-seven years old for adolescent outcomes and at ages twenty-five to twenty-nine for all other outcomes. Estimates for the conventional standardized coefficient control household size, race, parents' age at the birth of the child, and parents' education. Education equations control child's sex.

though the estimated effect of parental income on years of education for all twenty-four-year-olds drops dramatically when I control measured background characteristics, it does not drop much more when I control unmeasured parental characteristics.[12] The true effect of parental income on the educational attainment of high school graduates is greater than the conventional estimate.

Table 5.4 shows that the true effect of income on young men's wages and earnings is also greater than conventional estimates, though again these differences are small and the bias in Time 1 income is not statistically significant. These results suggest that the true effect of parental income is to increase male idleness, but the standard errors are large for this estimate.

Taken as a whole, Tables 5.1, 5.2, and 5.3 show that stable but unmeasured parental characteristics correlated with income have a greater

Table 5.4 The "true" effect of parental income on male labor-market outcomes

Estimate	Male earnings	Male wages	Male idleness
(1) Correlation with Time 1 income	.268	.247	−.043
(2) Correlation with Time 2 income	.168	.154	−.033
(3) Correlation between Time 1 and Time 2 income	.594	.594	.707
(4) Conventional standardized coefficient	.208	.195	−.039
(5) "True" standardized coefficient	.246	.230	.035
(SE)	(.079)	(.085)	(.087)
(6) Sample Size	674	674	835

Source: Computed from PSID data by Timothy Veenstra. See the text for a description of the model. Time 1 income is measured when children were thirteen to seventeen years old. Time 2 income is measured at ages twenty-five to twenty-nine. Estimates for the conventional standardized coefficient control household size, race, parents' age at the birth of the child, and parents' education, the county unemployment rate, and age of child in 1989.

influence on children's behavior problems, PIAT reading scores, teenage childbearing, dropping out of high school, single motherhood, and male idleness than previous researchers realized. But these unobserved traits have little effect on educational attainment, men's wages, or men's earnings.

Table 5.5 uses these results to estimate the true effect of increasing parental income from $15,000 to $30,000 on each outcome. For comparison, the first column shows the value of each outcome for a child in a family whose average income is $15,000. The second column shows the standard deviation for continuous outcomes. The third column shows the estimated change in each outcome due to increasing parental income from $15,000 to $30,000 from a conventional Ordinary Least Squares (OLS) or logistic regression model (from Table 4.2 or 4.3). The last column shows the estimated "true" change in each outcome due to such an income change. The last column is calculated by multiplying the change in column four by the ratio of the "true" coefficient to the observed coefficient (from Tables 5.2, 5.3, and 5.4).

Doubling parental income is likely to raise young children's PPVT and PIAT math scores a very small amount. It is unlikely to increase children's PIAT reading scores or reduce their behavior problems much. These results imply that doubling parental income from $15,000 to $30,000 would reduce the percentage of teenage girls who have babies from 38.5 to 27.7, the percentage of teenagers who drop out of

Table 5.5 The "true" effect of increasing parental income from $15,000 to
$30,000 on children's outcomes

Children's outcomes	Estimated value at $15,000	Standard deviation	Change due to income increase	
			Conventional estimate	True estimate
Test scores for five- to seven-year-olds				
PPVT	94.0	16.4	1.890	2.244
PIAT math	100.0	12.4	1.190	1.472
PIAT reading	104.0	12.2	1.970	.007
BPI	107.8	14.2	−1.960	−.095
Adolescent outcomes				
Probability of teenage childbearing	.385	NA	−.164	−.108
Probability of dropping out of high school	.307	NA	−.128	−.063
Young-adult outcomes				
Years of education	11.9	1.9	.546	.493
Years of education for high school graduates	12.67	1.7	.393	.619
Male workers' hourly wages (1992 dollars)	8.78	6.68	1.80	2.12
Male workers' annual earnings (1992 dollars)	17,009	15,048	4,401	5,205
Probability of male idleness	.122	NA	−.016	.014
Probability of single motherhood	.443	NA	−.178	−.085

Sources: Estimates for five- to seven-year-olds were computed from NLSY mother-child files by David Knutson. Estimates for adolescent and young-adult outcomes were computed from PSID data by Timothy Veenstra. The "conventional estimate" is the estimate from Table 4.2 or Table 4.3. The "true estimate" for continuous outcomes is calculated as $(b_t/b_c)(C_e)$, where b_t is the "true" standardized coefficient shown in Table 5.2, Table 5.3, or Table 5.4, b_c is the observed standardized coefficient also shown in the same tables, and C_e is the change in an outcome estimated from the conventional OLS model. When the outcome is dichotomous, the "true" estimate is $(b_t/b_c)(C_p)$, where C_p is the change estimated from a logistic regression model.

Note: NA = not applicable.

high school from 30.7 to 24.4, and the percentage of young women who become single mothers from 44.3 to 35.8. Doubling parental income is unlikely to have a large influence on whether sons are idle, but it could increase education and young men's wages and earnings. For example, these results imply that doubling parental income could increase the number of young adults who graduate from college by almost 10 percent.

I have already noted some potential problems with these estimates. Another potential problem is that the estimates in Table 5.5 might be too large because they do not take account of bias in the income coefficient resulting from parental traits that change over time. Suppose, for example, that Mrs. Smith loses her job, that this leads to both a loss of income and a loss of self-esteem, and that these changes in turn reduce her son's chances of finishing high school. If we have no measure of Mrs. Smith's self-esteem, we will attribute the entire effect of her unemployment to the loss of income. Yet if we sought to eliminate this adverse effect by providing unemployment compensation equal to 100 percent of her lost earnings, we might be disappointed to discover that they were not completely offset by generous benefits, because part of the problem was Mrs. Smith's self-esteem rather than her income. In this example the estimated effect of income is biased upward, even after accounting for bias resulting from unobserved stable characteristics.

Nonetheless, for most outcomes the results in Table 5.5 are consistent with the results from the estimates using "other" income. Both techniques for estimating the true effect of income show that conventional methods overstate the effect of parental income on children's behavior problems, teenage girls' chances of having a baby, teenagers' chances of dropping out of high school, young men's chances of being idle, and young women's chances of becoming single mothers. Both techniques also show that conventional estimates of the effect of income on children's PPVT scores, years of education, and earnings are not greatly biased. The results for the PIAT reading assessment and young men's wages differ depending on the technique.

Siblings

Imagine that the Smith children were born three years apart. In the year the first child was born, the Smith family's income was $15,000.

Each year their income increased by $2,000. Over the first five years of the oldest child's life, family income averaged $19,000 per year. Over the first five years of the second child's life, income averaged $25,000. The second child was raised with more money than the first. But there were also more family members to share the income when the second child was born. If this income increase was enough to offset the costs of an additional child, and if income improves children's life chances, the second child should fare better than the first. If the additional income is the result of Mrs. Smith's working more hours in the labor market, however, this might hurt both children's life chances.

Few studies have tried to compare the outcomes of siblings whose parents' income has changed. Surveys often do not include enough siblings for such comparisons, and when they do, siblings are often not different enough in age for their parental income to differ by much. When outcomes are dichotomous, like dropping out of high school and teenage childbearing, sibling comparisons are difficult to estimate.

I compared siblings' test scores and educational attainment (there are too few siblings to compare their wages or earnings). To do this I regressed the difference in the outcomes on parental income, controlling family size, parental education, age for the oldest child, and the difference in each of these factors between the older and the younger sibling. I also controlled changes in mothers' and fathers' hours of labor-market work and marital status.

These estimates show that changes in income between siblings have a very small and statistically insignificant effect on children's test scores and educational attainment at age twenty-four. For example, if a second sibling is raised with parental income that averages $15,000 more than it did for the first sibling, the second sibling's PIAT math score will be 1.035 points higher than the first sibling's score. The benefit of additional income is smaller for other test scores and is close to zero for educational attainment. This implies that additional income does not benefit siblings.

6

□ □ □ □ □

Income and Material
Well-Being

What I have called the investment theory holds that parental income influences children's outcomes because the things parents purchase as their income increases help their children succeed. If this is the case, then children from high-income families will succeed more often than children from low-income families. Figure 6.1 shows the part of my overall heuristic model that I examine in this chapter. It shows that parental income influences children's outcomes by increasing the goods and services available to children. Unfortunately, there is no agreement about what goods and services children need to succeed.

Some people believe that serious material hardships can hurt children's life chances, even though luxuries cannot help them. They imagine that children who do not get enough to eat, who do not get needed medical or dental care, and who live in crowded or dilapidated housing are at a disadvantage. But they do not think that rich children do better in school or avoid getting pregnant because they eat steak rather than hamburger, because they have a guest room in their home, or because their parents have a second car. As one Southern teacher put it, "After a certain level of comfort, and I mean comfort, the money just doesn't matter." When pressed about what she meant by comfort, she described "a house with basics such as heat that works, enough food, and in the South, air conditioning."

A teacher from an affluent neighborhood outside Chicago agreed that the extras do not help children at all, especially when they come at the price of having parents who work a lot. She put it this way: "They

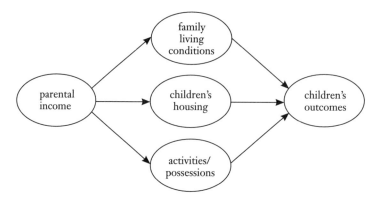

Figure 6.1 The mechanism through which income works: material well-being

[the parents] don't have to do it [work]. They do it for another TV, another redecorating, that kind of thing. They aren't there when the kids get home, and it's not because they need to work for the money. And the kid wants someone there. The parents say, 'Well, you wanted that new big TV,' but the kid didn't want it. He wanted a parent. The message is always 'You're not as important as the money.'" Another teacher explained that even poor parents can provide the basics for their children: "We were a lot poorer than my friends. We didn't have the fanciest clothes, and the fanciest this, and the fanciest that. You know . . . money might be tight, but some parents put the money on the wrong things."

Others seem to think that children need whatever goods and services are considered "normal" in their community. In making this point one teacher recalled, "I remember my first John Romain pocketbook. It was Christmas and, oh, I just cried. Then I fit in with everybody else." Another teacher, talking about the days when she was raising her children without much money, told me, "I used to argue with my mom. She'd say, 'Why do you buy them Izod shirts?' I'd say, 'Mom they were marked down twice. They have to have one or two to fit in.'" According to this view, children need not only warm clothing in the winter, but clothing that looks like what others are wearing.

Money can buy goods and services, but it can also buy experiences. One teacher put it this way: "Many of our children come to school with a real lack of different kinds of experiences. Then they have nothing to draw on when they read something. When I was young we didn't have much money, but we went to state parks, and we saw monuments and museums . . . and I had those experiences to draw on. A lot of our kids don't. A lot of kids have never been anywhere."

Ideally, we would like a single measure of the value of the goods and services available to children analogous to a measure of income. Then we could say that one child has "twice as much" as another. To construct such a measure we would need to either measure all the goods and services that are important to children or measure a random selection of such items and weight them by their importance to children. Social scientists usually assume that income is highly correlated with the goods and services available to children. Since it is much easier to measure income than to measure goods and services directly, they use income as a proxy for goods and services.

How Families Spend Additional Money

Table 6.1 shows how low-income and middle-income households spend their money. These data cover all households, not just those with children, so they are not ideal.[1] Nonetheless, they are revealing.[2] The poorest 20 percent of households report spending twice as much as they

Table 6.1 Household income and expenditures by income group, 1991

Expenditures	Poorest 20 percent	Middle 20 percent	Ratio of poorest/middle
Income	$5,981	$26,073	.229
Food at home	1,726	2,577	.670
Food away from home	617	1,368	.451
Alcoholic beverages	127	306	.415
Shelter	2,741	4,405	.622
Fuel and utilities	1,291	1,893	.682
Household operations	639	1,288	.496
Apparel	813	1,443	.563
Vehicles	670	1,960	.342
Other transportation	754	1,850	.408
Health care	1,041	1,580	.659
Pensions and insurance	296	2,224	.133
Other	2,044	3,851	.531
Total expenditure	13,464	26,144	.515

Source: U.S. Bureau of the Census, *Statistical Abstract of the United States, 1993*, table 708.

took in during 1991. This pattern reoccurs throughout the 1980s, too. Low-income families might be able to spend more than their income because they are only temporarily poor and can borrow or use savings to maintain their standard of living, or they may have a lot of unreported income. In either case, the consumption of high- and low-income households is more equal than their incomes.

Low-income households allocate a higher proportion of their expenditures to food eaten at home, shelter, and health care than middle-income households. Overall, low-income households spend just over half what middle-income households spend. But the outlays of low-income households on food eaten at home are two-thirds those of middle-income households, and the same is true for health care. Even in the case of housing, low-income households spend 62 percent of what middle-income households spend. Because the former devote a larger share of their resources to "necessities" than the latter, they often avoid serious material hardships. If material hardships hurt children's life chances but "luxuries" do not help, the fact that middle-income households spend more overall may not mean that their children fare much better.

Income and Material Hardship

The U.S. Department of Agriculture (USDA) has established food budgets for families of different sizes and for varying kinds of diets. Its lowest budget is the "thrifty" food budget. In 1993 the thrifty food budget for a family of three was $292 per month. The fact that a family spends $292 does not, of course, ensure that the children have a nutritious diet. That depends on how the family spends its money on food and how it prepares the food it buys. But the thrifty budget can in principle provide an adequate diet, and malnutrition is in fact quite rare in the United States. Using Consumer Expenditure Survey (CEX) data, I calculated the ratio of food expenditures to the thrifty food budget for households of various sizes. In 1990 the average low-income household spent 7 percent more than the thrifty food budget. The average middle-income household spent 21 percent more.

The most commonly reported food problem is not an inadequate weekly food budget, but occasionally running out of food. In a 1983–1985 survey, Christopher Jencks, Fay Cook, and I found that 18.6 percent of Chicago residents reported spending less than the USDA thrifty food budget on food (Mayer and Jencks 1989). But 25 percent reported that there had been a time in the last year when they needed food but could not afford to buy it. About half of the poorest 20 percent of households reported not being able to get needed food, compared with 18.3 percent of households with income twice the poverty line. This implies that lacking needed food is not the result of low income alone. In 1985, 7 percent of Chicago household heads reported that they or their children went hungry some time during the previous two years, compared with about a quarter of the heads of the poorest 20 percent of households.[3] But we have no way of knowing whether short-term food shortages of this sort affect children's outcomes.[4]

Table 6.2 shows the distribution of housing problems by income groups for children in the United States in 1991. It shows that the poorest 10 percent of children (I refer to these as poor children) are more likely than middle-income children to experience all the design and maintenance problems measured in the American Housing Survey (AHS). Children in the poorest 10 percent of the income distribution are very economically disadvantaged. Almost 20 percent of children were classified as officially poor in 1991, and about 13 percent of children receive AFDC. Thus it is not surprising that the poorest 10 percent of children experience housing problems. Many middle-income children experience at least one of these problem, but poor children are more likely than middle-income children to live in homes with multiple housing problems, although few have as many as four such problems. Poor children are also more likely to live in crowded homes and in neighborhoods that have abandoned buildings or that their parents see as having a crime problem.

Some readers will view the differences between poor and middle-income children as large, whereas others will view them as small. Those who wish to emphasize the differences between the rich and the poor usually cite the ratio of the proportion of poor children who experience a problem to the proportion of middle-income children who experience the same problem. Such a comparison leads to the conclusion that the homes of poor children are more than twice as likely as those of middle-income children to lack electrical outlets in a room or to have exposed wires, almost three times as likely to have cracks in walls or ceilings, and nearly four times more likely to have holes in the floor.

Table 6.2 Percentage of children living in homes with selected problems by parental income groups, 1991

Housing condition	Income decile		Income quintile				First–third
	First	Second	Second	Third	Fourth	Fifth	
Parental income	$3,918	$10,817	$21,097	$34,548	$51,941	$72,079	—
Design inadequacies							
Incomplete bathroom[a]	2.6	3.3	2.3	2.1	2.4	2.0	0.5
No central heat	32.3	34.7	28.1	21.4	14.9	9.6	10.9
No electrical outlets in one or more rooms	5.0	3.2	3.1	2.2	1.2	1.0	2.8
Exposed wires	5.5	5.0	2.4	2.1	1.4	1.0	3.4
Maintenance problems							
Holes in floor	5.0	5.7	2.4	1.3	0.8	0.5	3.7
Open cracks in wall or ceiling	18.9	15.2	8.7	6.5	3.6	2.7	12.4
Leaky roof	10.9	10.0	8.8	6.9	6.7	6.5	4.0
Signs of rats or mice	16.1	11.6	7.8	4.1	2.3	2.0	12.0
Multiple design or maintenance problems							
At least one problem	31.3	26.5	20.9	15.8	12.6	11.2	15.5
At least two problems	14.1	13.2	6.3	3.9	2.6	1.6	10.2
At least four problems	5.8	5.2	2.2	1.3	0.4	0.4	4.5
Neighborhood							
Crime problem[b]	39.6	32.4	26.7	23.9	21.4	19.9	15.7
Abandoned buildings	12.6	10.0	7.1	4.1	2.3	1.2	8.5
Crowding							
More than one person per room	19.0	20.0	20.0	11.0	6.2	5.3	8.0

Source: Computed from the 1985–1989 AHS by Timothy Veenstra. The unweighted sample size in the poorest decile is 4,027. The AHS income data are for families rather than households.

a. A complete bathroom includes hot and cold water, sink, toilet, and shower or tub for the exclusive use of household members.

b. Whether crime is a problem in the neighborhood is based on the respondent's judgment.

When the outcome is dichotomous, however, as most of these are, the size of this ratio depends on whether one considers the probability of having a problem or of lacking it. Those who want the ratio to sound large compare the likelihood of having a problem; those who want the ratio to sound small compare the likelihood of not having the problem.

The arithmetic difference between poor and middle-income households does not suffer from this problem. The last column in Table 6.2 uses this difference to compare poor and middle-income children. This difference ranges from a high of 15.7 percentage points for living in a neighborhood with a crime problem to a low of less than 1 percentage point for incomplete bathrooms. Most of the differences in housing problems seem modest, given that middle-income children have eight times as much income as poor children.

Table 6.3 shows the distribution of housing amenities, consumer durables, and telephone service in children's homes. Some of these amenities, such as dishwashers and second cars, might be considered "luxuries." Others, like having a telephone, are often considered necessities. If parents purchase goods and services in the order of their importance, families who have dishwashers or a second car are more likely to have met their basic material needs than families who do not.

Middle-income children are more likely than poor children to live in homes with all these amenities. The difference between poor chil-

Table 6.3   Percentage of children with selected consumer durables and telephone service by parental income groups

Amenity or durable	Income decile		Income quintile				First–third
	First	Second	Second	Third	Fourth	Fifth	
Housing amenities							
Air conditioning[a]	52.3	55.4	61.7	69.8	73.9	76.7	− 17.5
At least two bathrooms[a]	13.9	16.9	24.8	39.6	51.2	73.2	− 25.7
Durables							
Motor vehicle[b]	57.3	82.1	91.7	97.0	98.0	99.0	− 39.7
Two or more vehicles[b]	17.3	34.3	56.4	75.3	86.6	92.9	− 58.0
Clothes washer[c]	57.8	61.4	78.6	84.4	92.8	97.1	− 26.6
Clothes dryer[c]	37.5	38.0	62.0	75.2	88.9	94.6	− 37.7
Dishwasher[c]	16.5	16.0	25.8	41.6	58.2	79.7	− 25.1
Telephone[b]	68.7	79.7	90.8	96.5	98.3	99.5	− 27.8

a. Tabulations from the 1990 AHS by Timothy Veenstra.
b. Tabulations from the 1990 Census by David Knutson.
c. Tabulations from the 1988–1990 CEX by Judith Levine and Scott Winship using tapes prepared by John Sabelhaus.

dren and middle-income children is much greater for these amenities than for the housing conditions in Table 6.2, most of which are widely seen as necessities. It is hardly surprising that the difference between poor and middle-income children is greater for luxuries than for necessities. As we have seen, poor families spend a disproportionate amount of their economic resources on housing.

Table 6.4 shows the distribution of doctor visits over parental income groups for children younger than six years old and seven to eighteen years old in 1989. Poor children of all ages are less likely than middle-income children to have visited a doctor in the previous year. But the difference is less than four percentage points for children under seven, and it almost disappears for older children.

Among children with at least one doctor visit, the difference in the number of doctor visits between poor children and middle-income children is very small. Poor children tend to be sicker than affluent children, but even with extensive controls for health status poor children visit the doctor nearly as often as middle-class children (Mayer 1992). This does not mean that the quality of care is as high for poor children as for rich children. But when I control children's health status, poor children are almost as likely as middle-income children to visit a specialist (usually a pediatrician). Contrary to what many critics of the U.S. health care system claim, poor children are no more likely than middle-income children to have their visit in an emergency room once health status is controlled. Poor children are somewhat more likely to have their visit in a clinic, but it is not clear how this affects quality of care (Mayer 1992).

In summary, poor children clearly have worse living conditions than middle-income children. But serious housing problems are rare even among the poor, and poor children visit the doctor nearly as often as middle-income children. Poor families spend considerably less on food, but on average they still spend more than the USDA minimum food budget. The fact that few poor children experience serious housing problems, lack of medical care, or very low food expenditures is probably due to government programs such as Food Stamps and housing subsidies. A young student teacher told me, "When I was about ten, I can remember living off lima beans for like a whole month. I can remember when we went on Food Stamps having a meal other than beans and cornbread—it was tacos—and I remember that because I was so

Table 6.4 Children's annual doctor visits by parental income group, 1989

Age and measure of access	Income decile		Income quintile				First–third
	First	Second	Second	Third	Fourth	Fifth	
No doctor visit previous year (in percentages)							
Under seven	13.7	14.9	13.8	10.4	7.7	5.3	3.3[a]
Seven to eighteen	31.2	32.0	31.4	27.3	23.9	17.5	3.9[a]
Number of doctor visits in a year							
Under seven	3.6	3.7	3.6	4.0	4.0	4.7	0.9[b]
Seven to eighteen	2.6	2.6	2.1	2.3	2.5	3.1	1.1[b]

Source: Tabulations are by David Knutson using Health Interview Survey (HIS) public-use data tapes. Unweighted cell sizes range from 987 to 8,072.

a. The difference between the poorest decile and the third quintile.

b. The ratio of the poorest decile to the third quintile.

glad to have that meal." In the CEX, 60.6 percent of the poorest 20 percent of children's households report receiving Food Stamps. In the AHS, 36.3 percent of the poorest 10 percent of children's households either received housing subsidies or lived in public housing in 1991. In the same year, nearly 75 percent of poor children under the age of six received Medicaid (House Ways and Means Committee 1993, p. 1639).

The findings I have reported so far all come from surveys that cover a single domain, such as housing or medical care, and ask about income and living conditions in a single year. Families that are poor for only a year might not experience much material deprivation, because they can sometimes borrow or spend savings to maintain an adequate standard of living. In addition, none of these surveys includes information about goods and services specifically related to children, such as the number of books children have and whether they visit museums. To assess the effect of parental income on child-specific goods and services and the effect of persistent poverty on children's living conditions, I return to the PSID and the NLSY.

Between 1968 and 1972, the PSID asked families how much they spend on food consumed at home, food consumed away from home, rent, and mortgage payments. It also asked about the number of rooms in a family's home, the number of cars it owned, whether family members had health insurance, and how much the household spent on cigarettes and alcohol. Interviewers indicated whether a respondent's home needed major repairs and whether it was clean. I will refer to these measures as "household living conditions."

Because many people believe that material deprivations are especially likely to affect children's outcomes, I also created four measures of what I call material hardship: whether the child's housing was crowded, whether the family lacked a car, whether the family rented its home, and whether the family spent less on food than the USDA thrifty budget. I created a "household living conditions index" that weights living conditions in a way that maximizes the correlation of the index and parental income. The components of this index include both material living conditions and the hardships just described. Appendix D explains how this index was created.

The NLSY includes a few measures of possessions and activities that mainly benefit children. The possessions are how many books a child has and whether a child has a tape recorder or CD player. The activities are how often a child goes on an outing and how often a child visits a museum. I created a "possessions and activities" index by weighting these four measures in a way that maximizes their correlation with parental income.

NLSY interviewers were asked to record whether a child's home was safe, "dark and perceptually monotonous," "minimally cluttered," and "reasonably clean." Cheap apartments are presumably more likely than expensive apartments to be unsafe, dark, and monotonous. They are also likely to be small and therefore cluttered. Cleanliness might be a characteristic of the housing unit as well as its occupants. I created a "housing environment" index in a way that maximizes its correlation with income. Appendix D describes how I did this. The NLSY indexes are only available for four- and five-year-olds, because some of their components are not asked for older children.

Although these measures omit many potentially important goods and services, the measures for which I have information are probably highly correlated with those I omit. The household living conditions are especially likely to be correlated with whether families' basic needs are met. If households purchase goods and services in order of their importance, those who have a car and eat out often are likely to have met their basic needs for food and shelter. The activities and possessions index is probably correlated with other things parents purchase for their children. Parents who do not take their children on outings or buy them books are probably unlikely to provide music lessons, send their children to camp, or expose them to other stimulating activities.

Both income and living conditions change a lot from year to year. Table 6.5 shows average living conditions from 1969 to 1972 by average parental income group in those same years. Appendix D shows these living conditions measured in 1972 by parental income in 1972. The score on the living conditions index is about a third of a standard deviation lower for children whose families were poor for five years than for children whose families were poor in one year. Using annual data like that available in the national surveys I discussed earlier exaggerates income differences among families but understates the material deprivations of those who are poor for several years.[5]

Poor children are worse off than middle-income children on all household living conditions. The standard deviation for the household living conditions index is .439, so poor children's living conditions are more than a standard deviation worse than those of middle-income children.

Table 6.6 shows that poor children have fewer books, visit the museum less often, and go on fewer outings than middle-income children. Poor children's homes are also less likely than those of middle-income children to be clean, safe, and uncluttered and more likely to be dark and monotonous.

Even when I control a child's age and family size and parents' education, age, and race, the effect of parental income on all household living conditions is large and statistically significant. Table 6.7 shows that when I control these factors, doubling parental income increases expenditures on food eaten at home by $1,492 (.599 standard deviations) and expenditures on food eaten away from home by $472 (.714 standard deviations). Doubling income increases the living conditions index by nearly a standard deviation.

Table 6.8 shows that when I control family background characteristics, doubling parental income from $15,000 to $30,000 increases the activities and possessions index by .256 standard deviations. Doubling income increases the housing environment index by .271 standard deviations.

Table 6.5 Household living conditions by parental income group, 1969–1972

Living conditions	Poorest 10 percent	Middle 20 percent	Poorest/ middle	Poorest– middle
Income (1992 dollars)	18,723	45,130	41.5	—
Expenditures (1992 dollars)				
Food at home	4,879	7,059	69.1	—
Food away from home	146	414	35.3	—
Cigarettes	101	149	67.8	—
Alcohol	40	117	34.2	—
Value of dwelling	26,502	55,181	48.0	—
Number of cars	.75	1.51	49.7	—
Number of rooms	4.85	5.84	83.0	—
Years spending less than USDA budget	.59	.33	—	.26
Years with health insurance	2.11	3.65	—	−1.54
Years home needs repairs	1.66	1.11	—	.55
Years crowded	42.4	25.5	—	16.9
Household living conditions index	9.944	10.569	—	−.625

Source: Computed from PSID data by Timothy Veenstra. See Appendix D for a description of the living conditions.

Table 6.6 Activities, possessions, and housing conditions of four- and five-year-olds by parental income group

Living conditions	Poorest 10 percent	Middle 20 percent	Poorest– Middle
Number of books (1 to 10)	7.3	9.5	−2.1
Percentage with tape recorder	54.3	77.7	−23.4
Number of annual trips to the museum	3.2	3.0	0.2
Number of annual outings	82.9	109.7	−26.8
Activities and possessions index	9.87	10.13	−.260
Percentage with clean home	83.1	93.1	−10.0
Percentage with safe home	81.6	92.5	−10.9
Percentage with uncluttered home	78.9	81.4	−2.5
Percentage with home not dark and monotonous	77.3	94.6	−17.3
Housing environment index	9.97	10.10	−.130

Source: Computed from the NLSY mother-child files by David Knutson.

Table 6.7 The effect of doubling parental income from $15,000 to $30,000 on living conditions

Living conditions in 1969–1972	Mean (SD)	Effect of income increase
Household living conditions index	10.593 (.439)	.399
Expenditures (1992 dollars)		
Food at home	7,125 (2,491)	1,492
Food away from home	539 (661)	472
Cigarettes	133 (136)	28
Alcohol	95 (156)	31
Value of dwelling (1992 dollars)	60,521 (39,710)	26,183
Number of cars	1.48 (.71)	.353
Number of rooms	5.90 (1.24)	.518
Years owned home	3.39 (2.09)	.838
Years home needed repairs	1.13 (.70)	−.236
Years home dirty	1.43 (.93)	−.011
Years insured	3.44 (1.04)	.574
Years spending less than USDA budget	.33 (.35)	−.187

Source: Calculated from PSID data by Timothy Veenstra. Estimates in column two control parents' education and age, child's race, and family size.

Higher income leads to spending more on food, eating out, more roomy houses, and more automobiles. Thus when the government transfers cash or noncash resources to families, children are likely to be better housed and better fed. Parental income has a smaller effect on whether parents spend money on stimulating playthings and outings for their children and whether they create a safe and pleasant environment for their children.

Table 6.8   The effect of doubling parental income from $15,000 to $30,000 on four- and five-year-olds' activities, possessions, and housing environment

Living conditions	Mean (SD)	Effect of income increase
Number of books (1 to 10)	9.02	.56
	(2.56)	
Percentage with tape recorder	76.4	7.3
Number of annual trips to the museum	3.44	.57
	(5.68)	
Number of annual outings	103.89	2.67
	(96.70)	
Activities and possessions index	10.089	.072
	(.273)	
Percentage with clean home	93.8	3.9
Percentage with safe home	93.7	3.8
Percentage with uncluttered home	82.4	3.7
Percentage with dark and monotonous home	6.2	−4.6
Housing environment index	10.079	.052
	(.192)	

Source: Calculated from the NLSY mother-child files by David Knutson. Estimates in column two control mother's education, age, race, AFQT score, and child's sex.

Living Conditions and Children's Outcomes

The investment model suggests that the things parents purchase as their income increases actually improve children's outcomes. Table 6.9 shows the effect of a one standard deviation improvement in living conditions on each outcome. The first column controls only parents' income at the time that living conditions are measured, which is before the outcomes. The second column controls this same measure of income, but adds parents' age, race, and education. In the NLSY I also control the mother's AFQT score. For education outcomes and test scores, I also control the child's sex; and for labor-market outcomes I also control the county unemployment rate.

When I use the NLSY and control only parents' income, increasing the housing environment index by a standard deviation increases four- and five-year-olds' PPVT scores by 2.16 points. Its effect on the other test scores is smaller. Improving activities and possessions by a standard deviation increases PPVT scores by 6.21 points. This is a large effect—

Table 6.9 The effect of improving living conditions by one standard deviation

Index Outcome	Controlling income	Controlling observed parental traits and income
Housing environment index for four- and five-year-olds		
PPVT	2.16	1.47
PIAT math	1.92	1.48
PIAT reading	1.83	1.15
BPI	−.976	−.941
Activities and possessions index for four- and five-year-olds		
PPVT	6.21	3.44
PIAT math	2.90	1.58
PIAT reading	2.51	1.32
BPI	−1.98	−2.07
Living conditions index for adolescents and young adults		
Probability of teenage childbearing	−.073	−.038
Probability of dropping out of high school	−.050	−.035
Years of education	.296	.214
Years of education for high school graduates	.190	.142
Male workers' hourly wages (1992 dollars)	.729	.291
Male workers' annual earnings (1992 dollars)	951	−135
Probability of male idleness	.011	.026
Probability of single motherhood	−.087	−.023

Sources: Estimates for children's test scores were computed from the NLSY mother-child files by David Knutson. Estimates for other outcomes were computed from the PSID by Timothy Veenstra. To get the change in the outcome due to a standard deviation change in living conditions shown in column one for continuous outcomes, I estimate $O = b_1 L + b_2 I$, where O is an outcome, L is the living conditions, and I is income. Then I calculate the change in an outcome attributable to a standard deviation change in living conditions as $C = b'_1(SD_o)$, where b' is the standardized coefficient of living conditions and SD_o is the standard deviation of the outcome. When the dependent variable is dichotomous, I estimate $SD_L (b_p)$ where SD_L is the standard deviation of the living condition index and b_p is the partial derivative of coefficient for living conditions in an analogous logistic regression.

more than a third of a standard deviation. The second column shows that controlling observed parental characteristics cuts the apparent effect of living conditions on PPVT scores to 3.44 points.

Combining Tables 6.9 and 6.8, we can see that doubling parental income increases possessions and activities by .264 standard deviations, and increasing activities and possessions by a standard deviation increases PPVT scores by 3.44 points. Therefore, doubling income increases activities and possessions enough to increases PPVT scores by .908 points (.264)(3.44). The increase is smaller for other test scores.

For adolescent and young-adult outcomes, I measure income in 1969–1972, the same years in which living conditions are measured. Table 6.9 shows that when I control only parental income, a standard deviation improvement in the living conditions index reduces teenage childbearing by 7.3 percentage points, reduces single motherhood by 8.7 percentage points, and increases education by a fifth of a year. Improving living conditions also appears to increase the wages and earnings of males. But controlling family background characteristics reduces these effects.

Parental income has a large effect on the household living conditions index. Doubling parental income increases the index by .909 standard deviations. The living conditions index has an important effect on years of education. When we control other family background characteristics, children with a one standard deviation advantage on the living conditions index receive an extra .214 years of higher education. Therefore, doubling parental income increases household living conditions enough to increase years of higher education by .195 years (.909)(.214). The living conditions index includes home ownership, so it is not surprising that it influences children's chances of going to college. Parents who own their own homes can use the equity they have accumulated to borrow for their children's education. The living conditions index has a much smaller effect on other outcomes. For example, these results suggest that increasing living conditions by a standard deviation reduces teenage childbearing by 3.8 percentage points. Therefore, doubling income improves living conditions enough to reduce teenage childbearing by 3.45 (.909)(3.8) percentage points.

Observed parental characteristics account for some of the apparent effect of living conditions on children's outcomes. Unobserved parental characteristics might account for even more. I employed a technique similar to the one in Chapter 5 that uses Time 2 income to estimate the influence of stable parental characteristics on income and living conditions. This technique is described in Appendix C. In this case, however, controlling unobserved characteristics did not change these results much.

Because the activities and possessions I measure are inexpensive and not strongly related to income, they mainly reflect parents' tastes and values. Books appear to benefit children because parents who buy a lot of books are likely to read to their children. Parents who do not buy books for their children are probably not likely to read to them even if the books are free, and parents who do not take their children on outings may be less likely to spend time with them in other ways.

The activities, possessions, and housing environments that are important to children's outcomes are only moderately related to parents' income. Whether children have these amenities depends on parents' tastes and values. The household living conditions that are strongly related to parents' income are only moderately related to children's outcomes. This is probably because government programs targeted at helping poor parents make severe material hardships unusual even among the poor. Once basic needs are met, additional improvements in household living conditions do little to help children succeed.

Beyond the basics, therefore, cash plays a relatively modest role in assuring children's success. A school counselor put it this way: "Giving the family money can improve the standard of living, but it won't give the children the tools they will need for success." Her colleague added, "I think it is the parenting values—the parenting style—that matters more than the money." I turn to this idea in the next chapter.

7

□ □ □ □ □

Income, Psychological Well-Being, and Parenting Practices

One common explanation for why children from low-income families fare worse than children from more affluent families is that their parents experience more stress. Stress, in turn, is supposed to interfere with competent parenting. This hypothesis has considerable intuitive appeal. Worrying about money is common at all income levels, but one expects it to become more common as income falls. And almost all parents acknowledge that they are more apt to get angry and treat their children badly when they feel especially stressed. This model is shown in Figure 7.1.

Nonetheless, it is important to recognize that this model is at odds with "culture" theories, which imply that the long-term poor develop values, attitudes, and behaviors that reduce the stress associated with being poor. If these culture theories were true, we might not observe any more stress among the long-term poor than among the middle class. We would, however, still expect those who experience an income loss to undergo more stress. Yet Chapter 4 showed that income loss had little effect on most children's outcomes in this book once average income was held constant.

Income and Parental Stress

The empirical evidence that psychologists cite in support of the parental-stress hypothesis is largely indirect. Low-income adults are more likely than high-income adults to suffer from mental health problems.

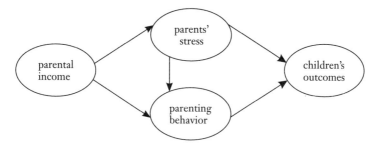

Figure 7.1 The mechanism through which income works: psychological well-being

Low-income adults are also more likely to experience stressful events, such as not being able to pay their bills or getting evicted. They are also more likely to have experienced a marital break-up, a job loss, the death of a relative or friend, or a residential move. And they are more likely to report that they worry about money. Experiences such as these are in turn associated with depression and other signs of stress.[1]

Poor parents are also more likely than other parents to use "power-assertive" disciplinary techniques, such as physical punishment, rather than reasoning, more likely to value obedience, and less likely to be supportive of their children. Psychologists often attribute these differences to the stress associated with poverty. Again, the link seems plausible. Parents who are depressed or who experience other negative emotional states are more likely than other parents to be punitive, inconsistent, and unresponsive toward their children. Both maternal depression and other forms of emotional distress are associated with physical abuse, aversive and coercive discipline, and diminished maternal sensitivity toward children. Because poverty is associated with symptoms of stress, and because symptoms of stress are associated with poor parenting practices, many researchers infer that poverty leads to bad parenting practices, which then cause worse outcomes among children.

Unfortunately, few studies provide empirical evidence about the causal links between parents' income, their psychological well-being, and parenting practices or about the links between children's outcomes and parenting practices. Most of the relevant work assesses children's social and emotional outcomes rather than the outcomes of interest in this book. Many of these studies use small and unrepresentative samples. Some cover only economically disadvantaged families, and others use samples of clinically depressed or mentally ill parents. Almost all these studies emphasize the statistical significance rather than the magnitude of effects. If parental income has a modest effect on parental stress, and stress has a modest effect on children's outcomes, the net result will be that income has a tiny effect on children's outcomes through its effect on parental stress. Thus the parental-stress hypothesis, though intuitively appealing, is not currently supported by strong empirical evidence.

One reason we know so little about the relationship between parental income, parental stress, and children's outcomes is that psychologists do not agree on how they should define or measure stress or distress. McLoyd's (1990) review of the literature, for example, includes studies that variously consider parental aggression, frustration, depression, anxiety, hostility, dissatisfaction with oneself, and somatic complaints.

Pearlin et al. (1981) argue that stress can arise from either discrete events, such as income loss, or from ongoing problems, such as persistent poverty. Life events and life strains intensify what they call "role strains," that is, one's ability to fulfill roles such as parent, spouse, or employee successfully. This in turn leads to diminished self-concept. When parents do not have resources available to mediate the impact of these "strains," they experience stress. Pearlin et al. conclude that stress can, at best, "be recognized as a generic term that subsumes a variety of manifestations" (p. 341).

Another reason we know so little about the stress-related consequences of low income is that while parental stress can be a result of low income, it can also be a cause of low income. Or other factors, such as marital dissolution or unemployment, can cause both stress and low income. Different measures of stress probably have different relationships to income. Bipolar disorder seems more likely to be a cause of low income than an effect. Feelings of frustration seem more likely to be a result of low income than a cause.

Corcoran et al. (1985) estimated the effect of changes in economic status on changes in adults' feelings of efficacy. Among low-income white men, changes in earnings were accompanied by changes in reported feelings of efficacy. Among black men, changes in hours worked and job-related geographical moves were associated with changes in efficacy. Among white women who headed their own households, changes in economic status seldom affected efficacy. Among black women, improving economic status appeared to lower feelings of efficacy.

Brooks-Gunn et al. (1991) find that maternal locus of control has a very small effect on the IQ and behavior problems of three-year-olds. Raising maternal locus of control by one standard deviation reduced the chances that girls ages fourteen to nineteen had an out-of-wedlock birth by 2.6 percentage points (from a mean of 10.6 percent) and reduced their chances of dropping out of high school by 4.4 percentage points (from a mean of 10.8 percent). But whereas maternal locus of control has an important effect on adolescent outcomes, income has only a modest effect on maternal locus of control. A one standard deviation increase in parents' poverty ratio increases mothers' locus of control by .10 standard deviations. Since the standard deviation of the poverty ratio is about 2, doubling income only raises mothers' locus of control by about .05 standard deviations, which would reduce teenagers' chances of dropping out by .22 percentage points and teenage childbearing by .10 points.

In one widely cited study about the relationship between income and stress, Pearlin et al. (1981) claim that job disruptions, such as being fired, demoted, or having to leave work because of illness, are likely to result in "economic strain." They argue that "as people experience an intensified strain, there is a substantial chance that they will also experience a heightened level of depression" (p. 345). To measure economic strain, they ask respondents whether they can afford a "suitable" home, whether they can afford furniture and household equipment that needs to be replaced, whether they can afford the kind of car they need, whether they have enough money for the medical care and clothing they need, how much difficulty they have paying their bills, and whether they have some money left over at the end of the month. Of course, this kind of economic strain is not necessarily associated with low income. Families' expectations change as their income increases, so a middle-income family's idea of a suitable home or car is different from a poor family's. Unfortunately, this study does not report the correlation between income and economic strain.

Pearlin et al. find that the correlation between disruptive job events and increased depression is .34 They argue that the change in income and the resulting change in economic strain that follow disruptive job events cause the change in depression. But the correlation between a change in income and a change in depression is only -.064. This does not suggest that parental income mainly affects children by influencing parental depression.

Glen Elder and his colleagues have also argued that income influences children's outcomes through its influence on parents' psychological well-being and behavior.[2] Once again, however, the relationships they report are weak. In a recent study, for example, the correlation between parental income and fathers' depression was $-.15$, and the correlation between fathers' depression and children's school performance (a composite of grade point average and getting along with teachers) was $-.18$. At most, therefore, increasing parental income by a standard deviation might reduce a father's depression enough to improve a child's school performance by $(-.15)(-.18)$ .027 standard deviations. The effect through mothers' depression was equally small. From this we can conclude that if income has an effect on children's school performance, it is not mainly through parents' depression. The idea that these paths are important comes mainly from focusing on their statistical significance while ignoring their size.

The PSID includes indexes of parents' aspirations, trust, efficacy, and anger. None of these indexes is ideal for measuring stress, but each taps a concept that psychologists have used to measure distress. Aspirations are a measure of a person's motivation to get ahead. The trust index measures optimism and how much a person takes others into account. The efficacy index tries to measure how much a person feels in control of events. The anger index subsumes both generalized anger and pessimism. To minimize random error, I average each measure of parents' psychological well-being over five years. (See Appendix D for details of the indexes.)[3]

Table 7.1 shows the effect of doubling income on the parents' psychological attributes in the PSID controlling parents' age and education, child's age and race, and household size. Parental income is the average for the five years when the attribute was measured. Doubling parental income appears to raise efficacy by about a third of a standard deviation, and trust by about a fifth of a standard deviation. It appears to reduce aspirations by a small amount. Income appears to have almost no effect on parental anger.

Table 7.2 shows the effect of a one standard deviation improvement

Table 7.1 The effect of increasing parental income on standardized measures of parents' psychological attributes, 1968–1972

Psychological indexes	Effect of doubling income	Effect of a standard deviation increase in income
Aspirations	−.121	−.094
Efficacy	.364	.284
Trust	.189	.148
Anger	.008	.006

Source: Calculated from PSID data by Timothy Veenstra. All the psychological indexes have a standard deviation of 1.00. The effect of income is statistically significant at the .05 level for all parental attributes except anger. Estimates control parents' age and education, child's race and age, and household size.

Table 7.2 The effect of improving parental psychological attributes by one standard deviation on children's outcomes

Children's outcomes	Aspirations	Efficacy	Trust	Anger
Probability of teenage childbearing	.021	−.019	−.024	−.001
Probability of dropping out of high school	.013	−.018	−.020	−.002
Years of education	−.025	.135	.168	.000
Years of education for high school graduates	.022	.070	.073	−.026
Male workers' hourly wages (1992 dollars)	.163	.357	.038	.202
Male workers' annual earnings (1992 dollars)	616	918	−109	143
Probability of male idleness	.006	.017	−.019	−.011
Probability of single motherhood	.022	−.029	−.040	−.023

Source: Calculated by Timothy Veenstra using the PSID.

in these measures of parents' psychological well-being on children's outcomes.[4] Parental anger has very little effect on children's outcomes. High parental aspirations appear to increase teenage childbearing, dropping out of high school, and single motherhood, although these effects are small. Improving parental trust by a standard deviation reduces teenage childbearing by 2.4 percentage points, dropping out by 2 percentage points, and single motherhood by 4 percentage points. It increases years of education by .168 years, but has a small effect on young men's labor-market outcomes. Parental efficacy has a greater effect than parental trust on male wages and earnings.

Combining the results in Tables 7.1 and 7.2, we see that doubling income only improves parental trust enough to reduce teenage childbearing by $(.189)(.024) = .005$ percentage points, and increase schooling by $(.189)(.168) = .03$ years. Income has a greater effect on parental efficacy than it does on parental trust. But parental efficacy has a smaller effect than parental trust on children's outcomes. Doubling income still improves efficacy enough to reduce teenage childbearing by $(.364)(-.019) = -.7$ percentage points. Doubling parental income does not reduce parental aspirations enough to have much of an effect on most outcomes.

No single measure captures all aspects of parents' psychological well-being. Income might influence some combination of these attributes more than any one attribute. But when I add all four measures of parental psychological well-being to equations predicting children's outcomes, they never explain more than a fifth of the income effect, and for most outcomes they explain less than 15 percent of the income effect. If parents' psychological attributes affect their income as well as the other way around, the stress-related effect of raising parental income on children's outcomes will be even smaller than these estimates imply.

Income and Parenting Practices

In the parental-stress model, stress affects children's outcomes by affecting the way parents treat their children. Some studies show, for instance, that mass unemployment increases the incidence of physical punishment and child abuse (Elder 1979; Lempers et al. 1989). This does not necessarily mean that income loss increases child abuse. When parents lose their jobs many things happen at once. They spend more time with their children, which creates the opportunity for abuse. They may turn to alcohol and drugs, which also increase the chances of abuse. If these changes were mainly the result of having more time rather than less money, we might find that job loss increased child abuse even if unemployment compensation replaced 100 percent of lost wages.

Conversely, income could affect parenting practices even if they had nothing to do with parental stress. If practices that are adaptive for the poor make it harder for children to escape poverty, as the culture of poverty hypothesis implies, low parental income could harm children even if their parents experienced no more stress than affluent parents. If poverty makes the poor reluctant to think carefully about the future, for example, this could have adverse effects on children that are unrelated to measures of stress.

The NLSY provides several measures with which we can test the relationship between income and parenting practices. It asked mothers what they would do if their children hit them—would they hit back, spank the child, send the child to his or her room, give the child a chore, talk to the child, or ignore the child? I created a "discipline-style" index that maximized the relationship between these responses and parental income. Higher scores on the index correspond to the responses given by affluent parents. Appendix D describes the index in detail.

NLSY interviewers also recorded whether the mother conversed with her child during the interview; caressed, hugged, or kissed her child; physically restricted her child; spanked her child; or answered her child's questions verbally. I used this information to create a "nurturing" index. My third index, the TV-Read index, is based on mothers' estimates of how often they read to their children and how many hours per day the television is on. Once again, both indexes were scaled to maximize their correlation with income, and higher scores were associated with the behavior of affluent parents.

The PSID also asked parents how much time they spent watching television and whether any adult had attended a PTA meeting in the last year. I use these to make a TV-PTA index for PSID respondents.

These measures of parenting practices are not ideal; they omit many things that influence the relationship between parents and children. Nor are they necessarily good proxies for unmeasured aspects of parenting. In the NLSY, a mother's discipline style is nearly unrelated to her nurturing ($r = .053$), and the TV-Read index is only moderately related to her discipline style ($r = .243$) or nurturing ($r = .111$).

Table 7.3 shows that when I control family background, doubling parental income has a small effect on the NLSY measures of parental practices, even though all these indexes are weighted so as to maximize their correlation with income. Doubling income has a somewhat greater effect on whether parents watch television and go to PTA meetings in the PSID.

Table 7.4 shows that all three NLSY measures of parenting practices have a substantial effect on PPVT scores and a smaller effect on other scores. The TV-Read index has the biggest effect on test scores. Table

Table 7.3   The effect of increasing parental income on standardized indexes of parenting practices

Psychological indexes	Effect of doubling income	Effect of a standard deviation increase in income
Discipline	.165	.159
Nurturing	.152	.146
TV-Read	.130	.125
TV-PTA	.229	.178

Sources: Estimates in the first three rows were computed from the NLSY mother-child files by David Knutson using a sample of four- and five-year-olds in 1986, 1988, and 1990. The last row was estimated from PSID data by Timothy Veenstra. Appendix D describes the construction of each index.

Table 7.4   The effect of improving parenting practices by one standard deviation on four- and five-year-olds' outcomes

Children's outcomes	Parenting index		
	Discipline	Nurture	TV-Read
PPVT	2.63	2.77	4.68
PIAT math	.75	1.77	1.98
PIAT reading	.22	1.14	2.05
BPI	− .87	− 1.23	− 1.87

Source: Computed from the NLSY mother-child files by David Knutson.

Table 7.5   The effect of reducing parental television watching and increasing PTA attendance by one standard deviation on adolescent and young adult-outcomes

Outcomes	Effect of improvement
Probability of teenage childbearing	− .023
Probability of dropping out of high school	− .010
Years of education	.207
Years of education for high school graduates	.125
Male workers' hourly wages (1992 dollars)	.122
Male workers' annual earnings (1992 dollars)	717
Probability of male idleness	− .018
Probability of single motherhood	− .030

7.5 shows that PSID children whose parents watch a lot of television and seldom attend PTA meetings have somewhat worse outcomes than other children.

Combining these tables, we can see that doubling parental income does not improve any of these parenting practices enough to improve children's outcomes substantially. Thus though a standard deviation improvement in the TV-Read index increases PPVT scores by 4.68 points, doubling parental income improves the TV-Read index by only .130 standard deviations. As a result, doubling income improves TV-Read enough to raise PPVT scores by (.130)(4.68) = .608 points. The other parenting practices have smaller effects on outcomes. Doubling income improves the PSID measure of TV-PTA by .229 standard deviations. A standard deviation improvement in TV-PTA increases years of education by .207. Doubling parental income improves TV-PTA enough to increase education by (.229)(.207) = .047 years. Its effect on other outcomes is also small.

When I regress children's test scores on all the parenting practices, controlling parents' income and age, child's race, age, sex, and family size, they always have large and statistically significant effects. Nonetheless, taken as a group, these parenting practices account for only 10 to 20 percent of the effect of income. This means that although parenting practices are important for children's outcomes, they do not account for much of the effect of income.

These correlations do not suggest that parental income influences children's outcomes primarily through its influence on parenting practices. Yet the correlations I report in this chapter are no smaller than those reported by advocates of this hypothesis. The widely cited study by Conger et al. (1992) concludes, for example, that economic pressures were associated with "depression and demoralization for both parents, which [were] related to marital conflict and disruptions in skillful parenting." The correlation matrix provided in that study shows that the standardized effect of per capita income on male seventh-graders' school performance through mothers' discipline style is .063.[5] Since the standard deviation of per capita income is about equal to the mean, these results suggest that doubling income per capita from its mean ($5,100 in 1989 dollars) improves school performance by .063 standard deviations. This does not control other characteristics of families, such as parental education, that are likely to influence parental income, parenting practices, and children's outcomes. Controlling such factors would reduce the apparent effect of income on school performance to less than .063. If one makes similar estimates based on the relationship of parental income to mothers' hostility or other measures of parenting style, their effect is even smaller in Conger et al.'s data.

Parent-child interactions appear to be important for children's success, but these results provide little evidence that parents' income has a large influence on parenting practices. Nor do the results in this chapter suggest that parental income has a large effect on parents' psychological attributes other than their feelings of efficacy. And parental efficacy has only a modest effect on children's outcomes.

8

□ □ □ □ □

More Evidence on the "True" Effect of Income

In this chapter I try to determine the true effect of income on children's life chances using two different approaches that depend on changes in income. First, I compare trends in parental income with trends in children's outcomes. Second, I compare the outcomes of children who lived in states that paid high AFDC benefits with the outcomes of children who lived in states that paid low AFDC benefits. I also review the evidence from the Negative Income Tax experiments.

Trends in Parents' Income and Children's Outcomes

If parental income has a substantial influence on children's behavior relative to other factors, trends in parents' income ought to produce parallel trends in children's behavior, at least if other major influences stay more or less the same.

The Median Child

Table 8.1 shows trends in the real household income of children (in 1992 dollars) between 1959 and 1989 using data from the two main sources of government statistics on income, the decennial Census and the CPS. I show Census data between 1959 and 1989 and CPS data between 1969 and 1989. The mean of the third quintile is approximately the median for all children, so both the Census and the CPS show that the median child's household income increased during the

Table 8.1 Mean income in 1992 dollars for children's households, 1959–1989, by income decile or quintile and year

Data set	Decile		Quintile			
Year	First	Second	Second	Third	Fourth	Fifth
Household income						
Census						
1959	3,844	10,752	17,995	25,071	33,112	58,608
1969	6,021	15,662	24,939	34,696	45,834	77,087
1979	5,330	14,527	25,244	37,812	51,155	85,535
1989	4,619	13,467	24,367	37,902	53,826	93,912
Percentage change						
1959–69	56.6	45.7	38.6	38.4	38.4	31.5
1969–79	−11.5	−7.3	1.2	9.0	11.6	11.0
1979–89	−13.3	−7.3	−3.5	0.2	5.2	9.8
1969–89	−23.3	−14.0	−2.3	9.2	17.4	21.8
CPS						
1969	8,085	16,871	25,338	34,668	45,262	74,449
1979	6,321	14,800	24,941	37,252	50,286	81,047
1989	5,217	13,049	23,490	37,320	53,414	91,292
Percentage change						
1969–79	−21.8	−12.3	−1.6	7.5	11.1	8.9
1979–89	−17.5	−11.8	−5.8	0.2	6.2	12.6
1969–89	−35.5	−22.7	−7.3	7.6	18.0	22.6
Per capita income						
Census						
1959	781	2,166	3,689	5,215	6,860	11,869
1969	1,353	3,326	5,268	7,217	9,408	15,365
1979	1,402	3,606	6,043	8,718	11,571	18,596
1989	1,247	3,428	5,961	8,988	12,664	21,468
Percentage change						
1959–69	73.2	53.6	42.8	38.4	37.1	29.5
1969–79	3.6	8.4	14.7	20.8	23.0	21.0
1979–89	−11.1	−4.9	−1.4	3.1	9.4	15.4
1969–89	−7.9	3.1	13.2	24.5	34.6	39.7
CPS						
1969	1,864	3,648	5,354	7,392	9,402	16,238
1979	1,663	3,679	6,026	8,711	11,491	17,399
1989	1,433	3,335	5,778	9,062	12,666	21,006
Percentage change						
1969–79	−10.8	0.9	12.6	17.8	22.2	7.2
1979–89	−13.8	−9.3	−4.1	4.0	10.2	20.7
1969–89	−23.1	−8.6	7.9	22.6	34.7	29.4

Source: Tabulations by David Knutson. Means for the top quintile are biased downward due to top-coding.

1970s and hardly changed during the 1980s. The Census also shows that the median child's household income increased very rapidly during the 1960s.

The average size of children's households declined from 4.25 to 3.39 members between 1960 and 1990, so the typical family needed less income in 1990 than in 1960. The estimates in the top half of Table 8.1 make no adjustment for such changes in household size. This strategy assumes that from a child's viewpoint the benefits of additional household members (who might be siblings, a second parent, a grandparent, a live-in boyfriend, or a roomer) exactly equal the costs. This is unlikely. The bottom half of Table 8.1 estimates the per capita income of children's households. This measure assumes that there are no economies of scale in larger households. Per capita income and unadjusted income set the upper and lower bounds of the "true" equivalence scale, which is somewhere between these extremes. In both the Census and the CPS, median per capita income increased substantially in the 1970s and less in the 1980s. Census data show that median per capita income increased very rapidly in the 1960s. In both the Census and the CPS, the increase in median per capita income was greater than the increase in median unadjusted income in both the 1970s and the 1980s. Much of the improvement in real per capita income is thus traceable to declining household size rather than rising income.

Regardless of how I adjust for household size, the trend in median household income is the same: the median child's real household income grew fastest during the 1960s, slower during the 1970s, and hardly at all during the 1980s. The trend in median household income is, however, sensitive to the way we adjust income for changes in prices. Different price indexes used by the federal government yield changes in the income of the median child's family that range from close to no change to an increase of 15.3 percent between 1969 and 1989.[1]

Inequality

If we compare 1989 with 1969 and do not adjust for household size, income rose for children in the top half of the income distribution and fell for those in the bottom half. Per capita income rose for the top four-fifths of the income distribution and fell for the bottom fifth.

Because income grew more at the top of the distribution than in the middle, the relative position of those in the middle deteriorated even though their absolute position improved. It is unclear whether the net result would be to make children in the middle better or worse off. That depends on whether relative or absolute economic well-being affects children more.[2] This is important because the gap between the middle and the top quintile grew by 40 to 80 percent between 1969 and 1989, whereas the absolute income of the middle quintile rose only 8 to 10 percent. Between 1959 and 1969, in contrast, parental income increased rapidly, whereas inequality declined slightly. Predictions about how these trends should affect the median child's outcomes clearly depend on whether relative or absolute income is more important.

For the poorest 20 percent of children, in contrast, the predictions are unequivocal. Their income rose both absolutely and relatively from 1959 to 1969, then fell both relatively and absolutely between 1969 and 1989.

Theories about the effect of parental income on children's outcomes are seldom explicit about whether relative or absolute levels of parental income matter for children. A discussion I had with two teachers illustrates this point. One argued that being poor was worse for white children than for black children because "the gap is so much bigger between the white that has and the white that doesn't." The other argued that being poor was worse for blacks because their absolute poverty was worse.

Children's Outcomes

Most children's outcomes are measured at a particular age. To assess trends in teenage childbearing, for instance, we must compare cohorts of twenty-year-olds, since we cannot tell whether a woman will become a teenage mother until she has had her twentieth birthday. Women who reach the age of twenty in a given year will not necessarily have had the same average family income as the average child under twenty in earlier years. Thus we cannot automatically assume that repeated cross-sections of parental income, such as those shown in Table 8.1, represent the experiences of cohorts of children. Nonetheless, because median income has increased over the entire period since 1959, we can assume that, on average, recent cohorts of children had higher real incomes during their childhood than earlier cohorts. Thus children's outcomes ought to have improved as well. If we track children born between 1940 and 1975, we might also expect to see more improvement in earlier cohorts than in more recent cohorts because income rose faster between 1940 and 1970 than after 1970.

National trend data are available for some of the outcomes I consider in this book. Table 8.2 shows trends in teenage childbearing rates, high school dropout rates, educational attainment, labor-market outcomes, and single parenthood. If real parental income affects children's outcomes and all else had remained the same, these outcomes ought to have improved because the income of each successive cohort of children has risen. High school dropout rates and years of education did improve

Table 8.2   Trends in children's outcomes

Children's outcomes	Year outcome is measured					Change 1970– 1980	Change 1980– 1990
	1970	1976	1980	1985	1990		
Births per 1,000 women ages fifteen–nineteen	68.3	53.5	53.0	51.0	59.6	− 15.3	6.6
Percentage of fourteen- to twenty-four-year-olds not graduated from high school and not enrolled	12.2	11.8	12.0	10.6	10.6	− 0.2	− 1.4
Outcomes at age twenty-four							
Mean years of education	12.4	12.9	12.8	12.8	12.9	0.4	0.1
Hours male worked last week	41.5	40.8	41.7	41.4	41.0	0.2	− 0.7
Male hourly wages (in 1992 dollars)	12.58	11.51	11.62	10.35	10.26	− .96	− 1.36
Percentage of males who are idle	6.5	13.4	11.4	13.7	11.6	4.9	0.2
Percentage of women who are single mothers	NA	11.2	10.2	14.1	16.5	NA	6.3

Sources: Information about births to teenage girls is from the *Statistical Abstract of the United States 1993*, table 93. All other estimates were tabulated by David Knutson using March CPS data

Note: NA = not available.

between 1970 and 1990. Births to teenage girls declined between 1970 and 1980, but they had increased again by 1990, even though the average family income of teenagers born in 1970 was higher than the average income of teenagers born in 1960. Educational attainment improved from 1970 to 1990, and improved more between 1970 and 1980 than between 1980 and 1990, when income growth slowed. The percentage of twenty-four-year-old men who were idle increased, young men's wages declined, and the percentage of twenty-four-year-old women who were single mothers increased between 1970 and 1990. Thus the overall pattern is mixed: some outcomes improved as income rose, but others did not.

Beginning in the early 1970s, income among poor families declined relative to the income of the median family. It declined even more relative to the income of affluent families. Thus the income of children near the bottom of the income distribution was worse in relative terms during the 1970s and 1980s than it was during the 1950s and 1960s. Absolute income also declined at the bottom of the income distribution during the 1970s and 1980s. Thus if income affects children's life chances, low-income children ought to have fared better in the 1970s than in the 1980s. Conversely, the outcomes of affluent children ought to have improved over this period, because their income improved both absolutely and relative to the mean.

We cannot use the Census or the CPS to estimate the distribution of children's outcomes over their parents' income groups. For this we need longitudinal data. I use the PSID to show the distribution of outcomes for children classified by their parents' income when they were fourteen years old. NLSY data on children's cognitive skills and behavior problems are not available until 1986, so we cannot use these data to assess the effect of income trends.

For comparison with the CPS and Census data, Table 8.3 uses PSID data to show trends in parents' median income and income for the poorest 20 percent and the richest 40 percent of fourteen-year-olds. Because the PSID oversamples low-income households, the number of unweighted cases in the richest 20 percent of the sample is sometimes too small to provide reliable estimates. Consequently, I show trends for the richest 40 percent of children. The PSID has too few cases to assess trends year by year, so I aggregate over four-year periods. Children

Table 8.3 Trends in parental income in the PSID

Years income is measured (years children turned twenty)	Median income	Poorest 20%	Richest 40%
1968–71 (1974–77)	$41,956	$16,390	$72,641
1972–75 (1978–81)	46,434	18,587	77,646
1976–79 (1982–85)	47,912	16,322	84,396
1980–83 (1986–89)	43,029	14,653	80,405

Source: Tabulated by Timothy Veenstra using PSID data. Income is measured when children were fourteen years old.

who were twenty years old between 1974 and 1977 were fourteen in 1968–1971, the first four years of the PSID. Children who were twenty-four years old between 1978 and 1981 were fourteen in 1968–1971.

After 1975, each successive cohort of PSID children experienced greater income inequality during adolescence than the previous cohort. Parental income among the poorest 20 percent of fourteen-year-olds fell from 40.0 percent of the median income in 1972–1975 to only 34.1 percent in 1980–1983. As in the Census and the CPS, the growth in inequality in the PSID results from both a decline in income near the bottom and an increase near the top.[3] Thus if income during adolescence affects children's well-being, success should have been redistributed from the poor to the rich over these years.

To see if the observed changes in children's outcomes correspond to the changes we would expect based on the changes in parental income, I used the "conventional" models in Chapter 4 to determine the expected effect of a 10 percent change in parental income on each outcome. The first column in Table 8.4 shows this estimate. Using this estimate, the second column shows the change in each outcome we would expect based on how the income of the poorest 20 percent of children actually changed over the 1970s and early 1980s. Because income fell for low-income children, we expect their outcomes to have worsened. The third column shows the expected change among the richest 40 percent of children. Because their income rose, we expect their outcomes to have improved.

The fourth and fifth columns show the observed changes over the same period. Two points are obvious from this table. First, the expected

Table 8.4 Expected change in each outcome for cohorts who turned twenty or twenty-four in 1978–1981 and 1986–1989

Children's outcomes	Predicted change for 10% income increase	Expected change Poorest 20%	Richest 40%	Observed change Poorest 20%	Richest 40%
Adolescent outcomes (in percentages)					
Girls who become teenage mothers	−1.70	3.60	−.60	−1.10	−9.60
Teens who drop out of school	−1.30	2.80	−.50	−5.60	−2.80
Outcomes at age twenty-four					
Years of education	.11	−.24	.04	−.002	.003
Years of education for high school graduates	.08	−.17	.03	−.28	.15
Male workers' hourly wages (1992 dollars)	.13	−.28	.05	−.10	−2.36
Male workers' annual earnings (1992 dollars)	355	−753	128	473	−2,401
Percentage of males who are idle	−.28	.60	−.10	−4.20	−8.60
Percentage of women who are single mothers	−2.20	4.70	−.79	4.70	−.20

Source: Computed by Timothy Veenstra using PSID data. In the poorest quintile, income decreased by 21.2 percent between 1972–1975 and 1980–1983. Income increased by 3.6 percent in the top 40 percent of the income distribution over the same period. Estimates of the effect of income are from equations in which outcome is regressed on (log)income when children are fourteen years old.

changes in these outcomes are relatively small. This is partly because the effect of income is modest and partly because the change in income, though historically large, is also modest. Second, the observed changes in the outcomes are almost unrelated to the changes we would predict on the basis of income data.

Taken together, these results imply that neither the trends in the overall level of children's outcomes nor the trends in their distribution parallel trends in parental income. Nonetheless, this does not prove that income had no effect at all. Changes in parental income may have been too small to produce large changes in children's outcomes, and the small changes that income did produce may be obscured by other, more powerful trends.

State Welfare Benefits and Children's Outcomes

In 1992 the maximum AFDC benefit for a family of three in the continental United States varied from a high of $680 in Connecticut to a low of $120 in Mississippi. If income per se helps children, then all else being equal, children should fare better in Connecticut than in Mississippi. The political debate over welfare has seldom focused on the potential benefits to children of increasing or reducing their families' incomes. Rather, it has focused on whether AFDC discourages parents from working, marrying, and controlling their fertility.

Political conservatives often claim that high welfare benefits actually hurt children by discouraging parental work and marriage. They also argue that high welfare benefits provide an incentive for teenagers themselves to become single parents, ruining their chances for subsequent success. Political liberals, in contrast, have usually argued that the additional income provided by AFDC allows parents to purchase the goods and services their children need to succeed and to have the peace of mind that allows them to be good parents.

As I discussed in Chapter 4, a family's income from welfare often appears to have a negative effect on children's outcomes. But this does not tell us that high welfare benefits hurt children. The amount of welfare income a family receives depends on many factors besides the state's benefit level, including how much time it spends on welfare, how much other income it has, its size, and other unmeasured parental traits. Unless we can control all the factors associated with both families' welfare income and children's outcomes, estimates of the effect of welfare income can be biased. The state benefit level does not depend on these characteristics, at least not in any obvious way. Thus its effect on children's outcomes is not biased by our inability to control some parental characteristics.

Previous Research

Most social scientists who study the effect of welfare benefit levels look at adult outcomes, such as the likelihood of parents' marrying or working. In many cases, moreover, researchers control variables that depend to some extent on benefit levels, so their estimates do not tell us the likely effect of an actual change in benefits. When Plotnick (1990) estimated the effect of state AFDC and Food Stamp benefits on teenage girls' chances of having an out-of-wedlock birth, for example, he found that higher benefits were associated with higher rates of out-of-wedlock teenage childbearing among white and Hispanic girls, though not among black girls. But Plotnick controlled total family income and welfare income when the girls were fourteen years old. Both these variables partly depend on the state's benefit level, so controlling them could mean that he underestimated the overall effect of state benefit levels.[4] By contrast, Plotnick's estimates fail to take into account many characteristics of states that are correlated with benefit levels and are likely to influence out-of-wedlock births, such as the availability of abortions, cultural attitudes toward illegitimacy, and so on. Omitting these characteristic of states could produce estimates that are too high.

Haveman and Wolfe (1994) also estimated the effect of state AFDC benefit levels when teenage girls were six to fifteen years old on their chances of having a baby. They found that the effect of the benefit level was close to zero, but their estimates are subject to many of the same biases as Plotnick's.

No study that I know of tries to estimate the effect of the welfare benefit level when girls were growing up on their chances of becoming single mothers after the age of twenty, though several studies have tried to estimate the effect of welfare benefit levels on adult women's chances of being married if they have children. Although political conservatives claim that high welfare benefits increase single motherhood and therefore hurt children, most research finds that welfare benefit levels have a surprisingly small effect on mothers' chances of marrying.[5]

Corcoran and Adams (1995) find that the combined state welfare and Food Stamp benefit level when boys were four to sixteen years old had a very small and statistically insignificant effect on their hourly wages when they were young adults. But Corcoran and Adams also controlled family income from welfare. Since welfare income is a product of the time a family spends on welfare and the monthly benefit levels, their estimate of the effect of state AFDC benefits is too low. When this bias is corrected, their results suggest that higher benefits lower both black and white men's earnings. Higher benefits also appear to lower hourly wages for whites, but slightly increase them for blacks.[6] Corcoran and Adams control neighborhood characteristics, the household head's average annual hours of work, and the percentage of time the child spent in a household headed by a female. Because these factors are likely to be influenced by state benefit levels, controlling them could bias the estimated effect of state benefit levels, though the direction of that bias is unpredictable.

Hill and O'Neill (1994) estimated that a 50 percent increase in the combined AFDC and Food Stamp benefit level raised the PPVT scores of children who had received welfare for at least two years by less than one half of one percentile point. This estimate is not reliably different from zero. But Hill and O'Neill also found that higher benefits were associated with higher PPVT scores for children in families that never received welfare. From this they concluded that states that provide high benefits must also provide "positive educational and cultural environments" that enhance children's vocabulary. Since no such benefit was apparent for children on welfare, one could infer that higher benefits could *lower* PPVT scores, although Hill and O'Neill do not test this hypothesis explicitly.

Butler (1990) estimated the effect of state benefit levels on the educational attainment of PSID children whose parents divorced, separated, or became widowed and whose income while married was no more than four times the official poverty threshold. She controlled parental education and income prior to the marital break-up, the county unemployment rate, the median county income, the state high school graduation rate, and the state college graduation rate. The last two variables were controlled to take account of state differences in the educational environment.

Butler found that a $100 increase (in 1988 dollars) in monthly AFDC benefits was associated with an additional .096 years of education for these children. The mean benefit level was $645, so her results imply that increasing the mean benefit by 10 percent would increase education by .059 years. This is consistent with conventional estimates of the effect of parental income on children's education. Most of the effect of welfare benefit levels was on years of completed post-secondary education. Welfare benefit levels had a small and statistically insignificant effect on completion of grades ten through twelve, but large and significant effects on completion of grades thirteen through sixteen. Welfare benefit levels had almost no effect on children whose parents stayed married.

Estimating the "True" Effect of AFDC Benefits

These studies underline the importance of selecting appropriate comparison groups when estimating the impact of welfare benefit levels on children. High welfare benefits are unlikely to have a detectable effect on mean outcomes for all children in a state, because only about one child in ten receives welfare. But we cannot just estimate the effect of benefit levels for families that receive welfare, because single mothers with higher skills and better marriage prospects are more likely to rely on welfare in high-benefit states than in low-benefit states. Since we cannot control all the characteristics of mothers that are correlated with both the state benefit level and the children's outcomes, estimates of how benefit levels affect children will be too large if they are based only on data for recipients.

Another problem is how to control all the state characteristics that are correlated with the welfare benefit level and children's outcomes. For instance, states with high welfare benefit levels might also spend a lot on schools, child care, or other amenities that help children. High-benefit states also tend to have a higher cost of living than low-benefit states. Ignoring such state-to-state differences could yield misleading estimates of the importance of welfare.

Since welfare mostly serves single-parent families, welfare benefit levels will mainly affect children living with one parent. Of course, benefit levels will also induce some parents not to marry, but research suggests that these effects are quite small, so this is not likely to be a serious problem. If higher parental income improves children's outcomes, and all else is equal, children living in single-parent families will have better outcomes in states with high benefits than in states with low benefits. Of course, all else is not equal across states. States with high benefit levels tend to spend more on education, have higher taxes, and so on. Thus we would expect children raised in these states to do better even if they grew up in two-parent families and never received welfare. But if these state-to-state differences influence all children in a state, whereas welfare mainly influences children raised in single-parent families, high welfare benefits should reduce the gap between children raised in one-parent and two-parent families.

The NLSY does not identify the state in which a child lives, so I cannot estimate the effect of state benefit levels on young children.

Instead I use PSID data to estimate the effect of the maximum AFDC benefit for a family of four on the gap in outcomes between children in single-parent families and children in married-couple families. The model I use for these estimates is explained in Appendix E. I average state benefit levels over the years when children were thirteen to seventeen years old. I do not include the value of Food Stamps. A family's Food Stamp benefit depends on its size and its income. As AFDC benefits increased, Food Stamp benefits decreased. Since Food Stamp benefits depended on AFDC benefits (and are therefore endogenous), I omit them from these estimates.

The first column in Table 8.5 shows that for children raised in married-couple families, all outcomes are better in states with high benefits than in states with low benefits. The second column shows that, with two exceptions, the same is true for children in single-parent families. The exceptions are that more young men are idle and more young women become single mothers in high-benefit states than in low-benefit states. But though almost all outcomes are better in high-benefit states, outcomes for children in single-parent families are less sensitive to benefit levels than outcomes for children in married-couple families. The gap between children in married-couple and single-parent families therefore increases as AFDC benefits increase (see column 3).

As I have noted, high welfare benefits are correlated with many other attributes of states that can influence children in both married-couple and single-parent families. But welfare mainly influences children in single-parent families. The apparent effect of high welfare benefits on children in married-couple families must therefore be largely attributable to these other factors. The effect of the welfare benefit level is measured by the change in the gap. The gap increases for teenage childbearing, dropping out of school, single motherhood, and male wages, earnings, and idleness. The increase is small for most outcomes, however, and it is reliably different from zero only for dropping out and single motherhood. (See Appendix E for the full model with standard errors.)

By estimating a confidence interval for each outcome, we can determine how likely it is that the true effect of welfare benefits will fall within a particular range. We can be fairly confident that higher benefits do not reduce the gap between children in one- and two-parent families with respect to high school dropout rates, male idleness, or single moth-

Table 8.5 The effect of doubling state AFDC benefit levels on outcomes of children in married-couple and single-parent families

Children's outcomes	Children in married-couple families	Children in single-parent families	Change in advantage of children with married parents
Probability of teenage childbearing	−.069	−.044	.025
Probability of dropping out of school	−.088	−.031	.057
Years of education	.495	.316	.179
Years of education for high school graduates	.257	.158	.099
Male hourly wages (1992 dollars)	1.73	.57	1.16
Male annual earnings (1992 dollars)	2,073	1,019	1,054
Probability of male idleness	−.034	.079	.113
Probability of single motherhood	−.065	.015	.080

Source: Estimates from PSID data by Timothy Veenstra.

erhood. We can also be fairly confident that higher benefits do not reduce the gap in young men's wages. For the other outcomes the effect of higher benefits is uncertain.

Because the PSID samples are relatively small, I also used the 1990 decennial Census to estimate the effect of state welfare benefits on the probability that fourteen- to twenty-four-year-olds who lived at home had dropped out of high school. There are many more cases in the Census sample that I used than in the PSID (110,331 cases versus 4,015). I controlled state characteristics using the same model I used with the PSID data. Doubling state AFDC benefit levels widens the dropout gap between children in single-parent and married-couple families by 1.2 percentage points. This estimate is statistically significant and consistent with the estimate in Table 8.5. I also used Census data to estimate the effect of state welfare benefit levels on the chances that fifteen- to nineteen-year-old women who lived with their parents had a baby. There were 35,323 cases for this estimate. Doubling state benefit levels increased the gap by about one percentage point.

This estimate was statistically significant, and it too is consistent with the results in Table 8.5.

Census data are not ideal for these estimates because many teenagers who drop out of high school and many who have babies leave their parents' home. The fact that higher welfare benefits result in more young single mothers' setting up their own households (Ellwood and Bane 1985) implies that these Census estimates are somewhat downwardly biased. Nonetheless, the results using Census data are similar to the results using the PSID.

The overall impression from these results is that increasing welfare benefits is unlikely to improve children's outcomes appreciably unless states also change other policies that affect children. But these results, like the others I report in this book, have some potential sources of bias.

As these results show, characteristics of states that are correlated with state welfare benefits influence children's outcomes. Welfare benefits vary in part because the cost of living varies across states. In fact, some people have argued that the purchasing power of AFDC and Food Stamps hardly varied at all once differences in the cost of living were accounted for. If this were the case, using the variation in state benefit levels to estimate the effect of changing the benefit level would be a mistake, because real benefits, adjusted for the cost of living, would hardly vary. I know of no good data on state-to-state differences in the cost of living, but housing costs are by far the most important source of state-to-state variation in the cost of living (Citro and Michael 1995), so we can get some idea of how much real benefits vary by looking at their relationship to rent. When I regress the maximum state AFDC benefit level for a family of four on the average annual housing costs of renters with children in the 1990 Census, I find that for each dollar increase in housing costs, benefit levels increase by $1.19.[7]

Low-income tenants' rent may, however, vary less than the average rent of tenants.[8] When I regress the state AFDC benefit level on the average rent paid by tenants with children in the poorest fifth of the state's income distribution, I find that AFDC benefits increase by $1.34 for each dollar increase in rents.[9] Put another way, each additional dollar in AFDC benefits is associated with a $.45 increase in rent. Food Stamp benefits decline by about $.30 for every dollar increase in AFDC benefits. If we take into account both the decrease in Food Stamps and the increase in rents, AFDC recipients in high-benefit states were only slightly better off than AFDC recipients in low-benefit states. Doubling AFDC benefits increased "disposable" income (AFDC benefits plus Food Stamps less rent) for single mothers receiving public assistance by only about 30 percent.[10] Consequently, we would not expect children to fare much better or worse in states with high benefits than in states with low benefits.

What Social Experiments Show

During the 1970s, the Office of Economic Opportunity conducted a series of NIT experiments to see whether income transfers discouraged work. There were four experiments: one in New Jersey and Pennsylvania, one in rural Iowa and North Carolina, one in Seattle and Denver, and one in Gary, Indiana. In each location some families received considerably more money than other.

The NIT experiments guaranteed participants a minimum income that ranged from 50 to 250 percent of the poverty line. A family's monthly check was then reduced by a set percentage (the "tax") as its income from other sources increased. After a family's income reached the so-called break-even point, that family received no NIT benefits. The tax on non-NIT income varied depending on the program. In some locations there was also a control group that received no NIT benefits. Members of the control group could, however, get benefits from other federal and state programs such as AFDC, for which they qualified. Initially, families were randomly assigned to either the control or the treatment group. Then they were randomly assigned to particular tax-and-transfer packages within the treatment group. Not surprisingly, members of the control group were much more likely to leave the experiment than members of the treatment group.[11]

In Gary, the income of NIT participants was about 50 percent higher than the income of the control group families. The difference in income between experimentals and controls was greater in Iowa and North Carolina, but I was unable to find out how much greater.[12] By comparing children in the NIT families with children in the control families, we can see if the additional income (or other factors associated with participating in the experiment) improved children's outcomes.

Studies that have tried to estimate the difference in standardized reading test scores between children in the NIT and children in the control groups have found different results in different locations. In rural North Carolina, elementary school children in the NIT group scored 8.4 percentile points higher than children in the control group. In rural Iowa, NIT elementary school children scored 7.7 percentile points lower than the controls. In neither case were the effects reliably different from zero. In the Gary NIT, children in grades four through six scored 22.3 percentile points higher in reading than control children, but children in grades seven though ten scored lower.

Two studies found that NIT children were less likely than control group children to drop out of high school, but the magnitude of the difference varied. Mallar (1977) found that among New Jersey teenagers living with both parents, those whose parents participated in the experiment were between 20 and 90 percent more likely to finish high school than the controls, depending on the parameters of the NIT plan. These same children also completed between .3 and 1.5 more years of school than the control group. Participants in the New Jersey plan that provided a guaranteed income equal to the poverty line with a 50 percent tax on other income were 25 percent more likely than controls to finish high school. Perversely, cutting the guarantee to 75 percent of the poverty line appeared to increase the advantage of participants over controls from 25 to 62 percent. With a 70 percent tax rate, a higher guarantee level also appears to reduce the advantage of NIT children over controls. The same pattern held for years of education. This study appears to show that low benefits help more than generous benefits, but that result is neither plausible nor statistically reliable. Indeed, none of these differences may be attributable to changes in parental income, since by year three of the New Jersey experiment, participants' weekly family income averaged only about 5 percent more than that of the control group (Watts, Poirier, and Mallar 1977).

The largest NIT study covered families in Seattle and Denver. There adolescents whose families received the NIT were only 11 percent more likely than controls to finish high school (Venti 1984). Unlike the New Jersey NIT, the Seattle and Denver samples included single-parent families and a greater number of black and Hispanic families, so the Seattle-Denver sample was more representative of low-income families than the New Jersey site.

Mallar (1977), Venti and Wise (1984), and others have shown that teenagers and young adults from NIT families were less likely to work at all and worked fewer hours than children in control families. But because these same children were more likely to be in school, NIT children were less likely than control children to be idle.[13] Because participants knew that generous income benefits were available only for a short time, they had a strong incentive to go to school during that time in order to improve their prospects once the benefits ended.

We can draw no firm conclusions about the effect of income transfers on children's cognitive test scores from the NIT experiments. For school enrollment, the NIT experiments suggest that generous short-term income transfers combined with high taxes on earnings could encourage enrollment in the short run, because they provide a strong incentive to go to school rather than work.

9

Helping Poor Children

Americans have not made much progress over the last two hundred years in thinking about how to address the needs of poor children. Today's debates are not very different from those conducted in the early nineteenth century. In Chapter 2 I argued that this was because we still do not agree on how important parental income is relative to other parental characteristics in shaping children's prospects. I have thus far tried to present the best evidence I could find that bears on this debate. In this chapter I summarize what I think the evidence shows and discuss its implications for helping poor children.

Raising Parental Income

My review of the evidence suggests three major conclusions. First, though the effect of parental income is nowhere near as large as many political liberals imagine, neither is it zero, as many political conservatives seem to believe. Second, though the effect of parental income on any one outcome appears to be fairly small, higher income has some effect on most outcomes, so its cumulative impact across all outcomes may be substantial. Third, one reason that parental income is not more important to children's outcomes is probably that government policies have done a lot to ensure that poor children get basic necessities most of the time. Each of these conclusions calls for some elaboration.

Modest Effects

If the results in this book are correct, young children's test scores are likely to improve by one or two points when their parents' income doubles. Both teenage childbearing and high school dropout rates might decline, but the magnitude of the expected decline is uncertain (between one-tenth and one quarter for teenage childbearing, and about half that much for dropping out). Doubling parental income probably raises a child's eventual years of education by about a fifth of a year. It might also improve male workers' wages and earnings, but it could increase men's chances of being idle. Doubling parents' income seems to reduce young single motherhood by between 8 and 20 percent. Increasing welfare benefits does not appear to improve children's outcomes.

To put these results in perspective, it is helpful to estimate what would happen to children's outcomes if we could double the household income of the poorest 20 percent of children through income transfers, tax credits, higher wages, guaranteed work, or some other strategy. The 1989 CPS suggests that this would require increasing the average income of the poorest quintile from about $10,000 to about $20,000 (in 1992 dollars). By historical standards, this would be a huge increase. The purchasing power of the poorest 20 percent of Americans has never been near $20,000. In absolute terms, such an increase would move almost all children above the poverty line and would move most of them above 125 percent of the poverty line, which was $14,228 for a family of four in 1992. For simplicity, I assume that we can accomplish this change by doubling income from all sources and that this leaves parents' choices about work, welfare, and fertility unchanged. This assumption is obviously not realistic, because all strategies for increasing income create incentives that alter people's choices. But this is still a useful mental experiment.

Among the poorest 20 percent of American teenage girls, about 40 percent have babies before they turn twenty years old. The largest estimate of the true effect of income suggests that doubling parents' income would reduce teenage childbearing by about 10 percentage points, from 40 to 30 percent. Given this change, the overall teenage childbearing rate in the United States would fall from 20 to 18 percent.

One reason the overall teenage childbearing rate would fall so little is that 60 percent of teenage births are to girls whose families are not low income. Raising the income of low-income families will not reduce teenage births to these families (and could actually increase them if redistributing income to low-income families required reducing the income of more affluent families). Doubling everyone's income should, of course, have a much greater effect on the teenage childbearing rate. But we do not know how to do that, and if what really matters is relative income, doubling everyone's income might not have any effect anyway.

Using these same assumptions, we can calculate that doubling low-income families' income would reduce the overall high school dropout rate from 17.3 to 16.1 percent, and increase the mean years of education from 12.80 years to 12.83 years. Male idleness would increase, and the percentage of young women who become single mothers would hardly change. From this we can conclude that any realistic income redistribution strategy is likely to have a relatively small impact on the overall incidence of social problems. For example, the EITC increases family income by at most about 10 percent. Nonetheless, the overall benefit to children from extra income could still be greater than the benefits of any other policy that costs the same.

Diverse Effects

In its 1964 annual report, the Council of Economic Advisors wrote, "[Poverty's] ugly by-products include ignorance, disease, delinquency, crime, irresponsibility, immorality, and indifference. None of these social evils and hazards will, of course, wholly disappear with the elimination of poverty. But their severity will be markedly reduced" (*Economic Report of the President*, 1964). As this list suggests, income-support policies are supposed to solve many social problems at once by changing one thing that seems common to them all. Income is the ultimate "multipurpose" policy instrument.

In contrast, what I call "targeted" solutions try to solve a narrowly defined problem, such as hunger, with one solution, such as Food Stamps. All noncash transfer programs are targeted policies. Another approach, which was characteristic of welfare policies at the local level until the 1960s and is still often used by state and local governments, is what I call "micro intervention." By this I mean one-on-one services for individuals or families. These services can include education, medical care, family therapy, homemaker services, school counseling programs, drug and alcohol treatment, and so on. Psychologists, who see problems in individual terms, tend to favor such programs. Most other social scientists dislike them because they are expensive, often pater-nalistic, and frequently create incentives for abuse.

Multipurpose solutions assume that one cause has many different effects. Changing that cause can thus solve many problems at once. Raising income is not the only candidate for this role. Just as many liberals believe that low income causes most of the problems that are correlated with poverty, many conservatives believe that single parent-hood causes most of the problems correlated with it. Conservatives therefore expect that getting parents to marry and stay married will solve the problems that liberals propose to cure with higher wages or more generous public assistance. Racism and racial discrimination often play a similar role in discussions of minority children's problems.

Multipurpose policies will only work if three conditions are met: a single cause must really affect many outcomes; we must correctly iden-tify this cause; and we must be able to change it. Yet even when mul-tipurpose policies meet all these conditions, they often fail politically because they are impossible to evaluate.

The biggest obstacle to evaluating multipurpose policies is that we cannot measure all their effects. I have estimated the effect of raising parental income on twelve outcomes for children, but I have omitted many other potentially important outcomes such as delinquency and suicide, and I have not considered any parental behaviors. After social scientists estimate the effect of multipurpose policies, we can always think of other outcomes that they neglected.

When advocates defend a policy, moreover, they often expand the effects it is supposed to have. Welfare-to-work policies illustrate this process. Work requirements for welfare recipients were originally in-tended to reduce the tax dollars required to support single mothers. In the late 1970s social critics began suggesting that work would not only reduce the welfare rolls but also improve the values and attitudes of recipients. As it became clear that getting welfare mothers to work was more expensive than transferring money, some people began to argue that requiring welfare mothers to work would improve the life chances of their children, because working mothers would become more socially integrated and be better role models for their children. Head Start is another example. It was initially supposed to raise children's test scores, and now it is supposed to have a dozen benefits.

A second obstacle to evaluating multipurpose policies is that when interventions affect multiple outcomes the outcomes tend to have many other causes. It follows that their effect on any one outcome is usually relatively small. Children's educational attainment, for example, is influenced by the children's own abilities, parental values and expectations, characteristics of schools, the availability of financial aid for college, and many other things. It is not surprising that even a large change in parental income does not greatly improve children's chances of graduating from college.

A third problem is that social scientists have relatively crude tools for measuring the effects of policies. When they have to rely on "natural experiments," as I have in this book, their estimates are subject to bias from mismeasurement, omitted variables, and other factors. Social scientists are rarely able to run social experiments. When they do, sample sizes are often small, and the experiments only approximate a true experimental design. So when the true effect of a policy is fairly small, we end up with conflicting and statistically unreliable estimates.

Even if it were possible to measure all the effects of multipurpose policies accurately, we would seldom agree on what weights to place on these effects. This is crucial if the effects go in opposite directions. Indeed, much of the political debate over welfare has been a debate over whether to give the small improvement in children's outcomes more weight than the small deterioration in parents' likelihood of marrying and working. This lack of consensus on the relative importance of outcomes is one reason multipurpose policies are attractive. It is hard to agree on targeted programs for all the problems we want government to solve because policy makers cannot agree on which problems are most important. Policies that do not require such a consensus are, therefore, more feasible.

When social scientists measure only a few of the potential effects of multipurpose policies, we must try to generalize from what they did measure to what they ignored. Because the effects for any one outcome are likely to be small, this approach often convinces us that the total effect of the policy is also small. Different constituencies then argue that these evaluations have not measured important potential effects of the program, and legislators assign their preferred ad hoc weights to these effects. No wonder there is much uncertainty about whether such policies "work."

How Much Is Enough?

I have argued that one reason income does not have a large effect on any one outcome is that programs such as Food Stamps, housing subsidies, and Medicaid have helped most American families meet their basic material needs. Once basic material needs are met, factors other than income become increasingly important to how children fare. But I have not tried to estimate how much money is enough to meet these needs.

It is not easy to decide how much is enough. The more resources families have, the less likely they are to face serious material hardships. But no one has found a breakpoint in the income distribution below which material hardship becomes much worse; nor are any of the material hardships for which I have data completely absent in the top half of the income distribution. This is because income is not the only determinant of material hardship. A family's income needs depend on its size, the health of its members, the efficiency with which it consumes goods and services, and the local cost of living. Tastes also vary from family to family.

Imagine again the two identical families headed by Mrs. Smith and Mrs. Jones. Mrs. Smith has all the attributes of an average middle-class American, but has fallen on hard times. When we give her $600 a month plus Food Stamps, she can find a way to shelter and feed her family. Mrs. Jones suffers from serious depression. She lacks the energy to search for cheap housing or travel to a cheap grocery store. Her depression may also have isolated her from friends and family who could help. The same resources do not buy as much for her children as for Mrs. Smith's children.

When the poor have the same values and skills as everyone else but cannot afford to buy food, housing, and other basic necessities, either income transfers or transfers of basic necessities can help their children substantially. But when the poor are considerably less competent than the middle class, income transfers may not help as much. Consequently, the important question for policy makers is not how much is enough, but rather what is the right kind of help. This depends on the social context of poverty.

If poverty occurred randomly, parental traits would by definition be unrelated to poverty. At least in the short run, the poor would be just like the middle class except that they would have less money. In the long run, however, poverty itself could alter parental traits.

But poverty is never completely random, even though it can sometimes be caused by more or less random events. When large numbers of fathers were killed in the Civil War, for example, poverty among their widows and children was not strongly associated with undesirable parental characteristics. Some Civil War widows escaped destitution because their husbands left them money, because they could work, or because they lived with relatives. Still, widowhood did plunge mothers from very different backgrounds into poverty. In the Great Depression, when unemployment was as high as 50 percent in some cities, poverty again struck all kinds of families. It was not completely random, but it was common enough for most people to think it could happen to them or to members of their family. Under such circumstances the poor were more like everyone else than they are today.

As countries get richer, they often implement policies that reduce poverty among families hit by random catastrophes such as the death of a spouse, protracted illness, or job loss. When countries do this, poverty declines. But those who remain poor also become less like everyone else. When barriers to work are lowered, as they have been for both women and racial minorities in this century, those who remain jobless are more exceptional than they were when these barriers were higher. When almost all employers discriminated against blacks, it was not surprising that blacks were more likely than whites to be poor. The fact that most blacks now escape long-term poverty leads to the suspicion that those blacks who remain poor today are different from those who do better.

A talented child born to bright, diligent, well-meaning parents who are too poor to feed the family might have trouble in school. When the government makes it possible for most parents to feed their children, other investments become more important in determining who succeeds and who does not. When poor children can get enough to eat but often cannot afford to go to school, variations in access to schooling rather than a nutritious diet will predict success. If the government then requires everyone to attend free public school up to age sixteen, variations in schooling after age sixteen will predict success. Thus if the state equalizes most important material and pedagogic investments in children, social and psychological differences between parents will explain a larger percentage of the variation in the success of their children. The marginal returns to additional market resources will also fall.

What Kind of Help?

Even in the United States today, however, millions of American families are poor for short periods of time. Students are often relatively poor while they are in college. Divorced mothers and their children are often poor for a short time when a marriage breaks up, and many families fall into poverty when a wage-earner loses his or her job. In the PSID, 20 percent of children were poor for at least one year between their ninth and fourteen birthdays. Only 5 percent were poor for all five years. Not surprisingly, those who were poor for only a year look a lot more like the nonpoor than those who were poor for all five years.

Most families that become poor are headed by competent parents who can care for their children quite adequately during normal times. When they fall on hard times due to unemployment, a change in family composition, or illness, they need short-term cash assistance just as they would if their homes were destroyed by a flood or an earthquake. Most of them will never need any other kind of help, so writing a government check on behalf of their children is quicker, cheaper, and more effective than any other form of help. Short-term cash help does not appear to create serious incentives for adults to behave in ways that hurt their children.

Unlike the short-term poor, the long-term poor tend to be quite different from the nonpoor. When families fall on hard times and stay there for years, this means they cannot or will not find a way to support themselves. The children in such families often need outside help that goes beyond economic support. This does not mean that the persistently poor are all lazy, ignorant, uncaring, or neglectful—they are not. Some are chronically ill or have children who are chronically ill. Some are depressed or disturbed. Some have very low cognitive abilities. As one sympathetic teacher in an impoverished school put it, "We should not confuse families' inability to do with their desire to do. That always bothers me. It makes me uncomfortable talking about these problems. It makes me feel like we are saying that folks don't care. One of the most astounding things to me since I've been here is how few parents there are—in fact I could only think of one or two if I thought real hard—that don't seem to care. Folks care. They want for their kids."

Some of the chronically poor are drug addicts and alcoholics. An assistant principal in an economically mixed elementary school in the South told this story:

> Drugs are a really big problem here. I had a little girl, a tough little girl who always had her guard up. One day she just let it all down and began to cry. When I asked her why she was crying, she said she just wanted everything to be like it had been in the third grade. I asked what it had been like in the third grade. She said she had gotten a certificate for good attendance and some other award and her mom had hung them up on the refrigerator. She said her mom had been so happy. That was before the crack. "Since the crack my mommy doesn't care any more," she cried. This mom was not a bad mom. She cared, and she had been good, but she just got into trouble and there is no help for her—no place for her to turn, and now this little girl is miserable.

It is hard to imagine that giving this girl's mother more money will help much. It is also hard to imagine that providing additional programs for this little girl will help her much unless we also find a way to help her mother.

Some persistently poor parents are shiftless and neglectful. The homes in which they raise their children attain neither the moral nor the material standards that most Americans believe children require. Political pressure to improve the behavior of these parents is an inevitable and appropriate response. Nonetheless, it seems clear that one thing we should not do is refuse to provide any help at all. That solution would give the most troubled parents less money to buy basic necessities for their children. It would also remove the most disorganized and incompetent families from the supervision of agencies that could potentially help the family follow community norms about how parents should raise their children. If the most vulnerable and inadequate families are deprived of any legal source of economic support, at least some will turn to illegitimate sources, such as prostitution, selling drugs, or other crimes, to make ends meet. Absent any state support, some women and children will be more likely to remain in abusive and destructive relationships with men. Others will turn to "social prostitution," serial relationships with men willing to help pay their bills.[1] Thus the fact that increases in parental income cannot be expected to improve any one outcome greatly does not mean that if we *reduce* cash or noncash transfers children will not suffer as a consequence.

Just as poverty alone is not synonymous with incompetence, a change in the number of poor does not necessarily imply a change in parental competence. In fact, my argument implies that as the poverty rate rises the average poor person becomes more like the average middle-class person than when poverty rates are low. This need not be the case, of course. If an epidemic of drug use were to drive up the poverty rate, the increase in poverty would be associated with an increase in incompetence.

Changing Parents' Noneconomic Characteristics

I have argued that the stable parental characteristics that affect children's outcomes are often the same characteristics that employers value. Based on my data, I can only guess what these might be. Indeed, even the use of the term "stable" may be misleading. These parental characteristics are only stable in the context of a particular person's life. They may be partly innate, but even then their expression depends on parents' own childhood experiences and their adult attitudes, values, goals, and predispositions, which are in turn influenced by social structure and institutions. The fact that a trait is relatively stable certainly does not mean we cannot change it. Height is stable in adulthood, but changing children's diets can change their adult height. Occupations are also quite stable, but they can still be changed.

With the exception of family size, I largely ignore parents' noneconomic characteristics, except insofar as controlling these characteristics allows me to estimate the effect of parental income more accurately. Yet if we want to improve children's outcomes we need to study the effect of these noneconomic characteristics as carefully as we study the effect of income. Parents' education, age when their children are born, and race account for up to half of the observed correlation between children's outcomes and parental income. Understanding each of these relationships would require careful study.

Parents' Education

We know that each additional year of parental education is associated with better outcomes for children. But, as with income, views about why parental education predicts children's outcomes fall on a spectrum. Liberals tend to believe that individuals learn skills in school that make them better workers and better parents. The extreme version of this "skills" model holds that if mothers who currently have, say, ten years of schooling had spent two additional years in school, their children's outcomes would be like those of children whose mothers had a high school diploma.[2]

Many conservatives believe that character and competence are primarily inherited from parents. They therefore see parental educational attainment mainly as a proxy for genetic propensities or effective upbringing. Parents pass these advantages on to their children. Children with these advantages get higher test scores, find school more rewarding, and stay in school longer than those with fewer advantages.[3] From this perspective, getting high school dropouts to stay in school longer will not appreciably improve either their job prospects or their children's outcomes. Almost no one believes the extreme version of this argument, but many believe that the benefits of schooling are considerably smaller than simple comparisons between dropouts and graduates imply. Empirical estimates also suggest that parental education has some important effects on children's outcomes even when many parental characteristics are controlled.[4]

Young Mothers

Children born to very young mothers have worse outcomes than children born to older mothers. Teenage mothers receive less education and earn less money than mothers who delay childbearing until they are at least twenty. Many people think that if we could get all teenage mothers to delay childbearing, their education and earnings would improve, which would help their children. Yet the best available evidence, based on comparisons between pregnant teenagers who have babies and those who have spontaneous miscarriages, suggests that delaying motherhood does not actually lead to much more maternal education or earnings (Hotz et al. 1995). Once again, the unobserved characteristics that cause teenagers to become pregnant also influence their education and wages. These same characteristics presumably influence children's outcomes, too.

Race

Black children fare worse than white children on all outcomes. But when I control parents' income, black children are less likely than white children to drop out of high school. Black children also receive more post-secondary education than whites with the same family income. Parental income also appears to account for some of the other differences between black and white children's outcomes, but the difference in PPVT scores, single motherhood, men's wages, and male idleness remains large.[5]

If low income is mainly a proxy for unmeasured parental characteristics that reduce parental income and hurt children, increasing the income of black parents through income transfers, child tax credits, child-support payments, or increased earnings would not by itself improve their children's life chances very much. The fact that income is lower among black parents implies that the unobserved parental characteristics that employers value and that affect such outcomes as children's test scores and teenage childbearing are more prevalent among white parents. These parental characteristics depend partly on parents' own childhood experiences. They also depend on the attitudes, values, and goals that parents acquire in the course of dealing with a predominantly white society. It should therefore come as no surprise that more black families than white families in the United States end up at a competitive disadvantage, both in the race for good jobs and in preparing their children for that race.

Values and attitudes are like habits: the longer one adheres to them, the harder they are to change. When the stakes are high enough, people can break many habits and acquire new ones. But because most government interventions are small compared with all the other things that influence parental behavior, policy makers who want to change adults' attitudes about work and family by changing the economic incentives built into government programs are usually disappointed. This is especially true if the attitudes they want to change are constantly reinforced by parents' relatives and friends.

Single Parenthood

Americans have always thought that growing up with only one parent is bad for children. The rapid spread of single-parent families over the past generation does not seem to have altered this consensus much. Many people see eliminating single parenthood as a panacea for children's problems.

I do not usually control parents' marital status in my estimates of the effect of income. Some evidence suggests that economic deprivation makes divorce more common and marriage less common among parents. To the extent that marital status really depends on prior income, controlling marital status would have led me to underestimate income's effect on children's outcomes. In practice, however, controlling marital status hardly changed the estimated effect of income.[6]

Estimating the effect of single motherhood with income controlled is even more problematic than estimating the effect of income with single parenthood controlled. Everyone agrees that when parents live apart their children are poorer. Once we hold income constant, moreover, the adverse effect of growing up in a single-parent family drops by roughly half (McLanahan and Sandefur 1994). This does not mean that we should control income when we estimate the effect of living arrangements. Low income is a direct consequence of single parenthood, so if we want to know the effect of single parenthood, we want to include the income effect. But the key role of income in accounting for the effect of single parenthood on children does imply that we could sharply reduce the adverse effect of single parenthood on children if we were to transfer large sums of money to custodial parents (or if we could devise a way of making absent parents do this).

As we have seen, however, it is risky to take calculations of this sort at face value. If income predicts children's later success because it is a proxy for other unmeasured parental characteristics, transferring money to single mothers will not help children as much as standard statistical models imply. Both low income and single parenthood may in fact be correlated with poor outcomes for children because they are proxies for unmeasured parental characteristics. This suspicion is bolstered by the well-established finding that when single parenthood is a by-product of death rather than divorce or failure to marry, children do about as well as children living with two parents who have comparable incomes (McLanahan and Sandefur 1994).

Where the Trouble Begins

Trying to figure out what the government can do to help poor children is not a task to be taken lightly. The results in this book suggest that although children's opportunities are unequal, income inequality is not the primary reason. Despite the fact that liberals have worked hard to reduce the influence of family income on children, they are unlikely to believe the claim that they have largely succeeded, much less greet the claim with a sense of accomplishment. Liberals worked hard for the cash and noncash transfers that have helped reduce the most serious material deprivations. These programs appear to have narrowed the gap between rich and poor children's material living conditions. Liberals also lobbied for Head Start, compensatory education, and guaranteed student loans for college in order to narrow the gap in educational opportunities. These programs appear to have reduced the impact of parental income on children's life chances; eliminating them could increase the effect of parental income on children's outcomes.

But if advantage comes from having parents whose depression is treated rather than left untreated, from having parents who speak English rather than another language, from having parents who love to read or do math, or parents who love rather than tolerate their children, it will be much harder to equalize opportunity. As a teacher who had taught in both the affluent north shore and the poverty-ridden west side of Chicago put it, "Money can ease the path, but it doesn't hit deep down where the trouble begins."

□ □ □ □ □

Appendixes
Notes
References
Index

Description of the
Samples and Variables

This appendix provides a description of the samples used throughout this book, followed by a description of the main variables used. Tables A.1 and A.2 show the means and standard deviations of these variables.

Samples

The Panel Study of Income Dynamics (PSID). The PSID is an ongoing longitudinal survey of U.S. households begun in 1968 by the Survey Research Center at the University of Michigan. Originally, the PSID was a stratified random sample of 5000 families, which included an over-sample of low-income families. The PSID follows the children of all the original families once they leave their parents' household. I use the 1989 wave of the PSID. For most analyses, I use a sample of children who have income data for the years when they were ages thirteen to seventeen and who remained in the sample until the outcomes were measured.

Given the duration of this longitudinal survey, it is not surprising that many of the original participants have dropped out. Attrition is not random, but the PSID tries to correct for differential attrition with sampling weights. Several studies of this attrition have been done. Becketti et al. (1988) and Duncan and Hill (1989) have compared PSID data with CPS data. PSID data are similar to CPS data on major demographic categories except that the PSID has fewer white families and fewer families that report very low incomes. Haveman and Wolfe (1994) also assess the representativeness of PSID samples. These stud-

Table A.1 Means (standard deviations) for variables used in model predicting
five- to seven-year-olds' test scores and behavior problems

Variable	PPVT	BPI	PIAT math	PIAT reading
Test score	94.629	106.622	100.670	105.060
	(16.235)	(14.306)	(12.376)	(12.185)
Log family income over five years	9.981	10.045	10.045	10.041
	(.633)	(.653)	(.652)	(.652)
Age of child	5.775	5.687	5.692	5.707
	(.785)	(.708)	(.708)	(.711)
Child is black	.212	.186	.189	.189
Child is Hispanic	.081	.078	.078	.079
Log family size	1.390	1.381	1.383	1.382
	(.282)	(.268)	(.269)	(.270)
Mother's highest grade completed	11.755	12.033	12.034	12.016
	(1.749)	(1.791)	(1.770)	(1.765)
Mother's age at child's birth	20.233	21.435	21.440	21.401
	(2.268)	(2.634)	(2.621)	(2.622)
Mother's AFQT score	37.570	38.839	38.841	38.694
	(25.856)	(25.821)	(25.873)	(25.715)
Sample sizes	1,175	2,890	2,942	2,901

Source: Estimated from NLSY mother-child files by David Knutson.

ies suggest that attrition has not caused the PSID to become seriously unrepresentative of the black and white nonimmigrant population of the United States. (See also Duncan et al. 1984.)

The PSID has developed weights to compensate both for over-sampling low-income households and for sample attrition. I use the 1989 person weight in all analyses, but sampling errors are estimated using the unweighted number of cases. In Appendix B I show that the results are not sensitive to whether I use weighted or unweighted data.

The National Longitudinal Survey of Youth (NLSY), mother-child files. The NLSY is a multistage stratified random sample of 11,406 individuals who were aged fourteen to twenty-one in 1979. The sample includes an over-sample of black, Hispanic, and low-income youth. These youths have been interviewed since 1979.

Beginning in 1986, women in the original NLSY sample who had become mothers were given the mother-child supplement to the NLSY, and their children were given cognitive and other assessments. In 1986, 3,053 women had 5,236 children. (See Chase-Lansdale et al., 1991, for an excellent description of this data set.) I use data from interviews in 1986, 1988, and 1990.

For most analyses, I use a sample of children who were aged five to seven in 1986, 1988, or 1990 or aged four or five in these same years. Children who were five to seven years old in 1986 had mothers who were fifteen to twenty-three years old at the time of their birth. Consequently, these children were born to rather young mothers. Children who were five to seven years old in 1990 had mothers who were four years older. With each additional cohort, the children become more representative of all children.

I weight the data by the Child Sampling Weights, which are intended to compensate for over-sampling. The weights are paired yearly with test scores, so when I predict test scores in 1986, I use the 1986 weight. Appendix B shows that the results are not very sensitive to whether I use weighted or unweighted data.

Definition of PSID Variables

Parental income. I convert all income amounts to 1992 dollars using the CPI-U-X1 price adjustment. Total family income includes all taxable and transfer income of the household head, spouse, and others. For most analyses, I count the face value of Food Stamps as income. The PSID contains no negative or zero values for income. Respondents report income for the year prior to the interview, so income reported in 1989 is for 1988.

Between 1968 and 1980, the PSID top-coded income at $99,000 (in nominal dollars). After 1980 it top-coded income at $9.9 million. For consistency, I top-code income in all years to $189,172, which is the value of $99,000 in 1972 converted to 1992 dollars.

For five-year income averages, a child must have at least three years of income data. Eighty-seven percent of children had all five years of data, 7 percent had four years, and another 6 percent had only three years. In Appendix B I test the sensitivity of my results to the number of years over which income is measured.

Table A.2 Means (standard deviations) for variables predicting adolescent and young-adult outcomes

Variable	Teenage childbearing	Dropping out of school	Years of education	Years of education for high school graduates
Dependent variable	.203	.173	12.793	13.320
	(.399)	(.380)	(1.940)	(1.663)
Log family income	10.671	10.687	10.687	10.761
	(.596)	(.588)	(.572)	(.565)
Log family size	1.623	1.611	1.647	1.630
	(.333)	(.331)	(.331)	(.336)
Parent is black	.157	.140	.141	.123
	(.361)	(.349)	(.347)	(.336)
Parent's age when child is fourteen	39.884	39.769	40.127	40.200
	(6.364)	(6.221)	(6.163)	(6.211)
Parent's education	12.613	12.747	12.590	12.966
	(2.671)	(2.648)	(2.722)	(2.636)
Child is a boy	—	.493	.481	.475
		(.502)	(.498)	(.512)
Sample sizes	2,121	4,003	3,275	2,586

I usually use the logarithm of parental income. Appendix B provides tests of the best functional form of income.

Teenage childbearing. To construct the teenage childbearing variable, I subtract the date of birth of each female child's oldest child from her own birth date. If the result is less than twenty, the mother is counted as a teenage mother and the variable is coded as one. If a woman has reported no birth or was twenty or older at the birth of her first child, teenage childbearing is coded zero. If data on either birth history or mother's birth date is missing, this variable is coded as missing. There were twenty-two cases with missing data for teenage childbearing.

Dropping out of high school. If a child has completed fewer than twelve years of schooling and is not enrolled in school at age twenty, he or she is counted as having dropped out of high school. If information on education or student status is not available when the child was twenty, I use information when the child was twenty-one or up to age twenty-five. If information on education is still missing, dropping out is counted as missing. There were 158 children with missing data on dropping out.

Table A.2   (continued)

Variable	Male hourly wages	Male earnings	Male idleness	Single motherhood
Dependent variable	11.557	23,728	.103	.237
	(6.684)	(15,084)	(.309)	(.419)
Log family income	10.682	10.682	10.682	10.679
	(.559)	(.559)	(.702)	(.572)
Log family size	1.665	1.665	1.639	1.656
	(.340)	(.340)	(.338)	(.328)
Parent is black	.086	.086	.117	.158
	(.287)	(.287)	(.326)	(.360)
Parent's age when child is fourteen	40.005	40.005	40.113	40.290
	(6.031)	(6.031)	(6.013)	(6.312)
Parent's education	12.547	12.547	12.744	12.447
	(2.690)	(2.690)	(2.790)	(2.731)
Child's age in 1989	31.602	31.603		
	(3.198)	(3.199)	—	—
County unemployment rate	5.447	—	—	—
	(2.048)			
Number of cases	954	954	1,355	1,741

Source: Estimated from PSID data by Timothy Veenstra.

Most children who received a GED are counted as having graduated from high school. After 1984, heads of households and spouses were asked whether they had a GED. Unfortunately, a quarter of the sample of children who turned twenty were not household heads or spouses of heads, so I have no way of knowing whether they have a GED.

Years of education. The number of years of completed schooling in the year a child turned twenty-four. Until recently, the PSID top-coded years of education at seventeen. For consistency, I top-code years of education to seventeen in all years. Forty-six children had missing education data.

Male earnings. The average annual hours of labor-market work times hourly wages in 1983 and 1984 for males who were not enrolled in school and who were at least twenty years old. This is calculated only for males who report at least one hour of work. Earnings are converted to 1992 dollars using the CPI-U-X1.

Male hourly wages. Total annual earnings divided by total annual hours worked and averaged over 1983 and 1984 for males who reported at least one hour of work and who were not enrolled in school. The top 1 percent and the bottom 1 percent of wages were trimmed. Wages are converted to 1992 dollars using the CPI-U-X1. There were 207 men with missing data on earnings and wages.

Because 1983 and 1984 were recession years and the effect of parental income on young men's labor-market outcomes could depend on the business cycle, I experimented with measures of male earnings and wages in different years. But the results were very similar to those reported in this book. Because I wanted to measure parental income for at least five years after the labor-market outcomes were measured, I show results for wages and earnings in 1983 and 1984.

Male idleness. A male who was not in school, not in the military, and who reported working fewer than 100 hours for the entire year when he was twenty-four years old is counted as idle. There were 207 males with missing idleness data.

Single motherhood. A woman is counted as a single mother if she had a baby and was not married any time before she turned twenty-five. If a woman did not have a baby or was married when she had a baby, she is counted as not having been a single mother. Seventeen women had missing data on single motherhood.

Parent's age. Age of the youngest parent when the child was fourteen years old.

Parent's education. The highest grade of school completed by the father or mother, whichever is greatest, reported when the child was fourteen years old.

County unemployment rate. Averaged over the years the child was thirteen to seventeen years old.

Child is a boy. Equal to one if the child's sex is male, zero otherwise.

Child's age in 1989. The child's age on December 31, 1989, constructed by taking the modal response to the birth date question in survey years 1983–1989.

Household size. Mean number of persons living in the child's household. The years over which household size is measured depend on the dependent variable and the specific estimation model. Household size is usually measured in the same years as income. For instance, for dropping out of high school, household size is usually averaged when the child was thirteen to seventeen years old. In all analyses I use the logarithm of household size.

Black. Equal to one if the head of the child's household is black, zero otherwise.

NLSY Variables

The *NLSY Child Handbook* by Baker and Mott (1989) provides extensive information on the reliability and validity of test scores. Chase-Lansdale et al. (1991) describe many aspects of the NLSY mother-child files.

Parental income. Total family income adjusted to 1992 prices using the CPI-U-X1. It is top-coded at $121,610 for reported incomes greater than $105,649. It includes cash income from all sources and the face value of Food Stamps.

When I measure income over five years, I require a valid measure of parental income for three of the five years. About 56 percent of NLSY children had a reported positive value for all five years. Another 30 percent had four years of data. When I replicate these estimates requiring all five years of income data, the sample size falls and the income coefficient increases somewhat. Table B.3 shows the change in each test score. The second column shows the same change for the smaller sample with all five years.

Income is usually averaged over five years. When this is the case, income must be nonmissing for at least three of the five years. When possible, I include income from opposite-sex partners. I usually use the logarithm of income. Appendix B provides a test of the best functional form.

PPVT (Peabody Picture Vocabulary Test Revised). A test of receptive vocabulary. I use the nationally standardized score. The PPVT was normed on a sample of 4,200 children in 1979 to have a mean of 100 and a standard deviation of 15. The NLSY eliminates scores less than forty. The PPVT was given once to each child at the first interview in which the child was eligible.

Behavior problems. The Behavior Problems Index (BPI) was developed for children aged four to seventeen. It includes twenty-eight items reported by mothers. It was normed on a same-sex sample in 1981 to have a mean of 100 and a standard deviation of 15.

PIAT math. An achievement test of math skills normed more than twenty years ago to have a mean of 100 and a standard deviation of 15. I use age-normed scores.

PIAT reading. A test of reading recognition. It was normed more than twenty years ago to have a mean of 100 and a standard deviation of 15. I use age-normed scores.

Age of child. The child's age at the time of the assessment.

Black. Equal to one if the mother is reported as black, and zero otherwise.

Hispanic. A variable equal to one if the mother is reported as Hispanic in the 1979 interview, zero otherwise.

Family size. The number of related people in the household. For most analyses, unrelated opposite-sex partners are treated like spouses. The length of time over which family size is measured usually corresponds to the length of time over which income is measured. In all models I use the logarithm of family size.

Mother's education. The mother's highest grade completed as reported up to and including the year in which the child's outcome is measured.

Mother's age at child's birth. The mother's reported age less the child's age. Since both mother's age and child's age are sometimes not consistently reported over time, this is the average of several years of data.

Mother's AFQT score. The mother's percentile score on the 1980 Armed Forces Qualification Test. The percentile is based on participants in the NLSY Profiles assessment. The overall mean percentile for women in the NLSY (including those without children) is 40.37. This is lower than the national mean of 50 percent. The mean for mothers is only slightly lower than the mean for all NLSY women.

APPENDIX B

☐ ☐ ☐ ☐ ☐

Conventional Estimates of the Effect of Income

The Measurement of Income

The functional form of income. In order to test the assumption that the effect of income on children's outcomes is linear, Table B.1 compares the predictive power of four different income measures. In all equations income is in constant 1992 dollars. The first equation uses family income in dollars. If this linear form of income provides the best fit to the data, then when we transfer money from the rich to the poor, the improvement in poor children's outcomes will exactly equal the deterioration in rich children's outcomes, leaving no overall change in the mean of the outcome. The next three models assume that parental income has a nonlinear effect and that a dollar of income makes more difference to the poor than to the rich. The first nonlinear model uses the cube root of income, which is a compromise between the linear and the logarithmic specifications. The next nonlinear model uses the logarithm of income. The last nonlinear model includes both the logarithm of income and four dichotomous variables. The first is equal to one if a family's income falls in the poorest income decile, the second is equal to one if income falls in the second poorest decile, the third is equal to one if income falls in the second to the richest income decile, and the fourth is equal to one if income falls in the richest income decile. This model tells us whether the logarithmic specification over or underestimates the importance of income at the extremes of the income distribution.

Table B.1 shows how well each form of income "fits" the observed

Table B.1 Comparison of goodness-of-fit statistics for various functional forms of income predicting children's outcomes

Children's outcomes	Linear	Cube root	Log	Log and decile	Number of cases
			Adjusted R^2		
Test scores for five- to seven-year-olds					
PPVT	.359	.358	.357	.356	1,112
PIAT math	.146	.147	.147	.148	2,736
PIAT reading	.145	.147	.147	.149	2,701
BPI	.046	.047	.045	.047	2,874
			Chi squared		
Adolescent outcomes					
Probability of teenage childbearing	1771.0	1773.9	1780.8	1766.1	2,121
Probability of dropping out of school	3164.9	3143.8	3143.3	3115.5	4,003
			Adjusted R^2		
Young-adult outcomes					
Years of education	.268	.268	.265	.267	3,268
Years of education for high school graduates	.199	.193	.188	.199	2,586
Male hourly wages	.195	.199	.199	.195	954
Male annual earnings	.223	.228	.228	.225	954
			Chi squared		
Probability of male idleness	898.7	898.8	897.9	875.8	1,355
Probability of single motherhood	1510.8	1510.9	1515.0	1505.4	1,741

Sources: Estimates for children's test scores were computed from NLSY mother-child files by David Knutson. Estimates for other outcomes were computed from PSID data by Timothy Veenstra. Income is averaged over five years. All equations control household size, race, parent's age at the birth of the child, and parent's education. Equations for labor-market outcomes also control the county unemployment rate and age of child. Education equations also control child's sex. Equations for assessment scores also control mother's AFQT score.

data. For continuous outcomes such as test scores, the goodness-of-fit statistic is R^2. For dichotomous outcomes such as teenage childbearing, the goodness-of-fit statistic is X^2. These two measures have opposite interpretations; a higher R^2 implies a better fit, whereas a lower X^2 implies a better fit.

The most obvious conclusion from this table is that these samples are not large enough to distinguish among these functional forms. In most cases the goodness-of-fit statistics are nearly the same for all specifications, but a nonlinear form usually provides a better fit than the linear form. These data suggest that different nonlinear transformations may be appropriate for different outcomes, but we would need much larger samples to be sure of this. Throughout this book I use the logarithm of income mainly because it is easy to interpret.

The number of years over which income is measured. Table 4.2 shows the effect of doubling income on five- to seven-year-old children's test scores for samples of children with one, three, or five years of income data. In that table, sample size varies depending on the income measures. When I estimate all models for the sample of children with five years of income data, the results are similar, but the income effect is generally somewhat smaller. For example, using the smaller sample the change in PPVT scores when family income doubles from $15,000 to $30,000 in one year is .62 compared with .72 when I use the larger sample of children with one year of income data.

Table 4.3 shows the effect of doubling parents' income from $15,000 to $30,000 on adolescent and young-adult outcomes for a sample of children with complete income data for five years during adolescence. Table B.2 shows the same estimates for a sample of children who have income data for ten years. These equations control family size measured during the same years as income, race, parents' education, and the youngest parent's age when the child was fourteen. In addition, the equations for labor-force outcomes control the county unemployment rate measured in the same years as income, and the education equations control the child's sex.

The estimated effect of income measured in a single year is smaller than the effect of income averaged over a longer period. Doubling income at age fourteen appears to reduce a teenager's chances of dropping out of high school by 18.1 percent. Doubling income over ten years reduces dropping out by 46.3 percent. For most outcomes the bias from

Table B.2 Effect of doubling parental income in one year and in ten years from $15,000 to $30,000 on adolescent and young-adult outcomes

Children's outcomes	Mean	$15,000	$30,000	Difference	Sample size
Adolescent outcomes					
Probability of teenage childbearing					
Income at age fourteen	.191	.266	.185	− .081	1,561
Ten-year income	.191	.381	.212	− .170	1,561
Probability of dropping out of school					
Income at age fourteen	.170	.182	.159	− .033	3,066
Ten year income	.170	.339	.182	− .157	3,066
Young-adult outcomes					
Years of education					
Income at age fourteen	12.81	12.52	12.72	.193	2,291
	(1.91)				
Ten-year income	12.81	11.68	12.43	.595	2,291
	(1.91)				
Years of education for high school graduates					
Income at age fourteen	13.33	13.16	13.27	.103	1,823
	(1.65)				
Ten-year income	13.33	12.45	13.00	.549	1,823
	(1.65)				
Male earnings (in 1992 dollars)					
Income at age fourteen	19,614	17,065	18,660	1,595	549
	(11,474)				
Ten-year income	19,614	13,800	17,682	3,882	549
	(11,474)				
Male hourly wages (in 1992) dollars					
Income at age fourteen	9.98	8.57	9.45	.88	549
	(5.59)				
Ten-year income	9.98	7.33	9.09	1.77	549
	(5.59)				
Probability of male idleness					
Income at age fourteen	.111	.123	.112	− .011	928
Ten-year income	.111	.145	.118	− .027	928
Probability of single motherhood					
Income at age fourteen	.233	.329	.232	− .096	1,213
Ten-year income	.233	.407	.254	− .152	1,213

Source: Estimated from PSID data by Timothy Veenstra. All equations control household size, race, parent's age at the birth of the child, and parent's education. Equations for labor-market outcomes also control the county unemployment rate and age of child in 1989. Education equations control child's sex. Time-dependent variables are averaged over the same period as income.

using only one year of income is quite large. Using income for ten years rather than five years makes far less difference.

When I estimated this same model for the larger sample with income at age fourteen, the results were similar to those in Table B.2, suggesting that the differences in the effect of income are mainly attributable to the differences in the income measure, not differences in the sample.

As in the NLSY, when I compute a five-year income average in the PSID, I require a valid income report for only three of five years. A large proportion of children have parental income for all five years, so requiring five years of income hardly changes the results. This is shown in Table B.3.

The effect of weighting data. The results reported in the text use sampling weights. I re-estimated the conventional models using un-

Table B.3 Effect of doubling parental income averaged over five years for weighted and unweighted data

Children's outcomes	Requiring three of five years (weighted)	Requiring all five years	
		Weighted	Unweighted
Test scores for five- to seven-year-olds			
PPVT	1.89	1.98	2.07
PIAT math	1.19	1.49	1.59
PIAT reading	1.97	2.91	2.88
BPI	−1.96	−2.33	−2.06
Adolescent outcomes			
Probability of teenage childbearing	−.164	−.153	−.123
Probability of dropping out of school	−.128	−.122	−.147
Young-adult outcomes			
Years of education	.546	.559	.494
Years of education for high school graduates	.393	.414	.313
Male hourly wages (1992 dollars)	1.80	1.26	1.32
Male annual earnings (1992 dollars)	3,310	3,033	3,473
Probability of male idleness	−.016	−.015	−.007
Probability of single motherhood	−.178	−.157	−.127

weighted data. For most outcomes, weighting the data makes little difference to the results. The last column in Table B.3 shows the effect of doubling income using unweighted data in both the NLSY and the PSID.

Tables B.4, B.5, and B.6 show the full regression models used to generate the estimates in Tables 4.2 and 4.3.

Income Change Models

I estimate three models of the effect of income changes on children's outcomes. In each model I include average income plus a measure of income change. I control the standard set of exogenous variables plus an indicator of changes in parents' marital status and changes in parents'

Table B.4 Unstandardized OLS regression coefficients (standard errors) for equations predicting five- to seven-year-olds' test scores

Variable	PPVT	BPI	PIAT math	PIAT reading
Intercept	67.067	145.743	75.210	97.465
	(8.117)	(5.378)	(4.382)	(4.269)
Log family income				
(five years)	2.721	−2.822	1.723	2.845
	(.746)	(.489)	(.397)	(.391)
Child's age	1.130	.395	1.019	−1.092
	(.506)	(.381)	(.308)	(.301)
Mother is black	−11.397	−1.187	−2.309	2.782
	(1.141)	(.797)	(.642)	(.634)
Mother is Hispanic	−8.663	−1.666	−2.699	−.821
	(1.485)	(1.019)	(.830)	(.815)
Log family size	−6.737	1.045	−3.758	−5.117
	(1.437)	(1.023)	(.823)	(.808)
Mother's highest grade				
completed	.875	−.344	.507	.554
	(.277)	(.186)	(.152)	(.150)
Mother's age at child's				
birth	−.526	−.414	−.107	−.702
	(.189)	(.113)	(.091)	(.090)
Mother's AFQT score	.178	−.028	.113	.128
	(.021)	(.014)	(.011)	(.011)
Sample size	1,174	2,890	2,942	2,901
R^2	.350	.044	.147	.157

Source: Estimated from NLSY mother-child files by David Knutson.

Table B.5 Logistic regression coefficients (standard errors) and partial derivatives for variables predicting adolescent and young-adult outcomes

Variable	Teenage childbearing	Dropping out of school	Male idleness	Single motherhood
Intercept	12.093	11.255	−1.106	11.187
	(1.278)	(.966)	(1.939)	(1.465)
Log family income (5 years)	−1.139	−1.025	−.224	−1.139
	(.129)	(.097)	(.195)	(.147)
	−.152	−.116	−.020	−.176
Log family size (5 years)	1.034	.832	.184	1.090
	(.181)	(.139)	(.267)	(.199)
	.138	.094	.016	.169
Parent is black	.015	−.362	.927	.933
	(.153)	(.125)	(.245)	(.160)
	.014	−.037	.109	.172
Parent's age when child was fourteen	−.039	−.017	.012	−.034
	(.009)	(.007)	(.015)	(.010)
	−.005	−.002	.001	−.005
Parent's highest grade completed	−.140	−.232	.033	−.084
	(.029)	(.021)	(.040)	(.029)
	−.019	−.026	.003	−.013
Respondent is a boy	—	.222	—	—
		(0.091)		
		.025		
Number of cases	2,124	4,003	1,355	1,741
Chi squared	1,780.8	3,143.3	897.9	1,515.0

Source: Estimated from PSID data by Timothy Veenstra.

hours of labor-market work because each of these presumably affects income changes as well as children's outcomes. Consequently, the number of cases for these analyses is smaller than the number of cases shown in Tables 4.2 and 4.3. The indicator of changes in marital status is the number of times marital status changed in the period over which income is measured. The measure of labor-force hours differs depending on the measure of income changes.

In the first model, the income-change variable is the slope of income. It is calculated by the typical formula for the slope of a line, namely:

APPENDIX B

Table B.6 Unstandardized OLS regression coefficients (standard errors) for variables predicting education and male wages and earnings

| | Outcomes | | | |
| | Years of education | | Male workers' | |
Variable	All	High school graduates	Wages	Earnings
Intercept	1.651	4.955	−44.566	−99,956
	(.652)	(.652)	(4.861)	(10,743)
Log family income	.784	.567	2.603	6,219
	(.065)	(.065)	(.435)	(961)
Log family size	−.714	−.507	−.683	−3,049
	(.091)	(.010)	(.603)	(1,332)
Parent is black	.257	.142	−1.150	−4,168
	(.091)	(.095)	(.729)	(1,603)
Parent's age when child was fourteen	.023	.019	.049	64
	(.005)	(.005)	(.033)	(73)
Parent's years of education	.235	.178	.126	153
	(.013)	(.014)	(.088)	(195)
Child is a boy	−.032	.025	—	—
	(.059)	(.058)		
County unemployment rate	—	—	.255	.122
			(.101)	(.222)
Age in 1989	—	—	.780	1,821
			(.066)	(145)
Number of cases	3,275	2,586	954	954
R^2	.265	.188	.199	.228

Source: Estimated from PSID data by Timothy Veenstra.

$$\frac{N\,(\Sigma xy) \;-\; (\Sigma x)(\Sigma y)}{N\,\Sigma\,x^2 \;-\; (\Sigma x)^2,}$$

where N is the number of years of income data, x is the age at which income is measured, and y is the logarithm of income. For the adolescent and young-adult outcomes in the PSID, a child must have at least seven out of ten years of parental income data to have a nonmissing value for the income slope. In this model, changes in labor-force hours are calculated as "work effort" by summing head and spouse labor-force hours and dividing by 4,000 if there are two parents or dividing by 2,000 if there is only one parent. I then estimate a slope for this measure of work effort.

I exclude families with an opposite-sex partner because I have no data on their work hours. I also exclude the top and bottom 1 percent of reported slopes, because of an apparent problem with outliers.

In the second model of income change, I assess the effect of a drop in income. I count children as having experienced an income drop if their parents' income fell by at least 35 percent in any two consecutive years over the five or ten years in which income is measured. The sample size for this estimate is smaller than for the slope model in the NLSY because I require all years of income data since I cannot interpolate an income drop. I calculated a second income-drop variable that counted children as having experienced an income drop if their parents' income fell by at least 50 percent in any two consecutive years. I estimate similar variables for a drop in parental work effort.

In the third model I estimate the standard deviation of the logarithm of income and work effort. The standard deviation of income is:

$$\sqrt{\frac{\Sigma(X-\bar{X})^2}{N}},$$

where X is income in a year and N is the number of years. I require all five years of income data in the NLSY and exclude families with opposite-sex partners. In the PSID I require seven of ten years of income data.

The "True" Effect of Income

This appendix describes the method used in Chapter 5 to estimate the "true" effect of parental income on children's outcomes. The text of Chapter 5 describes the intuition behind the method. To render this intuition more precisely, consider an outcome such as dropping out (O) that occurs between the first income observation (X_1) and the second (X_2). Assume that income in both periods depends on a vector of stable unmeasured variables, Z. The path diagram depicting this model is shown in Figure C.1.

If we convert all variables to means of zero and standard deviations

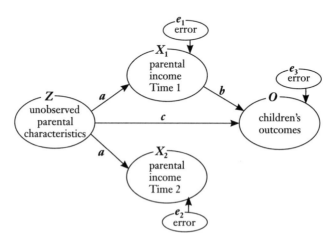

Figure C.1 The path model

of one, we have:

$$X_1 = aZ + e_1, \qquad (1)$$

where a is the correlation between income and its unmeasured determinants. Likewise,

$$X_2 = aZ + e_2. \qquad (2)$$

To estimate this model I assume that the error terms are uncorrelated:

$$E(e_1 e_2) = 0;$$
$$E(e_1 e_3) = 0;$$
$$E(e_2 e_3) = 0.$$

$E(e_1 e_2) = 0$ by definition, since all factors contributing to the correlation between X_1 and X_2, including nonrandom error, are subsumed in Z.

I also assume that $a_1 = a_2$, an assumption I relax later. Multiplying equation 1 by equation 2, dropping terms with an expected value of zero, and recalling that the correlation between two variables is equal to the product of their standardized values,

$$r_{x1,\, x2} = a2. \qquad (3)$$

The outcome, O, depends on Z and X_1 but not X_2, so:

$$O = bX_1 + cZ + e_3, \qquad (4)$$

where b and c are standardized regression coefficients. The correlation of O with X_1 is then:

$$r_{O,X_1} = b + cr_{z,x1} = b + ac, \qquad (5)$$

whereas the correlation of O with Z is:

$$r_{O,Z} = ab + c. \qquad (6)$$

Since X_2 does not affect O, the correlation of X_2 with O is simply:

$$r_{O,X_2} = a(ab + c)\ a2b + ac. \qquad (7)$$

Subtracting equation 7 from equation 5 yields:

$$r_{O,X_1} - r_{O,X_2}\ b(1 - a^2). \qquad (8)$$

Substituting from equation 3 and rearranging we get:

$$b = (r_{O,X_1} - r_{O,X_2}) / (1 - r_{X_1,\, X_2}). \qquad (9)$$

Clearly, when $r_{O,X_1} = r_{O,X_2}$, $b = 0$, which means that the entire effect of income is spurious. Likewise, if c is zero, making the observed coefficient of income unbiased, equations 3, 5, and 7 tell us that $r_{O,X_2} = r_{X_1, X_2} r_{O,X_1}$.

The estimated true effect of income in Tables 5.2, 5.3, and 5.4 assumes that parental characteristics have the same effect on Time 1 income and Time 2 income. Since the variance of income increases over time, this may not be the case. To test this assumption, I assume that the standardized effect of unobserved stable parental characteristics changes over time in the same way as the standardized effect of observed stable characteristics. To measure this change, I regress each income measure on the parental characteristics controlled in Tables 5.2, 5.3, or 5.4, using the appropriate sample for each outcome. If the multiple Rs in these two equations are the same, I assume that these observed characteristics have the same effect on income at Time 1 and Time 2. If the multiple Rs differ, I adjust the true effect to reflect this difference. The adjustment is:

$$b^* = \frac{r_{O,X_1} - r_{O,X_2}R}{1 - (r_{X_1, X_2}R)},$$

where $R = r_{Z,X_1} / r_{Z,X_2}$.

Estimates of the "true" standardized regression coefficient making this correction are:

PIAT reading: $b^* = -.067$ (.156)
BPI: $b^* = .363$ (.313)
Teenage childbearing: $b^* = -.204$ (.098)
Dropping out of high school: $b^* = -.078$ (.204)
Years of education: $b^* = .072$ (.228)
Single motherhood: $b^* = .021$ (.069).

Reliability of the income measures. I average income over five years. This average is more reliable than income measured in only one year. I experimented with LISREL models that provided different reliabilities for Time 1 and Time 2 income. But reliabilities as low as .95 produced results very similar to those shown in the text.

Standard errors. To estimate standard errors, I randomly assign the cases in each sample to ten nonoverlapping subsamples. I follow the procedure outlined above to estimate the true effect of income for each subsample. I calculate the standard deviation of these estimates and use this to calculate the sampling error of the estimates in the full sample on the assumption that increasing the sample size by a factor of ten lowers the sampling error of a given parameter by a factor of the square root of ten (3.15).

To check the robustness of these sampling errors, I repeated this procedure ten times for each outcome, each time using a different random procedure for assigning cases to samples. The standard errors shown in Chapter 5 are usually in the middle of the standard errors that are generated using different random assignments.

Additional estimation issues. An important assumption of my approach to testing the extent of bias due to unmeasured parental characteristics is that stable parental traits do not affect the transitory component of income. If they do, we cannot assume that future income is a proxy only for unmeasured stable characteristics, since stable parental characteristics could affect the transitory component of income by affecting either the variance of income or its trend. Imagine two parents. Parent A goes to graduate school. Her annual income is $10,000 for the five years she is in graduate school and $40,000 for the five years after she graduates. Her average income over the entire period is thus $25,000 per year. Parent B does not go to graduate school. She averages $20,000 in the first five years and $30,000 in the second five years, so she, too, has an average income of $25,000 per year. The difference between the income trend for Parent A and Parent B can easily be caused by a stable underlying trait, such as the value each parent places on education. More generally, if we observe a consistent upward or downward trend in income, we have reason to suspect that it reflects some stable attribute of the recipient.

We can test the hypothesis that the trend (or slope) in income is affected by stable parental traits by regressing the difference between Time 2 income and Time 1 income on observed parental traits. If the observed traits explain a substantial proportion of this difference, we must conclude that stable traits affect the slope of income. In fact, observed parental characteristics explain about 2 percent of the variance in the slope of income. The fact that observed traits explain so little of the variance in the individual income trends is strong, though not conclusive, evidence that stable unobserved characteristics do not greatly affect the trend either. Furthermore, if parental traits did have a large effect on both the trend of income and children's outcomes, we would expect the income trend to have a large effect on children's outcomes in models that omit these parental traits. But evidence presented in Chapter 5 showed that the slope of parental income measured before an outcome occurs has a small effect on children's outcomes. Thus there is little evidence that parental traits affect the transitory component of income.

The procedure I use to estimate the effect of income is similar but not identical to estimating a fixed-effect model in which we estimate the effect of the unstable component of X_1 on an outcome.

□ □ □ □ □

Index Construction

Procedures for Calculating the Household Living Conditions Index

There are at least two conceptually distinct ways to weight individual living conditions to create an overall index of living conditions. One is to weight the components by their importance to children's outcomes. The other is to weight them according to their responsiveness to parental income. Because I want to maximize the effect of income on living conditions, I choose the second option.

To create a measure of overall living conditions that maximizes the correlation between income and living conditions, I:

1. regress the logarithm of parental income averaged over 1968–1972 on the measures of living conditions measured in the same years;
2. use the unstandardized regression coefficient of each living condition as a weight to estimate each child's living condition score.

The resulting weights are shown in Table D.1. The index computed from these weights has a mean of 10.593 and a standard deviation of .439.

I used NLSY mother-child data to create the activities and possessions index and the housing environment index in the same way. The equations used to get the weights for these indexes are shown in Tables D.2 and D.3.

I also created indexes that maximized the correlation of household living conditions, activities and possessions, or the housing environment with children's outcomes. To do this, I regressed each outcome on the components of the index and used the unstandardized regression

Table D.1 Unstandardized OLS regression coefficient for living conditions in 1968–1972 predicting log parental income in 1968–1972

Living conditions in 1968–1972	Coefficient	Standard error
Intercept	9.171	.033
Food expenditures (in $1,000s)	.052	.003
Expenditures for eating out (in $1,000s)	.129	.009
Log cigarette expenditures	−.002	.002
Log alcohol expenditures	.015	.002
Years insured	.104	.005
Years house needed repairs	−.048	.007
Number of rooms	.025	.006
Number of cars	.159	.008
Years spent less than USDA food standard	−.036	.013
Years owned home	.010	.003
Value of dwelling (in $100,000s)	.347	.019
Sample size	3,609	—
Adjusted R^2	.684	—

Table D.2 Effect of activities and possessions on log five-year average parental income

Variable	Coefficient	Standard error
Intercept	9.049	.059
Number of books	.090	.006
No books	.332	.108
Number of museum visits	−.002	.002
No museum visits	−.071	.028
Number of outings	.001	.000
Less than two outings	−.022	.048
Has a tape recorder	.270	.028
R^2	.173	—
Sample size	2,583	—

coefficients as weights. The composite created using parental income correlates highly (.80 or better) with composites developed by weighting the components according to their effect on children's outcomes. Choosing a different index does not to lead to different conclusions.

Both the weighting scheme and, as discussed in the text, the components of the index are controversial. I tried many different weighting schemes and various combinations of components. None that I could find yielded substantially different conclusions from those in the text.

Table D.3 Effect of housing environment variables on log five-year average parental income

Variable	Coefficient	Standard error
Intercept	9.642	.059
Home is dark	−.397	.049
Home is safe	.238	.049
Home is cluttered	−.012	.035
Home is clean	.284	.055
R^2	.083	—
Sample size	2,519	—

Source: Estimated from NLSY mother-child files by David Knutson.

Nonetheless, better data and better theory about the relationship between parental income and families' material resources could yield different conclusions.

One Year versus Five Years of Income

Table D.4 shows living conditions in children's homes in 1972 by parents' income in that same year. Like more recent national cross-sectional data, the PSID data show that poor children experience more material hardships than middle-income children. But the data also show that poor children fare better than we would expect from their parents' income. Although income for poor children is only 45.1 percent of the income of middle-income children, poor children's families spend 76.5 percent as much as middle-income families on food eaten at home, and the value of their dwellings is 54.3 percent of the value of middle-income children's dwellings.

Average income is more equally distributed than one year of income: the difference in income between poor and middle-income children is smaller for five years of income than for one year of income. But the difference in expenditures is greater. Using one year of income, we find that poor families spend 76 percent as much as middle-income families on food eaten at home. Using five years of income, we find that poor families spend 69.1 percent as much on food eaten at home. Families whose income is low for a long time experience more material deprivations than those who have low income for only a single year. Families whose average income is low spend less on eating out and

Table D.4 Household living conditions by parental income, 1972

Living conditions in 1972	Income decile		Third income quintile	First/ third	First– third
	First	Second			
Income (1992 dollars)	16,359	24,395	36,282	45.1	—
Expenditures (1992 dollars)					
Food at home	4,651	5,024	6,076	76.5	
Food away from home	246	279	530	46.4	—
Cigarettes	125	126	163	76.7	—
Alcohol	59	77	123	48.0	—
Value of dwelling	33,221	40,310	61,128	54.3	—
Number of cars	.92	1.14	1.6	57.5	—
Number of rooms	5.15	5.64	6.01	85.7	—
Percentage spending less than USDA food budget	65.5	60.3	29.3	—	36.2
Percentage insured	88.5	91.9	99.2	—	− 10.7
Percentage needing home repairs	38.5	22.4	7.1	—	31.4
Percentage crowded	37.8	31.9	25.1		12.7
Percentage who own homes	42.3	51.6	79.3	—	− 37.0
Living conditions index score	10.093	10.224	10.580	—	− .487

Source: Calculated from PSID data by Timothy Veenstra.

more on eating at home than those whose income is low in any one year.

The Effect of Future Income on Living Conditions

In Chapter 5 I argued that parental income after a child's outcome had occurred was a proxy for stable parental characteristics. But standard economic theory holds that when families experience fluctuations around their "permanent" income, they borrow and save in such a way that they keep consuming at the level of their permanent income. If this theory were correct, Time 2 income would affect living standards at Time 1.

Most people believe that saving is virtuous. Yet parents who save for their own retirement when their children are young almost certainly lower their children's consumption. If consumption improves children's chances for success, saving may hurt rather than help children. Even parents who save for their children's college education may be making the children worse off if consumption during childhood is important and financial aid is available to college students.

To test the hypothesis that future income affects current living conditions, I regressed the living conditions on three measures of income: income measured at the same time as the living conditions (1969–1972), income measured soon after the living conditions are measured (1973–1976), and income measured almost a decade later (1978–1981). If parental income after living conditions are measured had a large effect on those living conditions, this would be evidence that parents anticipate future income and smooth it so that living conditions match their average income over the long run. In this case there would be no way to disentangle the effect of long-term parental income from the effect of stable parental characteristics correlated with income. If this stable component of income partly represents the purchasing power of future income, the "true" effect of income estimated in Chapter 5 will be too small, because what I attribute to stable parental characteristics will be partly due to parents' income. By contrast, if future income has a very small effect on current living conditions, we can conclude that the stable component of income is mainly a proxy for stable parental traits.

The second column in Table D.5 shows the effect of parental income in 1973–1976 (Time 2 income) on living conditions in the PSID controlling income in 1968–1972. The last column in Table D.6 shows the effect of income in 1988–1992 (Time 2 income) controlling income in 1981–1985 on the possessions, activities, and housing environment of NLSY children. The effect of Time 2 income is usually not statistically significant, but even when it is, its effect is much smaller than the effect of Time 1 income. One exception is that future income appears to affect whether families have a home that interviewers consider dirty. This effect is nearly as large as current income, though the effect of income in both periods is small. Future income appears to decrease current expenditures on cigarettes. The likely explanation for these exceptions is that a clean home and not smoking serve as proxies for parental characteristics that improve future job prospects.

If families anticipate income in the near future but not the distant future, the correlation between living conditions and future income will

Table D.5   Effect of doubling parental income on household living conditions

Living conditions in 1969–1972	Year income is measured		
	1969–1972	1973–1976	1978–1981
Living conditions index	.399	.011	.019
Expenditures (1992 dollars)			
Food at home	1,492	−51	86
Food away from home	472	55	31
Cigarettes	28	−18.8	−12.3
Alcohol	31	−5.9	4.2
Value of dwelling	26,183	1,745	1,648
Number of cars	.353	−.027	.003
Number of rooms	.518	−.004	−.025
Years owned home	.838	−.124	.202
Years home needed repairs	−.236	−.093	−.048
Years home dirty	−.011	−.008	−.010
Years insured	.574	.109	.112
Years spending less than USDA			
food budget	−.187	.013	−.013

Source: Calculated from PSID data from Timothy Veenstra. Coefficients in column one control parents' education and age, child's race, and family size. Coefficients in column two also control Time 1 income. Coefficients in column three control Time 1 income but not Time 2 income. Standard errors are in parentheses.

decline as income is measured further in the future. The last column in Table D.5 shows the effect of income in 1978–1981 (Time 3 income) on the living conditions in the PSID. The effect of Time 3 income is always much smaller than the effect of Time 1 income. The effect of Time 3 income is sometimes less than the effect of Time 2 income and sometimes greater, though the difference is usually small.

These results imply that living conditions are mainly influenced by current and past income, not by the purchasing power of income in the future. Thus if Time 2 income appears to influence children's behavior, this is probably because it serves as a proxy for stable parental traits that influence both parental income and children's outcomes, not because it is a proxy for unmeasured monetary resources at Time 1.

Economists who write about the permanent-income hypothesis note that predicting future income requires "intelligent, forward-looking behavior" (Hall 1978, p. 973). If this is the case, then families with high incomes should be able to act on their permanent income better than families with low incomes, since both cognitive ability and "forward-

Table D.6 Effect of doubling parental income on four- and five-year-olds'
activities, possessions, and housing environment

Index components	Mean (SD)	Income in 1981–1985	Income in 1988–1992
Number of books (1 to 10)	8.816 (2.557)	.563	.217
Owns tape recorder	.661	.072	.018
Annual trips to the museum	2.846 (5.574)	.449	.145
Annual outings	94.518 (96.695)	.944	.758
Activities and possessions index	10.033 (.293)	.073	.022
Home is clean	.913	.030	−.006
Home is safe	.902	.060	.005
Home is cluttered	.797	.039	.003
Home is dark and monotonous	.092	−.038	.010
Housing environment index	10.057 (.199)	.050	.005

Source: Calculated from the NLSY mother-child files by David Knutson. Coefficients in
column two control mother's education, age, race, AFQT score, and child's sex.
Coefficients in column three also control income in 1981–1985.

looking" behavior are positively correlated with income. But I find that
the patterns for high-income families are similar to those for low-income families.

Measures of Parents' Psychological Well-Being

All the measures of parental psychological well-being are constructed
variables in the PSID. Their means and standard deviations are shown
in Table D.7.

Efficacy index. This index is scored from zero to seven. It is constructed from responses to questions that ask respondents whether they
usually feel pretty sure that their lives will work out the way they want
them to, whether they are the kind of people that plan their lives ahead,
whether when they plan ahead they usually get to carry out their plans
as expected, whether they nearly always finish things they start, whether
they would rather spend their money and enjoy life or save more for
the future, and whether they think a lot about things that might happen
in the future.

Trust index. This index is scored between zero and five. It is constructed from responses to questions that ask respondents whether it matters to them what others think, whether they trust most people, whether they think the life of the average person is getting better, and whether they think there are a lot of people who have good things they don't deserve.

Aspirations index. This index is scored from zero to nine. It is constructed from respondents' answers to questions about whether they plan to get a specific kind of new job, whether they might quit their jobs because they are not challenging, whether they prefer a job with a chance for more money even if they dislike the job, whether they are more often satisfied or dissatisfied with themselves, and whether they spend a lot of time figuring out ways to get more money.

Anger index. This index measures the response to the question, Do you get angry fairly easily, or does it take a lot to get you angry? The responses are scored from zero to five.

Creating Parenting Practices Indexes

Discipline-style index. To create the discipline-style index, I use data from the HOME (Home Observation for Measurement of the Environment) assessment in the NLSY mother-child files. I use the mother's response to a question about what she would do if her child hit her. She could list as many of the following as she wished: hit back, spank the child, send the child to his or her room, give the child a chore, talk to the child, or ignore the child. I constructed dummy variables for every combination of responses given by mothers. For instance, I created a variable equal to one if a mother said she would do all of these, and another if she said she would hit back and spank the child but not

Table D.7 Means and standard deviations for psychological indexes

Psychological indexes	Mean	Standard deviation
Aspirations	2.879	1.178
Efficacy	3.612	1.292
Trust	2.505	.982
Anger	10.588	1.279

Source: Calculated from PSID data by Timothy Veenstra.

do any of the other things. Mothers gave forty-four different combinations of responses. I regressed the logarithm of income averaged over the five years before the assessment for all four- and five-years-olds in 1986, 1988, and 1990 on these forty-four categories. I used the unstandardized regression coefficients as weights for creating the discipline-style index.

Nurturing index. I used the same procedure to create the nurturing index. Interviewers recorded which of the following things the mother did during the interview: conversed with the child; caressed, kissed, and hugged the child; physically restricted the child; spanked the child; or answered the child's questions verbally. I created a dummy variable for each combination of responses. Mothers gave twenty-seven combinations. I regressed these on the logarithm of parental income averaged over five years and used the unstandardized coefficients as weights in constructing the index.

TV-Read index. This index is constructed in the same way as the other indexes. The weights for the variables are .001 for each day the mother reads to her child in a year, -.377 if she reports not reading at all, -.029 for each hour the television is on per day, and -.034 if she reports no television.

TV-PTA index. This index is also constructed in the same way as the others. The weights for the variables are .432 for each PTA meeting the respondent or spouse attended in the last year, and -.108 for each hour the household head watches television on an average weekday.

More Evidence on the "True" Effect of Income

I use the following model to estimate the effect of increasing state AFDC benefits on adolescent and young-adult outcomes:

$$O_i = b_1F_i + b_2F_iB_s + b_3 B_s + b_3R_i + b_4A_i,$$

where O is an outcome, F_i is a dummy variable equal to one if the family is headed by a single female, B_s is the state benefit level, R_i is the child's race, and A_i is the child's age in 1989. I count a child as living in a single-parent family if he or she was ever in such a family over a five-year period. For adolescent outcomes, this period is the five years prior to the event. For young-adult outcomes, it is when children were thirteen to seventeen years old. Thus this comparison implicitly takes into account any incentives provided by AFDC for parents to divorce or never marry. The AFDC benefit level is averaged over these same years.

Benefits vary both by year and by state. The child's age in 1989 controls trends in outcomes not accounted for by changes in state AFDC benefits. Therefore, benefit levels mainly reflect state differences. Because the benefit level is unique to a state for a cohort, this model is similar to using state dummy variables to estimate a state fixed-effects model. In fact, estimates from such a model are very close to the estimates from the model shown above.

In this model, b_3 is the effect of the state benefit level on children in married-couple families. Since I assume that AFDC benefit levels mainly influence children in married-couple families, this effect is spurious—it is attributable to other characteristics of states that are correlated with benefit levels and affect children's outcomes. In this model,

b_2 is the effect of the benefit level on the gap between children in married-couple and single-parent families. Thus $b_3 + b_2$ is the effect of the benefit level on children in single-parent families. Tables E.1 and E.2 show the estimates from this model.

This model for assessing the effect of AFDC benefit levels on children's outcomes depends on higher AFDC benefits increasing the income of single-parent families relative to the income of married-couple families. If a 1 percent rise in median income leads to a 1 percent rise in the combined value of Food Stamps, AFDC, and Medicaid, the income gap between one- and two-parent families will be constant in percentage terms and increase in dollar terms as AFDC benefits rise. In this case, higher AFDC benefits would not narrow the gap in children's outcomes. But, in fact, higher AFDC benefits do narrow the income gap. I regressed the ratio of income for single-parent families

Table E.1   Logistic regression coefficients for the effect of AFDC benefit levels on the probability of adolescent and young-adult outcomes

Variable	Coefficient (standard error) and partial derivative			
	Teenage childbearing	Dropping out of school	Male idleness	Single motherhood
Log AFDC benefit	−.619	−.914	.048	−.540
	(.165)	(.119)	(.272)	(.181)
	−.099	−.125	.005	−.094
AFDC × single-parent family	.226	.601	−.161	.654
	(.276)	(.213)	(.474)	(.324)
	.036	.082	−.016	.114
Single-parent family	−.705	−3.106	1.882	−3.608
	(1.775)	(1.367)	(3.103)	(2.108)
	−.101	−.264	.277	−.381
Child's age in 1989	.042	.043	.043	.010
	(.012)	(.009)	(.026)	(.016)
	.006	.006	.004	.002
Black	.700	.299	.628	1.433
	(.142)	(.115)	(.233)	(.152)
	.127	.044	.073	.303
Intercept	1.118	2.838	−3.989	1.596
	(1.047)	(.739)	(1.894)	(1.241)
Sample size	2,022	3,922	3,229	2,552

Source: Estimated from PSID data by Timothy Veenstra.

Table E.2 Unstandardized OLS regression coefficients for the effect of AFDC benefit levels on years of education, male wages, and male earnings

| Variable | Years of education | | Male wages | Male earnings |
	All	High school graduates		
Log AFDC benefit	.707	.367	2.469	2960.10
	(.098)	(.095)	(.551)	(1225.53)
Log AFDC × single-parent family	−.255	−.142	−1.657	−1506.91
	(.209)	(.210)	(1.349)	(2996.92)
Single-parent family	1.167	.689	9.549	6909.59
	(1.364)	(1.382)	(8.864)	(19690.60)
Child's age in 1989	−.019	−.012	.646	1629.97
	(.009)	(.008)	(.063)	(141.96)
Black	−.530	−.511	−2.171	−7314.23
	(.102)	(.101)	(.715)	(1589.10)
Intercept	8.943	11.408	−24.596	−45995.00
	(.667)	(.645)	(3.856)	(8565.00)
R^2	.045	.024	.155	.175
Sample size	3,229	2,552	938	938

to the income of married-couple families on the combined AFDC and Food Stamp benefit level for each state using 1990 Census data merged with data on state benefit levels. I find that for every 1 percent increase in benefit levels, the ratio declines by 1.35 percent, meaning that single-parent families have higher incomes relative to married-couple families in high-benefit states.

Notes

2. America's Response to Poverty

1. This chapter is a very brief summary of some aspects of the history of social welfare policy in the United States. Many other books provide more detailed histories. Among those I have consulted are Abbott 1941; Bell 1965; Berkowitz 1991; Folks 1902; Gordon 1994; Katz 1986b and 1989; Lynn and Whitman 1981; Patterson 1986; Piven and Cloward 1971; Skocpol 1992; and Trattner 1989, as well as specifically cited materials.

2. In the aftermath of the Civil War, America briefly instituted its first national social welfare program. Americans were willing to help widows of the war and families of wounded soldiers because their poverty was a result of the war effort. But these policies were short-lived. One of the best accounts of of them is in Skocpol (1992).

3. In 1900, orphanages housed about 100,000 children nationwide. There are no comparable estimates for children in foster care, but between 1853 and 1890 the New York Children's Aid Society alone removed more than 92,000 children from the slums of New York to family farms in the Midwest (Lindsey 1994, p. 13).

4. In 1959 Florida purged its welfare roles of more than 7,000 families with over 30,000 children, almost all black, because one or more of the children were illegitimate or because a social worker had reported that the mother's past or present sex life was unacceptable. Louisiana followed suit by purging its rolls of 20,000 children, again mostly black, because they lived in "unsuitable homes" (Piven and Cloward 1971, p. 149).

5. Opinions about whether a mother should work often depended on her race. Southern legislators argued that even low benefits would undermine the agricultural economy of the South and increase its tax burden. After the Social Security Act of 1935, most Southern states enacted rules that

allowed local authorities to deny benefits to "employable" mothers during periods of low unemployment. This meant that during the summer, when workers were needed in the fields, welfare offices routinely terminated benefits for black mothers, forcing them to accept the low wages paid to field hands. When the crops needed picking, Southern welfare officials assumed that black women, but not white women, were employable. In the 1960s, "employable-mother" rules, like suitable-home rules, were barred by the courts because they had been used to deny black mothers welfare.

6. For example, the 1988 *Children's Defense Fund Budget* recommended that the federal government require all states to provide combined AFDC and Food Stamp benefits equal to 75 percent (and eventually 100 percent) of the poverty line. But the main emphasis of the recommendations was "to reward parents who try to work." The recommendations included an increase in the minimum wage, creation of federal jobs, more money for training and education of welfare mothers, special incentives for teenage mothers to stay in school, a child care allowance for AFDC mothers who are in training or education programs, changes in child-support enforcement, and changes in the EITC and child care tax deductions (Children's Defense Fund 1988, pp. 108–110). It also recommended increasing government expenditures for child care, fully funding Head Start, increasing Chapter 1 funding, and increasing funding for school desegregation and community learning centers.

In its 1990 "steps toward reducing poverty and its damaging effects on young children," the National Center for Children in Poverty at Columbia University recommended universal health care coverage, increased child care subsidies, improving the quality and availability of child care, expanding Head Start, reforming unemployment insurance, a higher minimum wage, expansion of the EITC, creation of a child-support assurance system, and community-based services to help poor parents cope with "personal problems and parental responsibilities." It did not mention income support for families.

7. Head Start has always had some Republican support, especially from conservatives, who liked its emphasis on parental involvement. But in the past Republicans repeatedly voted to limit Head Start's appropriations. Conservatives attacked Head Start for being poorly run, excessively expensive, and, in its early days, for being a forum for registering black voters (Patterson 1986, p. 145).

8. In 1971 Nixon vetoed a bill to subsidize and regulate child care. But both Republicans and Democrats supported the child care provision of the 1988 Family Support Act, and in 1989 Orrin Hatch, a conservative senator from Utah, introduced another bill to provide funds for child care services. Hatch later switched to supporting a Democratic bill first proposed by a consortium of liberal child advocates (Hofferth 1993).

9. The expenditures in Table 2.1 reflect expenditures on poor children and their families. They do not include, for example, expenditures on Medicaid or Food Stamps that go to the elderly or to families whose income is greater than the official poverty line.

10. AFDC expenditures are from House Ways and Means Committee (1993), p. 679. Published AFDC expenditures prior to 1980 include foster care maintenance payments. Data on federal expenditures for foster care maintenance payments before 1981 are not available, but in 1980 federal expenditures for maintenance payments were $278.4 million, or 4 percent of the combined expenditure for AFDC and maintenance payments. Although legislation in 1980 made significant changes to the foster care program, these probably had little effect on maintenance payments in 1981. Therefore, I estimate that 4 percent of the 1980 benefit payments were for foster care maintenance, and I reduce the published AFDC expenditures for 1980 by this amount. Between 1970 and 1980 the foster care population grew from 1 percent of the AFDC population to 1.5 percent (House Ways and Means Committee 1993, p. 880), an increase of 50 percent. If the increase had been spread evenly over the decade, the proportion of AFDC children in foster care in 1975 would have been 25 percent greater than in 1970. If expenditures for foster care maintenance payments are proportional to the number of children served, 2.5 percent of the AFDC benefits in 1975 would have been for such payments. I therefore reduce the 1975 published AFDC expenditures by this amount.

11. This somewhat understates the growth in the number of recipients, because foster children were counted as recipients between 1971 and 1981.

12. Between 1975 and 1992, the maximum real monthly AFDC benefit for a family of three in the median state declined by 36.7 percent (from $578 to $372). The average real monthly benefit per AFDC family fell by 39.8 percent (from $644 to $388) over the same period. But the average monthly benefit *per person* fell by only 17 percent. In 1973 the average recipient family had 3.6 members. By 1990 it had 2.9 members (House Ways and Means Committee 1993, p. 696). As family size decreases, so do AFDC benefits. But benefits decline less than the total number of recipients because the benefit schedule assumes that a family of two needs more than half as much money as a family of four. Each state has a different adjustment for family size, but in 1992 in the median state a three-person family received $367, or $122 per person, whereas a four-person family received $435, or only $104 per person (House Ways and Means Committee 1993, p. 660). As family size declines, the per person transfer increases.

If the adjustments that states use to determine benefits are correct, the reduction in benefits over time for families of the same size would approximately reflect their decline in economic well-being. Thus the 36.7 percent decline in benefits for a three-person family would reflect a substantial decline in economic well-being. By contrast, if the "correct" equivalence adjustment is per capita, the decline in benefits for a particular family size overstates the reduction in economic well-being. In that case recipient families' economic well-being would have declined by 17 percent between 1975 and 1992. There is no way of knowing which is correct, but in either case expenditures on AFDC did not keep pace with the growth in the caseload.

13. Emergency assistance expenditures are from House Ways and Means Committee (1993), p. 654.

14. SSI expenditures are from House Ways and Means Committee (1993), pp. 842 and 815. To get SSI expenditures for children, I calculate Nc/Nt(Federal Expenditure), where Nc is the number of recipients under eighteen years old and Nt is the total number of recipients. The ratio for 1980 is interpolated from data in 1978 and 1983.

15. Medicaid expenditures are from House Ways and Means Committee (1993), p. 1646. In 1992, 15.2 percent of Medicaid expenditures were for AFDC children and 13.5 percent were for their parents (House Ways and Means Committee 1993, p. 1654). The amount in Table 2.1 is 28.7 percent of total Medicaid expenditures. This somewhat overstates the growth in expenditures on AFDC families, because their share of total Medicaid expenditures has shrunk from 33.5 percent of Medicaid payments in 1975 to 26 percent in 1992 (House Ways and Means Committee 1993, p. 1655).

16. Food Stamp expenditures are from House Ways and Means Committee (1993), p. 1609, and Bixby (1990), table 2. Since 1980, about 60 percent of households that received Food Stamps included children (House Ways and Means Committee 1993, p. 1620). In 1988 and 1990, 8 percent of households that received Food Stamps had incomes above the poverty line. To estimate Food Stamp expenditures for poor households with children, I calculate .92(.60) = .552.

17. Housing assistance expenditures are from House Ways and Means Committee (1993), p. 1675. Housing estimates are calculated as two-thirds of total outlays, because about a third of federal expenditures for subsidized housing go to the elderly. This may somewhat overstate the expenditures for poor households with children, because some nonelderly households without children get housing assistance. These are mainly low-income people with disabilities. This may also overstate the growth in expenditures for poor families with children, because the growth in expenditures for the nonelderly disabled may have outpaced the growth in expenditures for poor households with children.

18. Not all of this increase went to families with children. For instance, about a third of occupied public housing units are for elderly residents. But the proportion of public housing units occupied by the elderly has been fairly constant since 1980. Other subsidized housing units are for physically handicapped residents, most without children.

.19. WIC expenditures are from House Ways and Means Committee (1993), p. 1683. Because 73 percent of WIC recipients have incomes at or below the federal poverty threshold, this amount is 73 percent of federal expenditures for WIC. Funds for maternal and child health services are distributed in block grants to states for services associated with child health and nutrition, such as lead paint screening. Real expenditures on this program declined from $666.7 million in 1975 to $531.0 million in 1990. I was unable to find out how much was spent on this program in 1992.

20. Head Start expenditures are from House Ways and Means Committee (1993), p. 1690.

21. Compensatory Education expenditures are from the U.S. Bureau of the Census, *1982–83 Statistical Abstract of the United States*, table 216, *1988 Statistical Abstract of the United States*, table 210, and *1993 Statistical Abstract of the United States*, table 224.

22. Child care expenditures are from Robbins (1990), table 3. Child care expenditures include expenditures on AFDC work experience and WIN (Work Incentive Program). All years include expenditures on child care from Title XX. About 15 percent of Title XX block grant money goes for child care, and another 13 percent goes for substitute care and placement services for children (House Ways and Means Committee 1993, p. 875). After 1991, child care expenditures include AFDC transitional care, child care for at-risk children, and the Child Care and Development Block Grant. This omits many sources of federal child care expenditures because it is impossible to find them all.

23. Child nutrition expenditures are from the U.S. Bureau of the Census, *1990 Statistical Abstract of the United States*, table 210, and *1993 Statistical Abstract of the United States*, table 224.

24. Federal foster care expenditures are from House Ways and Means Committee (1993), p. 886. Expenditures for foster care and adoption prior to 1981, when new legislative rules took effect, are not published. Since 1975 the federal government has paid 50 percent of maintenance payments for children in foster care. Using the procedure explained above for AFDC expenditures, I estimate that in 1975 these payments amounted to $115.6 million. If the administrative costs were the same proportion of payments in 1975 as they were in 1981 (10.8 percent), administrative costs for these benefits would have been $12.5 million in 1975. If expenditures for adoptive services were the same proportion of expenditures for foster care services in 1981 and 1975, they would have been $.04 million in 1975.

25. The federal government does not collect data on the number of children in foster care, but estimates from other sources suggest that the number decreased from 326,000 children in 1970 to 302,000 in 1980, when 4.4 children per 1,000 were in foster care, then increased to 429,000 in 1991, when 5.9 children per 1,000 were in foster care (House Ways and Means Committee 1993, p. 940). It is unclear whether the increase in foster care

placement was due to a change in state policies concerning the removal of children from their parents or to changes in the need for foster care. Some people attribute the increase in foster care placements to the crack epidemic that hit the nation during the mid-1980s. Crack surely had an impact, but it is most likely not the whole story. Many states had increases in the foster care case load greater than those in New York (214.2 percent increase) or Illinois (161.1 percent increase), where the crack epidemic hit hard. Between 1985 and 1992, case loads increased dramatically even in states like Arizona (207.6 percent increase), Hawaii (322.9 percent increase), and Tennessee (261.2 percent increase), where the crack epidemic was barely felt (House Ways and Means Committee 1993, p. 943).

26. Child Welfare Services expenditures are from House Ways and Means Committee (1993), p. 886, and the U.S. Bureau of the Census, *1982–83 Statistical Abstract of the United States*, table 514.

3. How Rich and Poor Children Differ

1. There is a substantial theoretical literature on intergenerational mobility. See Becker and Tomes (1979 and 1986), Blinder (1976), and Conslick (1977).

2. See Dunn et al. (1981a and 1981b) for a discussion of these assessments.

3. Scores on the National Assessment of Educational Progress show that the average reading and math scores for nine-year-olds were higher in 1990 than in 1970 (House Ways and Means Committee 1993, pp. 1186–1187). The fact that the improvements were greater for black children than for white children and for disadvantaged urban children than for advantaged urban children suggests that disadvantaged children gained more than advantaged children over this period.

4. The NLSY also includes other assessments of young children's skills and temperament. I use no assessments for children younger than four years old because it is unclear how much these correlate with later outcomes. Nor do I use assessments of temperament or "self-worth." I did estimate the effect of parental income on a measure of "scholastic competence," but its effect was extremely weak. This assessment has not been normed on a national sample, and its correlation with other outcomes is less well known than for other assessments. The "memory for digit span" assessment was given to children seven years and older, but children this old have unusually young mothers.

5. I created two additional measures of dropping out of high school. The first treats as graduates students who get a General Equivalency Diploma (GED) after having dropped out. The second counts such students as dropouts. Some research suggests that individuals with GEDs earn little more than high school dropouts (Heckman 1994). Comparing these mea-

sures shows that more low-income than high-income children "graduate" by getting a GED. Therefore, treating GEDs as if they were high school diplomas could lead us to underestimate the impact of parental income on "bankable" schooling. These differences are relatively small, however. Among low-income children, 74.2 percent graduate from high school; of these, 13.6 percent have GEDs. Among middle-income children, 89 percent graduate and 12.4 percent receive GEDs. After 1985 the PSID asked heads of households and spouses whether they had graduated with a GED. This means that GED information is available for only a subset of PSID respondents who have turned twenty.

6. The "culture of poverty" hypothesis (Lewis 1968) is the version of the role-model hypothesis that has received the most attention from both academics and policy makers. More recently John Ogbu (1981) has emphasized that cultural traits are adaptations to poverty that reproduce poverty as well.

4. Conventional Estimates of the Effect of Income

1. I do not review the studies that try to estimate the effect of family socioeconomic status. Measures of socioeconomic status vary from study to study, sometimes including income as a component and sometimes not.

2. See Hauser and Daymont (1977); Hill and Duncan (1987); Kiker and Condon (1981); and Peters (1992).

3. None of the estimates I have described controls either parents' or children's cognitive skills. Hauser and Daymont (1977) found that the effect of a son's cognitive skills on earnings was small in the years just after high school graduation, but so is the influence of parental income on children's earnings. The importance of children's cognitive skills increases over time (see also Burtless 1994). Thus the extent of bias from omitting cognitive skills presumably varies with the age at which earnings are measured.

4. See Axinn et al. (forthcoming); Hauser and Daymont (1977); Hill and Duncan (1987); Jencks et al. (1983); Kiker and Condon (1981); Peters and Mullins (forthcoming); and Mare (1980).

5. It is unclear how important unemployment during adolescence is to employment as an adult, but idleness during adolescence appears to decrease future wages (Meyer and Wise 1982, Ellwood 1982). In addition, idle young men may be more involved in illegal and other socially costly activities than employed young men. Some studies find that family income has a positive effect on adolescents' employment (Meyer and Wise 1982), others find little effect of family income (Hall 1973, Rees and Gray 1982), and still others find a negative effect (Masters and Garfinkel 1977, McDonald and Stephenson 1979).

6. See Citro and Michael (1995), Mayer and Jencks (1989), and Ruggles

(1990) for a critique of the poverty thresholds and other criticism of the official poverty measure.

7. Few of these studies report the mean poverty ratio for families whose income is below the poverty line or families whose income is between one and two times the poverty line. This means that it is impossible to know how large an increase in income this represents. Using PSID data and averaging income over five years, I find that on average the poverty ratio of children whose family income was below the poverty line was .721, compared with 1.51 for children whose average family income was between one and two times the poverty line.

8. See Axinn et al. (forthcoming); Haveman and Wolfe (1994); Peters and Mullins (forthcoming); and Teachman et al. (forthcoming).

9. See also Haveman and Wolfe (1994) and Haveman et al. (forthcoming).

10. See Duncan et al. (1994) and Smith et al. (forthcoming). Brooks-Gunn et al. (1991) get much smaller income effects on IQ measures when children are only thirty-six months old. The same study estimates that raising income from the poverty line to twice the poverty line increases five-year-olds' scores on the Weschler Preschool and Primary Scale of Intelligence by 2.9 points, but this study controls neighborhood characteristics, which could downwardly bias the estimated effect of income.

11. Korenman et al. (1994) also show that children raised in poor families are more likely than children raised in nonpoor families to be short for their age and underweight for their age. But these factors do not account for the effect of income on cognitive test scores; nor do whether the mother smoked or drank alcohol during pregnancy, whether the baby was short at birth, or whether the baby had a low birth weight. This implies that poor nutrition is not the main mechanism through which parental income influences test scores.

12. Corcoran et al. (1987) control neighborhood economic mix, but they still found that increasing parental income by 10 percent increased a son's earnings when he was a twenty-five to thirty-two-year-old head of household by about 2 percent, which is similar to estimates that do not control neighborhood characteristics. When Datcher (1982) controlled average neighborhood income and the percentage of neighbors who are white, a 10 percent increase in black parents' income measured in 1968 improved the annual earnings of their sons by almost 5 percent, but the same amount of additional income increased white sons' annual earnings by only 1 percent.

13. To see if having a parent who dropped out of high school is especially harmful to children, I added a variable equal to one if a child's parent finished less than twelve years of school and zero otherwise. Having a parent who dropped out of high school never had a statistically significant effect once I controlled years of education. This means that completing

the twelfth year of schooling does not have an effect that is significantly different from finishing any other year of schooling.

14. Most people think that the benefit of a second adult in the household outweighs the costs, at least if that adult is a parent. A second adult can generate more income. If the results in Chapters 5 and 6 are correct, this is not likely to be a large benefit. Adults also provide supervision and other forms of home production, but they also consume resources. To see if an additional adult improves children's outcomes, I regressed each outcome on the logarithm of family size and the number of adults in the household as well as parental income and the other variables that I normally control. The effect of an additional adult on children's assessment scores and years of education, male wages, hours of work, and idleness, and single motherhood was not statistically different from the effect of an additional child. But an additional adult reduced teenager girls' chances of having a baby and teenagers' chances of dropping out of high school, whereas an additional child increased the risk of both outcomes.

15. Several important research literatures deal with these issues. For discussions of the effect of male earnings on the likelihood of single mothers' marrying, see the literature on the "male marriageability pool," including Jencks (1992), Mare and Winship (1992), and Wilson (1987).

16. To see if the cumulative influence of income grows as children get older, I estimated these same equations for children who were ten years old in 1990, except that income is averaged over ten years rather than six years. In general the effect of doubling parental income is greater for ten-year-olds than for six-year-olds, but even the effect for ten-year-olds is small. Many fewer children of NLSY respondents were at least ten by 1990 than were at least six, and those who were ten were less representative of all ten-year-olds than was the case for six-year-olds. This was because ten-year-olds' mothers had to be younger than the six-year-olds' mothers.

17. If children were already older than five when the survey began in 1968, we do not have information on their parents' income when they were as young as five.

18. Most research that tries to estimate the effect of parental income when children are different ages estimates a model of the form

$$O = b_1 I_1 + b_2 I_2 + b_3 X,$$

where I_1 is income at some young age of the child, I_2 is income at some older age, and X is a vector of observed parental characteristics. But the high correlation between I_1 and I_2 makes it difficult to tell if the difference between b_1 and b_2 is statistically reliable. Because the slope of income is correlated only .15 with mean income, colinearity is less of a problem using this approach.

19. The difference between young children's outcomes and adolescent outcomes does not arise because income is measured over a longer period for

adolescents. When I estimate the effect of the slope of parents' income over five years on adolescent and young-adult outcomes, the results are similar to those in Table 4.4.

20. I also assessed the effect of a 50 percent drop in parental income on these same outcomes, but the results were similar to those shown in Table 4.5.

5. The "True" Effect of Income

1. In the PSID, "other" income is also more weakly correlated with observed parental characteristics, but the differences are smaller. For example, parents' education is correlated .479 with earned income, -.270 with transfer income, and .209 with "other" income.

2. The fact that less "other" income than total income is reported does not necessarily mean that the effect of "other" income will be more biased than the effect of total income, since it is the variance of the error (relative to the true variance), not its mean, that results in bias.

3. Minarik (1975) found that in 1972 the PSID accounted for 95.7 percent of a measure of aggregate income that consisted of labor and asset income and several sources of transfer income. In the same year, the CPS accounted for 88.8 percent of the same measure of income (U.S. Bureau of the Census 1992). The CPS accounts for almost all labor income, and the PSID presumably does the same. Both the CPS and the Census account for very high proportions of Social Security income, which is the second largest single source of income after wages and salaries. Thus the higher income reported in the PSID probably results from respondents' reporting more welfare and "other" income rather than more labor income. When Duncan et al. (1984) compared income reports in the 1980 PSID with national aggregates of AFDC, SSI, Social Security, and other welfare sources, they found that the PSID accounted for 91.8 percent of welfare income compared with the CPS's 72.8 percent. But welfare income is only .6 percent of aggregate income, so better reporting on this measure alone cannot account for the higher level of income reported in the PSID. This implies that respondents report more interest, rents, dividends, alimony, and child support to the PSID.

In the PSID, 95.7 percent of total income, 92.8 percent of Social Security income, 91.8 percent of welfare income, and nearly all income from wages and salaries is reported. Assuming that the distribution of income by source is the same in the PSID and the CPS, 74.9 percent of income is from wages and salaries, 6.1 percent is from Social Security, .6 percent is from welfare transfers, and 18.4 percent is from "other" income sources, then

$$.957 = .749 + (.928 \cdot .061) + (.918 \cdot .006) + .184X,$$

where $X = .788$, which is the proportion of other income reported. If instead we assume that the distribution of income in the PSID is the same as the distribution from aggregate sources, the model is

$$.957 = .672 + (.928 \cdot .059) + (.918 \cdot .005) + .284X,$$

where $X = .852$.

This is a rough estimate because the distribution of income in the CPS and from independent sources is for 1987. The estimate of total income reported in the PSID is for 1972. The estimate for the amount of welfare income reported is for 1980. In addition, "other" income in these estimates includes some sources I count as transfer income, namely, workers' compensation and veterans' benefits. Although Duncan et al. estimate the proportion of SSI and social security and disability income reported in the PSID, I do not include these in the equations above because the proportion of all income from these sources is very small.

4. I use a linear specification for these estimates because I want to compare the change in an outcome for each dollar increase in total income with a dollar change in "other" income. Because a 10 percent increase in "other" income is a much smaller absolute increase in income than a 10 percent increase in total income, the log specification would not provide the right estimate.

5. The estimates in Table 5.1 are from the following model:

$$O = b_1 I_e + b_2 I_o + b_3 I_g + b_4 X,$$

where O is a child's outcome, I_e is family income from earnings, I_o is "other" income, I_g is income from government transfers, and X is a vector of observed characteristics. To see if the difference between the effect of I_o and total income (I_t) is statistically significant, I estimate:

$$O = b_5 I_t + b_6 I_o + b_7 I_g + b_8 X.$$

When b_6 is statistically significant, the effect of "other" income is significantly different from the effect of total income.

6. Although 1983 and 1984 were recession years, the results for young men's earnings and wages do not vary much depending on the years in which I measure them. For example, the coefficient of parental income is 2.245 when wages are measured in 1983–1984 and 2.653 for the same sample when wages are measured in 1987–1988. Since the sample is older in 1987–1988, the variance of income is somewhat greater, and so the standardized coefficient for wages in 1987–1988 is .176 compared with a standardized coefficient of .195 for wages in 1983–1984.

7. In the analyses that follow, I estimate different models with different assumptions about the reliability of the income measures I report these in Appendix C.

8. More generally, we can denote the correlation between income at Time 1

(I_1) and some outcome (O) as r_{O,I_1}. Using an analogous notation, r_{O,I_2} is the correlation between this same outcome and Time 2 income (I_2). Finally, r_{I_1,I_2} is the correlation between parental income in these two periods. Then we can show that the (standardized) effect of income after controlling all these unobserved factors (b) is

$$b = \frac{r_{O,I_1} - r_{O,I_2}}{1 - r_{I_1,I_2}}.$$

9. The estimates in Table 5.2 are based on smaller samples than the conventional estimates in Chapter 4, because fewer children have income at two points in time than at one point in time. As I discuss below, I use the estimates in this chapter to determine the degree of bias in the estimated effect of income, but I use the estimates from the larger sample to determine the point estimates.

10. The dichotomous variables are only moderately skewed: 20 percent of girls have babies as teenagers, 24 percent become young single mothers, and 15 percent of teenagers drop out of high school. Monte Carlo simulations suggest that these distributions will result in only modestly downward biased correlations (Hanushek and Jackson 1977).

11. To assess the robustness of the estimates in Tables 5.2, 5.3, and 5.4, I estimated six different models in which I changed the period over which both Time 1 and Time 2 income are measured. Time 1 income was measured at ages nine to ten, thirteen to seventeen, and the five years before the outcome. Time 2 income was measured at ages twenty-three to twenty-seven, and twenty-five to twenty-nine. The "true" partial correlation for teenage childbearing ranged from .009 to -.205. The range for other variables was much smaller.

12. For outcomes in young adulthood, I measure parental income during adolescence because I am interested in the effect of income when children are growing up on their future well-being. Arguably, parental income when children are twenty to twenty-five affects children's chances of going to college more than parental income when children are adolescents, because this is the time when parents must pay tuition. If true, the correlation between Time 2 income and educational attainment would be greater than the correlation between Time 1 income and educational attainment. This is not the case. Nonetheless, if, as I suggested in Chapter 4, income closer to an outcome is more important than parental income earlier in childhood, this method will overstate the influence of income per se on educational attainment.

6. Income and Material Well-Being

1. For some expenditure categories, I have used the Consumer Expenditure Survey public-use data files to estimate expenditures by income quintiles

for families with children. These are very similar to expenditures for the entire sample.

2. It is, of course, not necessarily true that if poor families' income increased they would spend their additional income in the same way that more affluent families now spend their money. If the tastes or needs of the poor differ from the tastes or needs of the more affluent, they will spend additional money differently. Using the PSID, I examined expenditures on food and rent for families whose income increased. As income increased, the proportion of expenditures going to food and rent declined to close to the average for families with their current income.

3. I thank Kathryn Edin for tabulating the estimates from the Chicago survey. When Edin interviewed low-income mothers for her own research (Edin and Lein, forthcoming), she asked those who reported going hungry what they meant by this. They usually meant that they or their children had to skip meals because there was no food in the house and they had no money.

4. Studies of the Negative Income Tax experiments find that nutritional intake (in North Carolina but not Iowa), consumption of clothing, and inventories of durable goods and cars increase with more generous benefit programs. See Michael (1978) for a good review of these studies.

5. For example, the CEX shows that the poorest 20 percent of households spend, on average, 7 percent more than the USDA thrifty food budget, compared with 21 percent more for the middle 20 percent of families. Using one year of expenditure data and one year of income data, the expenditures in the PSID are similar to those in the CEX. Using PSID data averaging over two years, food expenditures for the middle 20 percent of families are similar to those in the CEX, but the poorest 20 percent of respondents spend only 99 percent of the USDA thrifty budget.

6. For estimates using the living conditions index I control parents' income in 1969 to 1972 in order to maximize the effect of income on consumption. This means that both parents' income and their living conditions are measured when children were different ages. To see if the age at which these are measured affects the outcomes, I included a variable for the interaction between living conditions and child's age in 1989. This interaction term was statistically significant for teenage childbearing and single motherhood. In both cases the interaction was positive, implying that the older the child when living conditions were measured the more important they were for the outcome. This is consistent with the results in Chapter 4 showing that, for these same outcomes, income measured during adolescence is more important than income measured earlier.

7. Income, Psychological Well-Being, and Parenting Practices

1. This discussion is based on three excellent reviews of the literature on the relationship between poverty, parental stress, and children's outcomes:

McLoyd (1990); McLoyd and Wilson (1991); and Pearlin et al. (1981). See also Kessler (1982) and Vondra (1993).

2. See Conger et al. (1992); Conger et al. (forthcoming); Elder (1974); and Elder et al. (1985).

3. The studies cited in this chapter usually emphasize transitory psychological attributes. They are concerned with changes in psychological attributes that arise from changes in economic well-being. But the correlations of the psychological attributes measured in one year and income measured in the same year are much smaller than the correlations for the five-year averages of income and psychological attributes. The correlations of a measure of parents' psychological attributes in one year with children's outcomes are also much smaller than the correlations using psychological attributes averaged over several years. This suggests that the stable component of parents' psychological attributes, not the transitory component, influences children's outcomes.

4. To get the change in an outcome due to a standard deviation change in psychological traits *(C)* for continuous outcomes, I estimate $O = b_1P + b_2I + b_3X$, where O is an outcome, P is the psychological trait, I is income, and X is a set of controls including household size, child's race, and parents' education and age. Then I estimate $C = b'_1(SD_O)$, where b' is the standardized coefficient of living conditions and SD_O is the standard deviation of the outcome. When the dependent variable is dichotomous, I estimate $SD_P(b_p)$, where SD_P is the standard deviation of the psychological attribute and b_p is the partial derivative of coefficient for the attribute in an analogous logistic regression. I use this same procedure in Tables 7.4 and 7.5 to estimate the effect of changes in parenting practices.

5. The correlations are as follows:

Variable	Income	School performance
Mother's discipline score	.25	.24
Mother's hostility score	.20	.05
Mother's nurturant parenting score	.21	.30
Child's school performance	.21	—

See also Conger et al. forthcoming.

8. More Evidence on the "True" Effect of Income

1. The estimates in Table 8.1 use the CPI-U-X1 to adjust for changes in prices over time. This yields a 9.7 percent increase in the real household income of the median child between 1969 and 1989. If we substitute the

CPI, the median income of children's households hardly changed between 1969 and 1989. If instead we use the implicit price deflator for Personal Consumption Expenditures (PCE) in the National Income and Product Accounts, the real income of the median child's household rose 6.7 percent. Using the fixed-weight PCE index for the market basket that consumers bought in 1987, the median child's household experienced a 15.3 percent increase in purchasing power between 1969 and 1989. Most economists who study these matters also believe that standard price adjustments underestimate the value of qualitative improvements in the goods and services consumers buy. If this bias means that the true rate of inflation was one point less than the fixed-weight PCE index implies, the purchasing power of the median households with children would have risen by 42 percent between 1969 and 1989. See Jencks and Mayer (1996) for a discussion of how different price adjustments affect trends in the income of the median child and trends in child-poverty rates.

2. For this time period, trends in annual income appear to parallel trends in income measured over longer periods, implying that income volatility has not increased over this period, though it may have been different in earlier periods (Duncan, Smeeding, and Rodgers 1995; Mayer and Jencks 1993).

3. There is less inequality within years in these PSID cohorts than for all households with children under eighteen years old in the CPS and the Census. This is largely because the poorest 20 percent of families are richer in the PSID than in the Census or the CPS. The poorest 20 percent of children's families reported incomes averaging $10,867 in 1969 in the CPS, but $16,390 between 1968 and 1971 in the PSID (both in 1992 dollars). Income is higher for these PSID cohorts partly because the income of parents of fourteen-year-olds tends to be higher than the income of all parents, partly because the PSID sample excludes Hispanics, partly because the PSID might be better than the CPS or the Census at getting low-income respondents to report their income, and perhaps partly because attrition in the PSID at the bottom of the income distribution is not fully offset by reweighting. In all data sets, income at the bottom of the distribution declined after the early 1970s.

4. Plotnick estimated the following:

$$O = b_1 W_i + b_2 W_s + b_3 I_o + b_4 X,$$

where W_i is a family's income from welfare when the child is fourteen years old, W_s is the state combined AFDC and Food Stamp benefit level when the child is nineteen, I_o is a family's income from sources other than welfare, and X is a vector of other family background characteristics. If W_i is a family's welfare benefit level and W_s is the state welfare benefit level, $W_i = W_s T_w$, where T_w is time on welfare. Then

$$O = b_1(W_s T_w) + b_2 W_s + b_3 I_o + b_4 X = W_s(b_1 T_w + b_2) + b_3 I_o + b_4 X.$$

Thus the effect of the state benefit level is a combination of b_1 and b_2. In Plotnick, b_2 is positive. The effect of family welfare income is also positive. This implies that the effect of state benefit levels on out-of-wedlock births is also positive, but downwardly biased in this model. We cannot tell from this exercise whether the effect of the benefit level would be statistically significant in a reduced-form model.

5. Several studies used data from the 1960s and 1970s to estimate the effect of welfare benefit levels on the number of unwed mothers (see Groenveld et al 1983). More than half these studies found either that the state welfare benefit level had no effect on marriage or that higher benefit levels decreased the number of unwed mothers. In the studies where higher benefits increased single parenthood, the effects were generally small in magnitude or not reliably greater than zero.

Ellwood and Bane (1985) found that a $100 increase in benefits (in 1975 dollars, which was equivalent to a standard deviation change in benefits) increased the fraction of ever-married mothers who divorced or separated by 5 to 10 percent. They also found that a $100 increase in benefits was associated with a 5 percent increase in births to unmarried women, but this estimate was not statistically significant.

Robert Moffitt (1990) used CPS data for 1969, 1977, and 1985 to see if marriage or out-of-wedlock births were more prevalent in states with generous total welfare packages (the value of AFDC, Food Stamps, and Medicaid) than in states with less generous benefits. When he controlled several characteristics of women, the size of the total welfare package had only a small and statistically insignificant effect on the probability of marriage among either black or white women.

6. Corcoran and Adams (1993b) estimate the effect of the state welfare benefit level controlling the family income-to-needs ratio and the proportion of family income from welfare, both of which were recoded into categorical variables. If we simplify this model and assume that these variables are continuous, Corcoran and Adams are in principle estimating:

$$O = b_1 W_i + b_2 W_s + b_3 X,$$

where W_i is income from welfare, W_s is the state welfare benefit level, and X is a vector of family background and neighborhood characteristics. Since $W_i = W_s T_w$, where T_w is time on welfare,

$$O = b_1(W_s T_w) + b_2 W_s = W_s(b_1 T_w + b_2) + b_3 X$$

Thus the effect of the state benefit level is a combination of b_1 and b_2. For black men's earnings and hours of labor-market work, b_2 is negative. The effect of the proportion of family income from welfare is also negative. This implies that the effect of state benefit levels is also negative. For white men the effect of the state welfare benefit level is negative for labor income, hours worked, and hourly wages. Getting more than 15 percent of family income from welfare is also negative. This too implies that the effect of the state welfare benefit level on sons' future labor-market success is negative. For black men the effect of the state benefit level on hourly wages is positive, but the effect of the percentage of income from welfare is negative. Since the positive effect of the benefit level is greater than the negative effect of the percentage of income from welfare, this implies a positive, though very small, effect of the benefit level on black men's hourly wages. We cannot tell from this exercise whether the effect of the benefit level would be statistically significant in any of these models.

7. The housing costs of renters include utilities.

8. Recipients in states in which the purchasing power of the AFDC benefit is low are likely to find ways to supplement the benefits. Edin and Lein (forthcoming) find that AFDC recipients often get income from family members, friends, and work that they do not report as income. If welfare recipients in states with low real benefits are more likely to have unreported income, reported income would be a worse measure of the resources available to families in these states than in high benefit states. As a test of this hypothesis, I used the 1990 Census data to regress the percentage of the poorest 20 percent of renters who reported paying rent greater than their income on the maximum AFDC benefit for a family of four, controlling the average low-income renter's housing costs as a measure of cost of living. The AFDC benefit level had no effect on the percentage reporting rent greater than income.

9. To estimate the effect of rent levels on AFDC benefits, I use a 5 in 1,000 Census sample. I first estimate the twentieth percentile cut-point for the income distribution within each state. I then estimate the mean gross rent for renters whose income falls below that cut-point. I then regress the AFDC benefit level on this mean rent. I use data from states with at least 100 renters in the poorest income quintile.

10. Using a 5 in 1,000 1990 Census sample, I selected single mothers receiving public assistance and regressed the (log) state AFDC benefit level on a measure of (log) disposable income. Disposable income was computed as the maximum AFDC benefit for a family of three plus the Food Stamp benefit for such a family less the average rent paid by public assistance recipients in that state. I use only states with at least 100 single mothers receiving public assistance.

11. Currie (1995) reviews NIT results for other outcomes related to children's well-being, including health outcomes.

12. Maynard and Murnane (1979) report that the annual income of NIT families was $800 greater than that of control families in North Carolina, and $500 greater in Iowa. But they do not report the mean income for either group.

13. See McDonald and Stephenson (1979) and West (1980).

9. Helping Poor Children

1. See Edin and Lein (forthcoming). The phrase "social prostitution" was used by a welfare recipient interviewed by Edin and Lein to describe her relationships with men, which were not for love, but not just for money either.

2. See Angrist and Krueger (1991); Ashenfelter and Krueger (1994); Ashenfelter and Rouse (1995); and Becker (1993) for discussions of this debate and support for the "skills" hypothesis.

3. See Herrnstein and Murray (1994); Plomin et al. (1988); and Scarr and Weinberg (1978) for support of the "hereditarian" view.

4. The full equations from the conventional model, which controls both maternal education and maternal AFQT scores, are shown in Appendix B. They show that, controlling mothers' AFQT scores, each additional year of maternal education increases test scores by between one half and one point.

5. The PSID sample I use does not include Hispanic respondents, but in the NLSY, children of Hispanic parents score lower than children of white parents on the three cognitive assessments. In fact, the scores of Hispanic children are similar to the scores for black children once parental characteristics and family size are controlled.

6. For instance, the partial derivative for the effect of income on teenage childbearing is $-.165$ when I control parents' marital status and $-.177$ when I omit marital status. For dropping out of high school, the partial derivatives are $-.113$ and $-.124$ respectively.

References

Abbott, Grace. 1941. *From Relief to Social Security*. Chicago: University of Chicago Press.

Altonji, Joseph, and Thoman Dunn. 1991. "Relationships among the Family Incomes and Labor Market Outcomes of Relatives." Cambridge, Mass.: National Bureau of Economic Research, Working Paper no. 3724.

Altonji, Joseph, and Aloysius Siow. 1987. "Testing the Response of Consumption to Income Changes with (Noisy) Panel Data." *Quarterly Journal of Economics* 102(2):293–328.

Angrist, Joshua, and Alan Krueger. 1991. "Does Compulsory Schooling Attendance Affect Schooling and Earnings?" *Quarterly Journal of Economics* 56(4):979–1014.

Ashenfelter, Orley, and Alan Krueger. 1994. "Estimating the Returns to Schooling Using a New Sample of Twins." *American Economic Review* 84:1157–1173.

Ashenfelter, Orley, and Cecilia Rouse. 1995. "Income, Schooling, and Ability." Unpublished manuscript.

Axinn, William, Greg Duncan, and Arland Thornton. (Forthcoming). "The Effect of Parental Income, Wealth, and Attitudes on Children's Completed Schooling and Self-Esteem." In Jeanne Brooks-Gunn and Greg Duncan, eds., *The Consequences of Growing Up Poor*. Russell Sage Foundation.

Baker, P. C., and F. L. Mott. 1989. *NLSY Child Handbook*. Columbus, Ohio: Ohio State University Center for Human Resource Research.

Becker, Gary. 1981. *A Treatise on the Family*. Cambridge, Mass.: Harvard University Press.

———. 1993. *Human Capital: A Theoretical and Empirical Analysis with Special Reference to Education*. Chicago: The University of Chicago Press.

Becker, Gary, and Nigel Tomes. 1979. "An Equilibrium Theory of the Distribution of Income and Intergenerational Mobility." *Journal of Political Economy* 87(6):1153–1189.

———. 1986. "Human Capital and the Rise and Fall of Families." *Journal of Labor Economics* 4(2), part 2:S1–S139.

Becketti, Sean, William Gould, Lee Lillard, and Finis Welch. 1988. "The Panel Study of Income Dynamics after Fourteen Years: An Evaluation." *Journal of Labor Economics* 6(4):472–492.

Behrman, Jere, Zdenek Hrubec, Paul Taubman, and T. Wales. 1980. *Socioeconomic Success: A Study of the Effects of Genetic Endowments, Family Environment, and Schooling.* New York: North-Holland.

Behrman, Jere, and Paul Taubman. 1990. "The Intergenerational Correlation between Children's Adult Earnings and Their Parents' Income: Results from the Michigan Panel Study of Income Dynamics." *Review of Income and Wealth* 36(2):115–127.

Bell, Winifred. 1965. *Aid to Dependent Children.* New York: Columbia University Press.

Berkowitz, Edward. 1991. *America's Welfare State: From Roosevelt to Reagan.* Baltimore: The Johns Hopkins University Press.

Bernanke, Ben S. 1984. "Permanent Income, Liquidity, and Expenditure on Automobiles: Evidence from Panel Data." *Quarterly Journal of Economics* 49 (August): 587–614.

Bixby, Ann Kallman. 1990. "Public Social Welfare Expenditures, Fiscal Years 1965–87." *Social Security Bulletin* 53(2):10–26.

Blau, David. 1995. "The Effect of Income on Child Development." Department of Economics, University of North Carolina, unpublished manuscript.

Blinder, Alan. 1976. "Inequality and Mobility in the Distribution of Wealth." *Kyklos* 29:607–638.

Brooks-Gunn, Jeanne, Greg Duncan, Pam Kato, and Naomi Sealand. 1991. "Do Neighborhoods Influence Child and Adolescent Behavior?" Unpublished manuscript.

Burtless, Gary. 1994. "The Employment Prospects of Welfare Recipients." Brookings Institution, unpublished manuscript.

Butler, Amy. 1990. "The Effects of Welfare Guarantees on Children's Educational Attainment." *Social Science Research* 19:175–203.

Campbell, John, and Angus Deaton. 1989. "Why Is Consumption So Smooth?" *Review of Economic Studies* 56:357–374.

Carroll, Christopher. 1994. "How Does Future Income Affect Current Consumption?" *Quarterly Journal of Economics* 109(1):111–147.

Chase-Lansdale, P. L., Frank Mott, Jeanne Brooks-Gunn, and Deborah Phillips. 1991. "Children of the National Longitudinal Survey of Youth: A Unique Research Opportunity." *Developmental Psychology* 27(6):918–931.

Children's Defense Fund. 1988. *A Children's Defense Fund Budget.* Washington, D.C.

Citro, Constance, and Robert T. Michael. 1995. *Measuring Poverty: A New Approach*. Washington, D.C.: National Academy Press.

Conger, Rand, Katherine Conger, and Glen Elder, Jr. (Forthcoming). "Family Economic Hardship and Adolescent Adjustment." In Jeanne Brooks-Gunn and Greg Duncan, eds., *The Consequences of Growing Up Poor*. Russell Sage Foundation.

Conger, Rand, Katherine Conger, Glen Elder, Jr., Frederick Lorenz, Ronald Simons, and Les Whitbeck. 1992. "A Family Process Model of Economic Hardship and Adjustment of Early Adolescent Boys." *Child Development* 63:526–541.

Conslick, John. 1977. "An Exploratory Model of the Size Distribution of Income." *Economic Inquiry* 15:345–366.

Corcoran, Mary, and Terry Adams. 1993a. "Family and Neighborhood Welfare Dependency and Son's Labor Supply." University of Michigan, unpublished manuscript.

Corcoran, Mary, and Terry Adams. 1993b. "Race, Poverty, Welfare, and Neighborhood Influences on Men's Economic Outcomes." Report to the Rockefeller Foundation.

———. 1995. "Race, Sex, and the Intergenerational Transmission of Poverty." Unpublished manuscript.

Corcoran, Mary, Greg Duncan, Gerald Gurin, and Patricia Gurin. 1985. "Myth and Reality: The Causes and Persistence of Poverty." *Journal of Policy Analysis and Management* 4(4):516–536.

Corcoran, Mary, Roger Gordon, Deborah Laren, and Gary Solon. 1987. "Intergenerational Transmission of Education, Income, and Earnings." Ann Arbor: University of Michigan, mimeo.

———. 1992. "The Association between Men's Economic Status and Their Family and Community Origins." *Journal of Human Resources* 27(4):573–601.

Currie, Janet. 1995. "Welfare and the Well-Being of Children." In James P. Smith and Finis Welch, eds., *Encyclopedia of Labor Economics*. Newark, N.J.: Harwood Academic Press.

Datcher, Linda. 1982. "Effects of Community and Family Background on Achievement." *Review of Economics and Statistics* 64:132–141.

Davis, Ada J. 1929. "The Evolution of the Institution of Mothers' Pensions in the United States." *American Journal of Sociology* 35:573–587.

Duncan, Greg. 1994. "Families and Neighbors as Sources of Disadvantage in the Schooling Decisions of White and Black Adolescents." Unpublished manuscript.

Duncan, Greg, Jeanne Brooks-Gunn, and Pamela K. Klebanov. 1994. "Economic Deprivation and Early-Childhood Development." *Child Development* 65:296–318.

Duncan, Greg, and Daniel H. Hill. 1989. "Assessing the Quality of Household Panel Data: The Case of the Panel Study of Income Dynamics." *Journal of Business and Economic Statistics* 7(4):441–452.

Duncan, Greg, Daniel Hill, and Michael Ponza. 1984. "How Representative Is the PSID? A Response to Some Questions Raised in the Unicon Report." University of Michigan, Survey Research Center, unpublished manuscript.

Duncan, Greg, and Saul Hoffman. 1990. "Welfare Benefits, Economic Opportunities, and the Incidence of Out-of-Wedlock Births among Black Teens." *Demography* 27(4):519–535.

Duncan, Greg, Timothy Smeeding, and Willard Rodgers. 1995. "Household Income Dynamics in the 1970s and 1980s." Unpublished manuscript.

Duncan, Greg, and Wei-Jun J. Yeung. 1994. "Extent and Consequences of Welfare Dependence among America's Children." Unpublished manuscript.

Dunn, Lloyd, and Leota Dunn. 1981a. "Peabody Individual Achievement Test." Circle Pines, Minn.: American Guidance Service.

———. 1981b. "Peabody Picture Vocabulary Test-Revised." Circle Pines, Minn.: American Guidance Service.

Economic Report of the President. 1964. Washington, D.C.: Government Printing Office.

Edin, Kathryn, and Christopher Jencks. 1992. "Reforming Welfare." In Jencks, *Rethinking Social Policy.* Cambridge, Mass.: Harvard University Press.

Edin, Kathryn, and Laura Lein. (Forthcoming). *Making Ends Meet: How Single Mothers Survive Welfare and Low-Wage Jobs.* New York: Russell Sage Foundation.

Elder, Glen. 1974. *Children of the Great Depression: Social Change in Life Experience.* Chicago: The University of Chicago Press.

———. 1979. "Historical Change in Life Patterns and Personality." In P. B. Baltes and O. G. Brim, Jr., eds., *Lifespan Development and Behavior,* vol. 2. New York: Academic Press.

Elder, Glen, Tri Van Nguyen, and Avshalom Caspi. 1985. "Linking Family Hardship to Children's Lives." *Child Development* 56:361–375.

Ellwood, David. 1982. "Teenage Unemployment: Permanent Scars or Temporary Blemishes?" In Richard Freeman and David Wise, eds., *The Youth Labor Market Problem.* Chicago: University of Chicago Press.

Ellwood, David, and Mary Jo Bane. 1985. "The Impact of AFDC on Family Structure and Living Arrangements." In R. Ehrenberg, ed., *Research in Labor Economics.* Greenwich, Conn.: JAI Press.

Folks, Homer. 1902. *The Care of Destitute, Neglected, and Delinquent Children.* New York: MacMillan Co.

Garfinkel, Irwin, and Sara McLanahan. 1986. *Single Mothers and Their Children.* Washington, D.C.: Urban Institute Press.

Gordon, Linda. 1994. *Pitied but Not Entitled: Single Mothers and the History of Welfare.* New York: The Free Press.

Gottschalk, Peter. 1992. "The Intergenerational Transfer of Welfare Participation: Facts and Possible Causes." *Journal of Policy Analysis and Management* 11(2):254–272.

Graham, John, Andrea Beller, and Pedro Hernandez. 1994. "The Effects of

Child Support on Educational Attainment." In Irwin Garfinkel and Sara McLanahan, eds., *Child Support and Child Well-Being*. Washington, D.C.: Urban Institute Press.

Groenveld, Lyle, Michael Hannan, and Nancy Tuma. 1983. "Marital Stability: SIME/DIME Final Report Part V." In *Design and Results: Final Report of the Seattle-Denver Income Maintenance Experiment*, vol. 1. Menlo Park: SRI International.

Hall, Robert. 1978. "Stochastic Implications of the Life Cycle–Permanent Income Hypothesis." *Journal of Political Economy* 86(6):971–987.

Hanlan, Archie. 1966. "From Social Reform to Social Security: The Separation of ADC and Child Welfare." *Child Welfare* (November): 493–500.

Hanushek, Eric, and John Jackson. 1977. *Statistical Methods for Social Scientists*. New York: Academic Press.

Hauser, Robert, and Thomas Daymont. 1977. "Schooling, Ability, and Earnings: Cross-Sectional Findings Eight to Fourteen Years after High School Graduation." *Sociology of Education* 50 (July): 182–206.

Haveman, Robert, and Barbara Wolfe. 1994. *Succeeding Generations: On the Effects of Investments in Children*. New York: Russell Sage Foundation.

———. 1995. "The Determinants of Children's Attainments: A Review of Methods and Findings." *Journal of Economic Literature* 33 (December): 1829–1878.

Haveman, Robert, Barbara Wolfe, and Kathryn Wilson. (Forthcoming). "Intergenerational Determinants of High School Graduation and Teen Nonmarital Births: Reduced Form and Structural Models." In Jeanne Brooks-Gunn and Greg Duncan, eds., *The Consequences of Growing Up Poor*. Russell Sage Foundation.

Hayes, C., ed. 1987. *Risking the Future: Adolescent Sexuality, Pregnancy, and Childbearing*, vol. 1. Washington D.C.: National Academy Press.

Heclo, Hugh. 1992. "Alms without End." *The World and I* (September): 60–75.

Herrnstein, Richard, and Charles Murray, 1994. *The Bell Curve: Intelligence and Class Structure in American Life*. New York: The Free Press.

Hill, Martha, and Greg Duncan. 1987. "Parental Family Income and Socioeconomic Attainment of Children." *Social Science Research* 16:39–73.

Hill, Martha, and Michael Ponza. 1983a. "Intergenerational Transmission of Poverty: Does Welfare Dependency Beget Dependency?" Paper prepared for the Southern Economic Association Meeting, November.

———. 1983b. "Poverty and Welfare Dependence across Generations." *Economic Outlook, USA* 10(3):61–64.

Hill, M. Ann, and June O'Neill. 1994. "Family Endowments and the Achievement of Young Children with Special Reference to the Underclass." *Journal of Human Resources* 29(4):1064–1100.

Hofferth, Sandra. 1993. "The 101st Congress: An Emerging Agenda for Children in Poverty." In Judith Chafel, ed., *Child Poverty and Public Policy*. Washington, D.C.: Urban Institute Press.

Hofferth, Sandra, and Cheryl Hayes, eds. 1987. *Risking the Future: Adolescent Sexuality, Pregnancy, and Childbearing*, vol. 2. Washington D.C.: National Academy Press.

Hotz, V. Joseph, Susan Williams McElroy, and Seth Sanders. 1995. "The Costs and Consequences of Teenage Childbearing for Mothers." In *Kids Having Kids: The Consequences and Costs of Teenage Childbearing in the United States.* Report to the Robin Hood Foundation.

House Ways and Means Committee. *1993 Green Book*. Washington, D.C.: U.S. Government Printing Office.

Houston, Aletha, Vonnie McLoyd, and Cynthia Coll. 1994. "Children and Poverty: Issues in Contemporary Research." *Child Development* 65:275–282.

Jencks, Christopher. 1992. *Rethinking Social Policy: Race, Poverty, and the Underclass.* Cambridge, Mass.: Harvard University Press.

Jencks, Christopher, James Crouse, and Peter Muesser. 1983. "The Wisconsin Model of Status Attainment: A National Replication with Improved Measures of Ability and Aspiration." *Sociology of Education* 56:3–19.

Jencks, Christopher, and Susan E. Mayer. "Do Official Poverty Rates Provide Useful Information about Trends in Children's Economic Welfare?" Northwestern University Center for Urban Affairs and Policy Research Working Paper no. 96-1.

Kammerman, Sheila B., and Alfred Kahn. 1995. *Starting Right: How America Neglects Its Youngest Children and What We Can Do about It.* New York: Oxford University Press.

Katz, Michael. 1986a. "Child-Saving." *History of Education Quarterly* 26(3):413–424.

———. 1986b. *In the Shadow of the Poorhouse: A Social History of Welfare in the United States.* New York: Basic Books.

———. 1989. *The Undeserving Poor: From the War on Poverty to the War on Welfare.* New York: Pantheon Books.

Kessler, Ronald. 1982. "A Disaggregation of the Relationship between Socioeconomic Status and Psychological Distress." *American Sociological Review* 47:752–764.

Kiker, B. F., and C. M. Condon. 1981. "The Influence of Socioeconomic Background on the Earnings of Young Men." *Journal of Human Resources* 16(1):92–105.

Knox, Virginia, and Mary Jo Bane. 1994. "Child Support and Schooling." In Irwin Garfinkel and Sara McLanahan, eds., *Child Support and Child Well-Being.* Washington, D.C.: Urban Institute Press.

Korenman, Sanders, Jane E. Miller, and John E. Sjaastad. 1994. "Long-Term Poverty and Child Development in the United States: Results from the NLSY." Institute for Research on Poverty Discussion Paper no. 1044-94.

Korenman, Sanders, and David Neumark. 1992. "Marriage, Motherhood, and Wages." *Journal of Human Resources* 37(2):233–255.

Lazear, Edward, and Robert T. Michael. 1988. *Allocation of Income within the Household.* Chicago: The University of Chicago Press.

Leff, Mark. 1973. "Consensus for Reform: The Mothers' Pension Movement in the Progressive Era." *Social Service Review* 47(3):397–417.

Lempers, J., D. Clarke-Lempers, and R. Simons. 1989. "Economic Hardship, Parenting Practices, and Adolescent Distress." *Child Development* 60:25–39.

Lewis, Oscar. 1966. "The Culture of Poverty." *Scientific American* 215(4):19–25.

Lindsey, Duncan. 1994. *The Welfare of Children.* New York: Oxford University Press.

Lynn, Laurence Jr., and David Whitman. 1981. *The President as Policymaker.* Philadelphia: Temple University Press.

Mallar, Charles. 1977. "The Educational and Labor-Supply Responses of Young Adults in Experimental Families." In Harold Watts and Albert Rees, eds., *The New Jersey Income Maintenance Experiment*, vol. 2. New York: Academic Press.

Mare, Robert. 1980. "Social Background and School Continuation Decisions." *Journal of the American Statistical Association* 75(370):295–305.

Mare, Robert, and Christopher Winship. 1992. "Socioeconomic Change and the Decline of Marriage for Blacks and Whites." In Christopher Jencks and Paul Peterson, eds., *The Urban Underclass.* Washington, D.C.: The Brookings Institution.

Masters, S., and I. Garfinkel. 1977. *Estimating the Labor Supply Effects of Income Maintenance Alternatives.* New York: Academic Press.

Mayer, Susan E. 1992. "Are There Economic Barriers to Visiting the Doctor?" The University of Chicago, Harris School Working Paper no. 92–6.

Mayer, Susan E., and Christopher Jencks. 1989. "Growing Up in Poor Neighborhoods: How Much Does It Matter?" *Science* 243:1441–1445.

———. 1993. "Recent Trends in Economic Inequality in the United States: Income vs. Expenditures vs. Material Well-Being." In Edward Wolff and Demitri Popademitrious, eds., *Poverty and Prosperity in America at the Close of the Twentieth Century.* New York: St. Martin's Press.

Maynard, Rebecca. 1977. "The Effects of the Rural Income Maintenance Experiment on the School Performance of Children." *American Economic Review* 67:370–375.

Maynard, Rebecca, and Richard Murnane. 1979. "The Effects of the Negative Income Tax on School Performance: Results of an Experiment." *Journal of Human Resources* 14(4):463–475.

McDonald, J. F., and S. Stephenson. 1979. "The Effect of Income Maintenance on the School-Enrollment and Labor-Supply Decisions of Teenagers." *Journal of Human Resources* 14(4):530–555.

McLanahan, Sara. 1985. "Family Structure and the Reproduction of Poverty." *American Journal of Sociology* 90:873–901.

———. 1986. "Family Structure and Dependency: Early Transitions to Female Household Headship." University of Wisconsin, Institute for Research on Poverty Discussion Paper no. 807–86.

McLanahan, Sara, and Gary Sandefur. 1994. *Growing Up with a Single Parent.* Cambridge, Mass.: Harvard University Press.

McLoyd, Vonnie. 1990. "The Impact of Economic Hardship on Black Families and Children: Psychological Distress, Parenting, and Socioemotional Developement." *Child Development* 61:311–346.

McLoyd, Vonnie, and Leon Wilson. 1991. "The Strain of Living Poor: Parenting, Social Support, and Child Mental Health." In *Children in Poverty: Child Development and Public Policy.* New York: Cambridge University Press.

Meade, Lawrence. 1986. *Beyond Entitlement: The Social Obligations of Citizenship.* New York: The Free Press.

Meyer, Robert H., and Davis Wise. 1982. "High School Preparation and Early Labor Force Experience." In Richard Freeman and David Wise, eds., *The Youth Labor Market Problem.* Chicago: The University of Chicago Press.

Michael, Robert. 1978. "The Consumption Studies." In John Palmer and Joseph Pechman, eds., *Welfare in Rural Areas.* Washington, D.C.: Brookings Institution.

Minarik, Joseph. 1975. "New Evidence on the Poverty Count." In *Proceedings of the Social Statistics Section, American Statistical Association*, pp. 554–559.

Moffitt, Robert. 1990. "The Effect of the U.S. Welfare System on Marital Status." *Journal of Public Economics* 41:101–124.

———. 1992. "Incentive Effects of the U.S. Welfare System: A Review." *Journal of Economic Literature* 30 (March): 1–61.

Ogbu, John. 1981. "Origins of Human Competence: A Cultural-Ecological Perspective." *Child Development* 52:413–429.

Parker, Steven, Steven Greer, and Barry Zuckerman. 1988. "Double Jeopardy: The Impact of Poverty on Early Child Development." *Pediatric Clinics of North America* 35(6):1227–1240.

Patterson, James. 1986. *America's Struggle against Poverty, 1900–1985.* Cambridge, Mass.: Harvard University Press.

Pearlin, Leonard, Elizabeth Menaghan, Morton Lieberman, and Joseph Mullan. 1981. "The Stress Process." *Journal of Health and Social Behavior* 22:337–356.

Peters, H. Elizabeth. 1992. "Patterns of Intergenerational Mobility in Income and Earnings." *Review of Economics and Statistics* 74(3):456–466.

Peters, H. Elizabeth, and Natalie Mullins. (Forthcoming). "The Role of Family Income in Adolescent Achievement." In Jeanne Brooks-Gunn and Greg Duncan, eds., *The Consequences of Growing Up Poor.* Russell Sage Foundation.

Piven, Francis Fox, and Richard A. Cloward. 1971. *Regulating the Poor: Functions of Public Welfare*. New York: Vintage Books.

Plomin, Robert, John DeFries, and David Fulker. 1988. *Nature and Nurture during Infancy and Early Childhood*. New York: Cambridge University Press.

Plotnick, Robert D. 1990. "Welfare and Out-of-Wedlock Childbearing: Evidence from the 1980s." *Journal of Marriage and the Family* 52 (August): 735–746.

Rainwater, Lee. 1974. *What Money Buys*. New York: Basic Books.

Rees, Albert, and Wayne Gray. 1982. "Family Effects in Youth Unemployment." In Richard Freeman and David Wise, eds., *The Youth Labor Market Problem*. Chicago: The University of Chicago Press.

Robbins, Phillip K. 1990. "Federal Financing of Child Care: Alternative Approaches and Economic Implications." *Population Research and Policy Review* 9 (1):65–90.

———. 1991. "Child Care Policy and Research: An Economist's Perspective." In David Blau, ed., *The Economics of Child Care*. New York: Russell Sage Foundation.

Ruggles, Patricia. 1990. *Drawing the Line: Alternative Poverty Measures and Their Implications for Public Policy*. Washington, D.C.: Urban Institute Press.

Sameroff, Arnold, and M. Chandler. 1975. "Reproductive Risk and the Continuum of Caretaking Casualty." *Review of Child Development*, ed. F. D. Horowitz, M. Hetherington, S. Scarr-Salapateck, and G. Seigel. Chicago: University of Chicago Press.

Sameroff, Arnold, and Ronald Seifer. 1983. "Familial Risk and Child Competence." *Child Development* 54:1254–1268.

Scarr, Sandra, and Kathleen McCartney. 1983. "How People Make Their Own Environments: A Theory of Genotype -> Environment Effects." *Child Development* 54:424–435.

Scarr, Sandra, and Richard Weinberg. 1978. "The Influence of 'Family Background' on Intellectual Attainment." *American Sociological Review* 43:674–692.

Sewell, William, and Robert Hauser. 1975. *Education, Occupation, and Earnings: Achievement in the Early Career*. New York: Academic Press.

———. 1980. "The Wisconsin Longitudinal Study of Social and Psychological Factors in Aspirations and Achievements." In Alan Merckhoff, ed., *Sociology of Education and Socialization*, vol. 1. Greenwich, Conn.: JAI Press.

Shaw, Lois. 1982. "High School Completion for Young Women." *Journal of Family Issues* 3(2):147–163.

Shea, John. 1995. "Does (Parents') Money Matter?" Department of Economics, University of Wisconsin, unpublished manuscript.

Sherman, Arloc. 1994. *Wasting America's Future*. Boston: Beacon Press.

Skocpol, Theda. 1992. *Protecting Soldiers and Mothers: The Political Origins of Social Policy in the United States*. Cambridge, Mass.: Harvard University Press.

Smith, Judith, Jeanne Brooks-Gunn, and Pamela Klebanov. (Forthcoming).

"The Consequences of Living in Poverty for Young Children's Cognitive and Verbal Ability and Early School Achievement." In Jeanne Brooks-Gunn and Greg Duncan, eds., *The Consequences of Growing Up Poor.* Russell Sage Foundation.

Solon, Gary. 1992. "Intergenerational Income Mobility in the United States." *American Economic Review* (June): 393–408.

Teachman, Jay, Kathleen Paasch, Randal Day, and Karen Carver. (Forthcoming). "Poverty during Adolescence and Subsequent Educational Attainment." In Jeanne Brooks-Gunn and Greg Duncan, eds., *The Consequences of Growing Up Poor.* Russell Sage Foundation.

Trattner, Walter. 1989. *From Poor Law to Welfare State: A History of Social Welfare in the United States.* New York: The Free Press.

U.S. Bureau of the Census. 1990. *Statistical Abstract of the United States, 1990 (110th edition).* Washington, D.C.: U.S. Government Printing Office.

———. 1992. *Money Income of Households, Families, and Persons in the United States, 1991* (Current Population Reports P-60, no. 180). Washington, D.C.: U.S. Government Printing Office.

———. 1993. *Statistical Abstract of the United States, 1993 (113th edition).* Washington, D.C.: U.S. Government Printing Office.

U.S. House of Representatives, Committee on Ways and Means. 1993. *1993 Green Book.* Washington, D.C.: U.S. Government Printing Office.

Van der Gaag, Jacques, and Eugene Smolensky. 1981. "True Household Equivalence Scales and Characteristics of the Poor in the United States." *Review of Income and Wealth* 28(1):17–28.

Vaughn, Denton. 1984. "Using Subjective Assessments of Income to Estimate Family Equivalence Scales: A Report of Work in Progress." Washington, D.C.: Social Security Administration, offset.

Venti, Steven. 1984. "The Effects of Income Maintenance on Work, Schooling, and Non-market Activities of Youth." *Review of Economics and Statistics* 66(1):16–25.

Venti, Steven, and David A. Wise. 1984. "Income Maintenance and the School and Work Decisions of Youth." Report prepared for the U.S. Department of Health and Human Services, Washington, D.C.

Viard, Alain. 1993. "The Productivity Slowdown and the Savings Shortfall: A Challenge to the Permanent Income Hypothesis." *Economic Inquiry* 31:549–563.

Vinovskis, Maris. 1992. "Schooling and Poor Children in Nineteenth-Century America." *American Behavioral Scientist* 35(3):313–331.

Vondra, Joan. 1993. "Childhood Poverty and Child Maltreatment." In Judith Chafel, ed., *Child Poverty and Public Policy.* Washington, D.C.: Urban Institute.

Watts, Harold, Dale Poirier, and Charles Mallar. 1977. "Sample, Variables, and Concepts Used in the Analysis." In Harold Watts and Albert Rees, eds.,

The New Jersy Income-Maintenance Experiment, vol. 2. New York: Academic Press.

West, Kenneth D. 1988. "The Insensitivity of Consumption to News about Income." *Journal of Monetary Economics* 21:17–33.

West, Richard. 1980. "The Effects of the Seattle and Denver Income Maintenance Experiments on the Labor Supply of Non-heads." *Journal of Human Resources* 15(4):574–590.

Wilson, William Julius. 1987. *The Truly Disadvantaged: The Inner City, the Underclass, and Public Policy*, Chicago: The University of Chicago Press.

Wise, Yorum, Arden Hall, and Fred Dong. 1980. "The Effect of Price and Income on Investment in Schooling." *Journal of Human Resources* 15(4):611–640.

Zimmerman, David. 1992. "Regression toward Mediocrity in Economic Stature." *American Economic Review* (June): 393–408.

Index

Abbott, Grace, 16

Adams, Terry, 134–135, 208–209n6

Adolescent(s): deviant behavior among, 40; labor-force participation of, 40

Adolescent outcomes: vs. parental income, 44–45; income and, 75; "true" effect of parental income on, 91–92

Adult behavior, effects of, 13

Adults, benefit of, in households, 201n14

Adult well-being, 58

Age, child's, as variable, 164, 166; mothers', 153–154; parental, as variable, 164, 166

Aid to Dependent Children (ADC), 5, 25–26; goal of, 27

Aid to Families with Dependent Children (AFDC), 11–12, 27–28; federal expenditures for, 31–32; state expenditures for, 32–33, 80; controversy over effects of, 133; estimating "true" effects of, 136–140; benefit levels of, 190–192; expenditures of, 195n10; and family size, 195–196n12; and rent levels, 209n9

Alimony, 80, 82, 83

Almshouses, 19; children removed from, 19–20

Amenities, importance of, 10

American Housing Survey (AHS), 101, 105

Anger index, 118, 119, 188

Angrist, Joshua, 210n2

Annual income, components of, 9–10, 63, 87. See also Family income; Future income; Income; Other income; Parental income; Permanent income, hypothesis

on; Transitory income; Wages; Welfare income

Armed Forces Qualification Test (AFQT), 61; mothers' score on, 82, 83, 110; mothers', as variable, 166; mothers', and education, 210n4

Ashenfelter, Orley, 210n2

Aspirations, and doubling parental income, 118, 119

Aspirations index, 188

At-Risk Child Care Program, 36

Axinn, William, 200n8

Bad-parent theory, 17

Baker, P. C., 165

Bane, Mary Jo, 208n5

Becker, Gary, 46, 47, 198n1, 210n2

Becketti, Sean, 159

Behavior: deviant, 40; dysfunctional, 50

Behavior problems: children's, 40; and parental income, 57–58; and raising income, 66–69; income slope and, 74, 75

Behavior Problems Index (BPI), 44, 165; "true" effect of parental income on, 90–91

Black mothers, 23, 166

Blau, David, 57, 58

Blinder, Alan, 198n1

Brace, Charles Loring, 20

Brooks-Gunn, Jeanne, 64, 68, 71, 117, 200n10

Bushnell, Horace, 19

Butler, Amy, 135